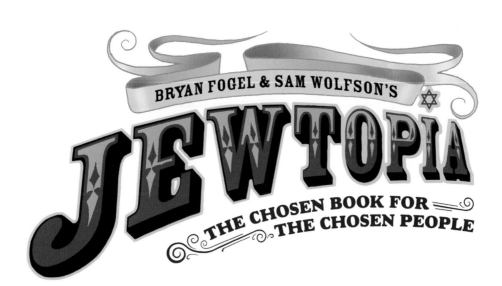

BRYAN FOGEL & SAM WOLFSON'S

JEWTOPIA

THE CHOSEN BOOK FOR THE CHOSEN PEOPLE

Warner Books

Hachette Book Group USA
1271 Avenue of the Americas, New York, NY 10020

Warner Books is a trademark of Time Inc. Used under license.

Printed in Singapore

First Edition: September 2006
10 9 8 7 6 5 4 3 2 1

ISBN: 0-446-57954-8
ISBN-13: 978-0-446-57954-4
LCCN: 2006921367

JEWTOPIA

THE CHOSEN BOOK FOR THE CHOSEN PEOPLE

Written and Edited by
Bryan Fogel
Sam Wolfson

Additional Writing
Amy Shearn

**Original Drawings
and Illustrations**
Drew Beam

Layout and Design
Amy Marrin
Kim Schuman

Additional Material
Aryeh Cohen-Wade
Adam Markowitz
Deirdre MacNamara

Research
Hannah Seligson

Special Thanks
Ralph Bishop, Tim Zeller

WARNER BOOKS

NEW YORK   BOSTON

Contents

CHAPTER 1:
History—Part 1:
Where It All Began...

1

CHAPTER 2:
History—Part 2:
Oh for Christ Sakes!

21

CHAPTER 3:
Holidays:
Cel-e-brate Bad Times!

45

CHAPTER 4:
Food: Anyone Have Some Zantac?

71

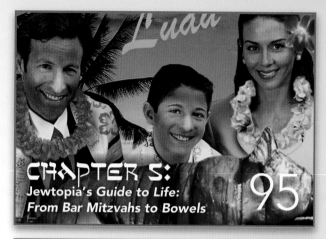

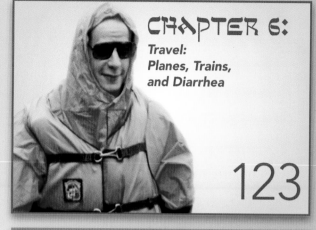

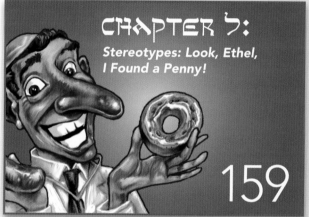

Introduction

In 2001, we were two struggling actors/writers in Hollywood. Bryan was a prop comic doing 1:00 AM sets at the Improv pulling foot-long plastic alligators out of his pants. Sam was a gopher for the *Jeff Foxworthy Show*, getting daily phone calls from his mother saying, "We spent eighty grand for you to go to Northwestern and you're doing WHAT?!"

Desperate to get a break, Bryan came up with an idea to produce an industry one-act festival, where actors and writers could perform material to an audience of Hollywood agents, managers, casting directors, and producers. For the festival, the two of us decided that we would write and perform an original scene. The scene, which would later become Act One, Scene One of *Jewtopia*, was the highlight of the night and the two of us felt that we were on to something special.

Over the next year, *Jewtopia* the play was created. Once we finished a first draft, we did a reading of the play for friends and family, then spent another six months rewriting. During this time, we were promised money from investor after investor to mount the production, but in the end none of them coughed up the bucks. In an act of final desperation, we maxed our credit cards and borrowed the rest from our parents to raise the $80,000 that we needed to open the show.

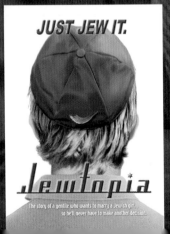

Jewtopia premiered on May 8th, 2003, at the Coast Playhouse in Los Angeles under the amazing direction of Andy Fickman. The stakes were high: if it didn't work out, we promised ourselves we would finally give up the Hollywood dream and find something else to do with our lives...not to mention never hearing the end of it from our parents.

We opened to rave reviews and the show immediately found an audience. Unfortunately, we were also the sole producers on the play, so not only were we performing and extensively rewriting the show nightly, we were handling the box office, placing the advertising, doing group sales, casting and rehearsing understudies, and doling out paychecks to the crew. Seventeen months later, we had become the longest-running original comedy in the history of Los Angeles theater and were being courted by just about every New

But we didn't want to sell it! We wanted to find somebody we could partner with and still retain ownership and creative control. We met Tamar Climan, a New York general manager who believed in the show and introduced us to established Broadway producer and really cool guy Bill Franzblau. We joined hands and together raised $625,000 to put up the show in New York City. We opened on October 21st, 2004, to sold-out houses and recouped the entire investment in a record 16 weeks!

The show is still running in New York and has also had long runs in Chicago, Florida, and is currently on a 35-city national tour. International productions are being planned for Israel, Australia, London, France, Toronto, and if things keep going as they have been, *Jewtopia* Rwanda should be opening around 2008.

The past three years have been a dream come true for us. And now we're getting to write our very own book for Time Warner. TIME FREAKIN' WARNER!!! So to anyone who might take offense at our brand of crazy, wacked-out humor, we swear we're just a couple of nice Jewish boys with way too much time on our hands. We love our families. We love being Jewish. We were Bar Mitzvahed and everything.

So sit back, laugh, enjoy the book, and we'll see you next year in Jerusalem. (Can anybody tell us why we say that when we have absolutely no intention of going there?)

Love,

Bryan and Sam

Foreword

You're probably asking yourself right now, "Why is Herbert Hitler, grandson of Adolf, writing the foreword to Bryan and Sam's *Jewtopia* book?" Don't feel silly, because when Bryan and Sam arrived at my Kinkos in Freidrichshain, Berlin, I asked myself the very same question. And then it struck me. They couldn't get Mel Brooks.

You know, it's not easy being the grandson of Adolf Hitler. You should see the dirty looks I get when people come into Kinkos and read the nametag on my apron. I'm like, "Yeah, my last name's Hitler, and no, these copies aren't going to be ready by five o'clock! Gut können Sie *dies* kopieren, Weibchen!"[1] I don't think anyone can imagine how hard it is to live in the shadow of the most infamous evil tyrant in the history of mankind! Sure, I just got promoted to assistant manager, and no one undoes a paper jam like me, but come on! I'm seventy-five years old and I'm the assistant manager at a frickin' Kinkos because nobody else would hire a Hitler! I don't even get any royalties from *Mein Kampf*! You know who does? The state of Bavaria. Bavaria! Das bindet nur meinen Penis in Knoten![2]

What would my Pop-Pop Adolf say if he knew about *Jewtopia*? He'd say, "Herbie, Jews are filthy mongrels out for world domination and are conspiring to keep our master race from rightfully ruling the world by diluting its racial and cultural purity. Now be a good grandson and pull your Pop-Pop's finger."

But that's my Pop-Pop—Not me!!!

When I start thinking about all the crazy bad stuff my Pop-Pop did to the Jews, I'm so totally amazed that you guys are still around! Not only that, but every time someone was trying to rain on your parade, you Jews just got all Gloria Gaynor on their asses and were like, "I will survive! You can't keep me down, girlfriend!" I'm just saying it's kind of fabulous!

And there's no Jew more fabulous than Hymie Bernstein, my life-partner of 12 years. Yes, you heard me, world! Herbert Hitler Ist ein Jude, der Homosexuellen liebt![3] I've known I was gay ever since my Pop-Pop sat me down and showed me my first Nazi propaganda film. All those strong officers with their chiseled frames and tight pants…let's just say their arms weren't the only things rising up! And not to be a Chatty Cathy, but I wouldn't be surprised if my Pop-Pop was pitching for the Heidelberg Homos, if you know what I'm saying. I mean, come on people, anyone who was so insecure that the only way he can feel good about himself is by trying to wipe out an entire race of people had to be

hiding something. Maybe the fact that he had one ball? Oopsy! Did I say that out loud?

I'll never forget the first time I met Hymie. I had just started working here. He came in to make bulk copies for his dance troupe's performance piece at the local community center. There was just something about him: the way his tufts of curly chest hair puffed out from above his pink baby-T; the way the shimmering light from the copy machines glistened against his bulbous nose; the way his beady little Jew eyes peered into my soul. I don't know what came over me, but at that moment I was Glücklicher als ein Schwein in Scheiße.[4] I gave him my employee discount, and he invited me to his dance performance that night. After drinking seven Apple-Tinis at the cast party, I finally had enough courage to whisper in his ear, "Ich möchte Ihren Kugeln glauben."[5] From that moment on we were inseparable.

So here I am, Adolf Hitler's really, really gay Jew-loving grandson, writing the foreword to what will be the greatest, most fantabulous book ever written about the Jewish people!!! It's just as good as *Mein Kampf*, but funnier and with more pictures! And Bryan and Sam are such Heiße Stücke von Juden Esel![6] So I hope you enjoy these crazy Jews as much as I enjoy mine! Speaking of which, I better punch out so I can go home and get the house ready for Hymie's surprise 75th birthday party tonight. When he comes in, I'm going to jump naked out of an enormous hamentaschen! And guess what he's getting for his birthday? A brand-new hardcover edition of Mein Cock!

Auf Wiedersehen! xoxoxoxoxoxoxo,

---

1 Translation: "But you can copy *this*, bitch!"
2 Translation: "That really ties my penis in a knot!"
3 Translation: "Is a Jew-loving Homosexual!"
4 Translation: "Happier than a pig in shit."
5 Translation: "I want to grab your balls."
6 Translation: "Hot pieces of Jew ass!"

Media-controlling Moishe goes for a walk.

HISTORY—PART 1:
WHERE IT ALL BEGAN...

Are you a Jew? Think about it before you answer. Really think about it. If both of your parents are Jewish, you had a Bar (or Bat) Mitzvah, you go to a Passover Seder every other year, and you go to synagogue every three years, your knee-jerk answer might be, "Yeah. I'm a Jew. You got a problem with that, pal?"

But look deep into your heart. Are you a true-blue Jew? If so, you kvetch about your multitudinous allergies. You send your food back at every restaurant you set foot in. If so, you don't know how to fix a car engine—or, for that matter, open a car's hood.

Even if you are a true-blue Jew, it's impossible to fully understand yourself without looking back—way back. How did we become the bank-owning, media-controlling, economy-manipulating, world-dominating peoples that have been despised since the beginning of time? One simply needs to examine our history—a history of death, destruction, neuroticism, and overbearing, painfully intrusive parental love—to make sense of where it all came from. Unless you don't care and you're one of those self-hating Jews who doesn't read Hebrew, wears leather pants, has six-pack abs, and not only owns power tools...but knows how to use them (Figs. 1.1 and 1.2).

We shudder to think...

CHAPTER ONE

Fig. 1.1

The gleaming abs of a non-Jew.

Fig. 1.2

This book was originally written in Hebrew. If any of the jokes don't seem funny, blame the shoddy translators.

IN THE BEGINNING, GOD CREATED THE HEAVENS, THE EARTH, AND ANXIETY

The story of Creation is told in Genesis, the first book of the Torah (Fig. 1.3). While there are many theories as to who actually transcribed the Torah from what was allegedly God's word, it is apparent that they had no access to a library and a very hazy understanding of science. The Torah claims that God created the world in six days, less time than it takes most people to return a phone call. God then mashed together a bunch of earth and blew the "breath of life" into it, creating the first human, Adam. Adam lived in the lush paradise of Eden and spent his days hanging out with all the animals God had created. God even let Adam take care of all the animals and name them, which is why in biblical times rabbits were called BouncyFurryBalls and male donkeys (i.e., jackasses) were called George W. Bush.

But Adam was lonely with no one but animals to talk to all day, so God created him a female mate, Eve (Fig. 1.4). God said to Eve, "Your desire shall be for your husband, and he shall rule over you." Eve responded, "Righhhhht, got it," and rolled her eyes. For the next several years, Adam and Eve lived in their heavenly paradise with low real estate taxes and plentiful parking. One fateful day, while they were out in the garden naming the weasels Dick Cheney, a serpent offered to hook them up with some primo fruit from the Tree of Knowledge. Adam refused because God had previously told him that if he ate the fruit he would die. Eve egged Adam on, saying, "Just try it, you never do anything fun!" Adam, in the first instance of a man being pussy-whipped, ate the forbidden fruit. For their sins, God expelled them from the garden. According to a famous bit of biblical apocrypha, this is when Adam turned to Eve and said, "I told you we should have ordered in!" Jews have been living in exile and blaming things on their wives ever since.

And as if that wasn't bad enough, by disobeying God Adam and Eve brought sin into the world. No longer would it be easy to harvest fruit, as thorns and weeds would make farming hard labor, women would give birth in pain, and the animals, which were once kind and gentle, became dangerous and carnivorous, especially the George W. Bushes and the Dick Cheneys.

Fig. 1.3

The coolest part of the Torah.

Fig. 1.4

And Eve said unto Adam, "Does this fig leaf make me look fat?"

3

Exiled from the Garden, things only got worse. Adam and Eve's 56 children spawned a whole race of wicked, evil, corrupt inbreeds that populated the Earth. They grew wickeder and wickeder, until they were wicked wicked. This was when God decided to sweep the earth clean in an enormous flood, declaring the world's largest Do-Over. God entered a covenant with the least wicked spawn he could find, Noah, promising to save him and his inbred family from the flood if they would build an ark and save the world's animals. Noah built the ark, and has since gone down in the annals of history as the last known Jew to have a boat and actually use it.

ABRAHAM: THE UR-JEW FROM UR

Judaism itself didn't get going for another couple hundred years after the flood, during which the world repopulated itself in a new, slightly less-wicked way. Around 1800 B.C.E., Abraham was born in Ur, which is somewhere in Mesopotamia. One day, young Abraham had a revelation that this whole idol-worshipping society was totally messed up. He took to playing his lyre really loudly in his room and smashed his father's idols. Finally God came to him, and in distinct *Godfather* fashion made him an offer he couldn't refuse. If Abraham left his home and family and agreed to believe in only one God, then God would make him the founder of a great nation. "Ibiza?!" Abraham asked. "No, Israel," answered the Lord. "Oh... okay...I guess." They performed an ultra-secret handshake, and thus began the covenant between God and the Jewish people. "Oh, and did I mention that you have to circumcise yourself?" asked the Lord. But they'd already shook on it.

Fig. 1.5

Steven Polansky spends some quality time with his brothers from another mother, Achmed and Mohamed.

ISLAM ALERT: The religion of Islam originated with the Arab people, who are descendants of Ishmael, the daughter of Hagar. Hagar was the Egyptian servant of Abraham, Ishmael's baby daddy. Now that's some Thomas Jefferson-style shit! So Jews should embrace our Muslim friends—even the ones always trying to kill us—as they are, after all, our brothers from another mother (Fig. 1.5).

God promised the land of Israel to Abraham's descendants and said that they'd have no trouble claming it when the time came. But he and his wife were growing old and

4

Abraham soon began to worry about whether they would have any descendants. Finally, when Abraham was 100 and Sarah was 90, God promised them a son. Sarah laughed, saying, "Chaacch! No thank you! I'm 90, all I want to do is play mahjong, you crazy man!" Soon afterwards, Sarah gave birth to Isaac, whose name means "These varicose veins are murder."

Fig. 1.6

Isaac spent the rest of his life in strict Freudian analysis.

But being circumcised wasn't enough and God needed to test Abraham's faith yet again, asking him to sacrifice Isaac (Fig. 1.6). Abraham was about to shank the little fellow when God stopped him, saying, "Dude, I was totally kidding. Jeez. Here, do the ram instead." While Abraham had passed his test with flying colors, after this incident Isaac was known to wake up in the middle of the night screaming, "Dad, I promise I'll clean up my room! Please don't kill me!!!!"

CHILLIN' WITH THE CHILDREN OF ISRAEL

Isaac lived to marry Rebecca, who bore him twin sons, Jacob and Esau. Esau was born first, which meant that he would inherit more. Jacob was born holding on to Esau's heel, trying to pull Esau back so that he, Jacob, would be born first—shrewdly thinking of his investments even as a youngster. Esau grew up to be a big strapping hunter, while Jacob was a sensitive, scholarly, girly-man. Can you guess which one the Jews are descended from?

Fig. 1.7

As it says in the Bible, "Hey, hey, hey, Joseph; you're doing fine! You and your dreamcoat ahead of your time!"

One day, desperate for attention, Jacob tricked his father into blessing him by dressing in hairy goatskins so that his father mistook him for Esau. Isaac wasn't amused, and Jacob, sick of playing second fiddle to Esau, ran away from home. One night, Jacob had a dream in which he saw a ladder with angels moving up and down. He climbed to the top of the ladder, where God was perched. God promised to protect Jacob and give him a large family. God then warned Jacob, "Be careful, that thing you're standing on there is not a step." Later in his journeys, Jacob was walking down the road at night when he encountered an angel. And, as any man in his right mind would, he immediately began to wrestle it. At dawn, the angel finally relented and blessed Jacob, changing his name to Israel. So basically, Judaism can trace its roots back through the ages to a hallucinating hobo. Eventually Jacob, a.k.a. Israel, married Rachel and her hot sister Leah, fulfilling every young man's dream of getting to bang two sisters at the same time. They had twelve sons, all with funny names, and then Joseph. These sons would one day form the Twelve Tribes of Israel. Joseph was prone to having dreams that he would one day overshadow and rule his father and brothers. Not wanting to take any chances of being ruled by their baby brother, his older brothers all ganged up and sold Joseph into slavery in Egypt, where he got to wear flamboyant, colorful clothing, interpreted the Pharaoh's dreams, and hosted a celebrity interview/variety show called *Joey Live!* (Fig. 1.7).

During this time there was a terrible famine, and Joseph's brothers came to Egypt, looking for food. They didn't recognize him at first with his new *Queer Eye* makeover, but Joseph forgave his whole family and invited them to live with him in Egypt (Fig. 1.8). Soon all the Jews were flocking to Egypt, because Joseph, the toast of Tutankhamen-town, made being a slave look great. But slavery turned out to not be much fun, after all.

Fig. 1.8

Joseph said to his father, "Look at my hat! It's me, it's me, and I'm fabulous!"

Who's your favorite Moses?

- Moses, who led the children of Israel through Egypt to the Promised Land?
- Moses Maimonides, who wrote *The Guide to the Perplexed*, the most important work of medieval Jewish thought, in 1195?
- Moses Mendelssohn, the great Jewish Enlightenment scholar who lived from 1729–1786?
- Moses Malone, the third-leading rebounder and sixth-leading scorer in NBA/ABA history, and one of the greatest NBA centers of all times?

A BEHIND THE ARK EXCLUSIVE LOOK:

Everyone knows the story of Noah's Ark: Noah was an ordinary 600-year-old man, minding his own business in a crazy mixed-up world when God ordered him to build an ark and save all the animals from the upcoming flood. Noah said, "Even Bouncyfurryballs and George W. Bush?" to which God responded, "Yes, but let's start calling them rabbits and jackasses, okay?" Here are some things about the ark that they didn't tell you in Sunday School:

Noah strictly enforced the rules about no running by the pool, much to the dismay of the cheetahs.

Noah knew that civilization had returned when his dove brought back a double venti vanilla soy latte.

Shuffleboard was available on deck 2.

The monkeys dominated the stateroom Bingo tournaments.

ENCHANTMENT OF THE

Stegosaurus offered scuba-diving lessons to the other dinosaurs. (Noah later learned that Stego wasn't a licensed instructor.)

The ark was originally called *Enchantment of the Bloody, Body-Infested Seas*.

The elephants loved to frequent the Gomorrah Nights Disco club.

▶ **ARK-TOID**

According to some stories, a giant Og named King Bashan sat on the roof of the ark during the whole flood. They believed in giants! How stupid is that?

Chinchillas were used for skeet shooting.

Noah liked to "Pimp His Ship" with spinning porthole covers.

Noah had his own special chamber with a heart-shaped bed, and passed the time with his "special friend" Sir Cherokee.

BODY, BODY-INFESTED SEAS

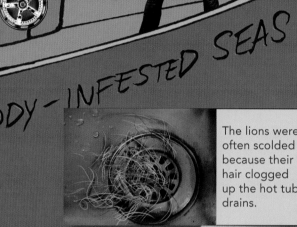

The lions were often scolded because their hair clogged up the hot tub drains.

Noah's sons, Ham, Shem, and Japheth entertained the animals with their boy band.

I think we're alone now doesn't seem to be anybody around

Moby Dick

Giraffes did karaoke in the evenings, and oddly they liked Tiffany songs.

Manicures were performed by teams of chipmunks in the Biblical Beauties salon.

ENTER "THE MOSENATOR"

So, after only 400 years or so, God decided to free his children from Egypt under the leadership of a lisper named "Motheth" who wore dresses. For more on this, check out the Passover story in Chapter 3, or just pay attention at your next Seder for once in your life. Basically, Moses led his ragtag bunch of Israelite misfits through the desert for 40 years, only to reach Mt. Sinai and find the all-you-can-eat buffet already closed. As a means of conciliation, God offered them the Ten Commandments, and dictated the Torah to Moses. God then spoke and told everyone to worship only him and to follow his commandments. Overwhelmed with joy, the entire Apple Dumpling Gang responded, "Everything that the Lord has spoken we will do!"

As we now know, there was a group of Reform Jews in the back, crossing their fingers beneath their cloaks.

ISRAEL: THE PEOPLE'S COURT

After all the good times they shared during those 40 years wandering the desert, the 12 tribes of Israel were thrilled to arrive at the Promised Land and immediately split up, heading their separate ways while talking trash about each other. After Moses died, the Jews spent the next 400 years being judged all the time. Literally—it was the time of the Judges. The scattered tribes were occasionally ruled by a series of wise and honorable judges, including Deborah, Samson, Samuel, Ito, Judy, and Wapner. Without a king, the Jews just kind of acted however they felt was right, which was usually very, very sinful. When things got way too sinful, some outside enemy would generally attack, and God would appoint a judge to lead the people into repentance, winning physical victory over the enemy and saving the Jews once more. Then everything would be tranquil for a few years. But left to their own devices, the Jews would all start sinning again. Again, God would prove his unending forgiveness by appointing another judge to

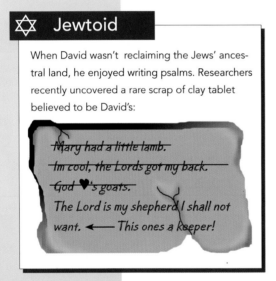

✡ Jewtoid

When David wasn't reclaiming the Jews' ancestral land, he enjoyed writing psalms. Researchers recently uncovered a rare scrap of clay tablet believed to be David's:

~~Mary had a little lamb.~~
~~I'm cool, the Lord's got my back.~~
~~God ♥'s goats.~~
The Lord is my shepherd I shall not want. ← This one's a keeper!

lead them back to righteousness. Either that, or he was too lazy to wipe everyone's wicked ass out with another flood.

SAUL, DAVID, AND SOLOMON: DOING THE KING THING

If it takes a Jewish family 45 minutes to decide on a Chinese take-out order, you can imagine what a mess it was having 12 tribes scattered around Israel with no central authority to say, "That's it! You're all getting the Kung Pao Chicken." So in 1020 B.C.E., after the era of Judges, the Israelites held a contentious election that was marred by confusion at the ballots. Although many were skeptical about the integrity of the democratic process, Saul, who ran on the "I'm backed by God" platform, was narrowly elected leader after three recounts and his reign was beset by mishandled wars. Luckily this would never happen again in the history of the world.

Fig. 1.9

An inspection of King David's palace uncovered this weapon of mass destruction.

Saul's daughter married David, the warrior famous for killing Goliath with his sling-shot (Fig. 1.9). At first, King Saul and his wife were ecstatic that their daughter had finally married a nice strong Jewish boy. This, of course, was before their son-in-law David turned out to be not so nice, overthrowing his in-laws to become King of Israel in 998 B.C.E.

Soon after David became king, he made a plan to take back the city of Jerusalem, which the Jews had not controlled for 450 years. Between playing the harp and writing psalms, David—a cunning warrior who created a deadly new weapon, the "Ninja Throwing Star-of-David"—somehow found the time to breach the heavily fortified city-state. Soon after this victory, David brought the ark back to Jerusalem. The ark was later misplaced when the Temple was destroyed, only to be found 2000 years later by Harrison Ford.

YIDDISH LESSON #1

Chochem (CHAW-chum)—a wise man.

Proper usage: King Solomon was such a *chochem* that when two women came to him with a dispute over a baby, he was somehow able to convince them to make out with each other in front of him.

Just before David died, he appointed his 12-year-old son Solomon the new King of Israel. This was a lot of responsibility for a kid who was busy preparing for his Bar

10

Mitzvah and had still memorized only half of his Torah portion. Luckily, Solomon had a "magic stick" that he used to land himself 700 royal wives and 300 concubines. After ruling for ten years, Solomon built his famous temple, originally called Sol's Babe-a-torium (Fig. 1.10).

Fig. 1.10

If this Temple's rockin', don't come a knockin'!

Solomon's Temple was the focal point for the Jewish Kingdom until 587 B.C.E., when Babylonians led by Nebuchadnezzar destroyed it. It wasn't until 539, when Cyrus of Persi conquered Israel (then Babylonia), that the Jews were allowed to return to Jerusalem and rebuild the Temple. Some changes were made to Solomon's original design—the Second Temple had fewer trampolines and no naked posters of Bo Derek.

During the next few centuries the Jews once again became divided. The land of Israel was conquered again and again by the empires of Babylonia, Persia, Greece, and Rome, tossed to and fro like a sandy sphere in the beach volleysphere game of antiquity.

Then in the first century B.C.E., Herod became governor of Judea and ordered the Second Temple to be renovated, including the addition of an outer retaining wall. His plans for an adjoining casino, which he claimed would convince the Messiah to appear at last, were eventually thwarted. The western part of what he did build still stands, and is now cleverly called The Western Wall.

✡ Jewtoid

The land now known as Israel has at various times also been called Canaan, Palestine, Judea, Babylonia, and this unpronounceable symbol:

WHY TODAY'S JEWS ARE LEAVING THEIR RELIGION

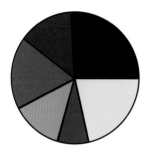

- **8%** Died while fasting on Yom Kippur
- **10%** Started doing yoga and became Jew-Bu's
- **13%** Can't find yarmulkes to match their Hugo Boss suit
- **19%** Their hot Asian girlfriends made them convert (**Fig. 1.11**)
- **24%** Refuse to eat gefilte fish
- **26%** Feel that blowing a ram's horn is not politically correct

WHY YESTERDAY'S JEWS STAYED WITH THEIR RELIGION

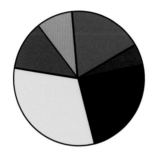

- **4%** Pope, shmope
- **7%** Couldn't fathom reading left to right
- **12%** Heard if you stood near the Burning Bush you'd catch a wicked high (**Fig. 1.12**)
- **17%** Didn't have anywhere else to go
- **24%** Loved seeing a ram's horn get blown
- **36%** Masturbation? Not a problem

Fig. 1.11

Yumi, a great danger to the Jewish people.

Fig. 1.12

"Dude, do you ever wonder if, like, cats are really aliens?"

MOSES' LOST DIARY

Everyone knows the story of how Moses freed the Israelites from slavery and led them across the desert for forty years. However, what is not known is how Moses fared psychologically during these forty years. In 2001, an archaeologist in Jordan uncovered what is believed to be Moses' personal diary.

June 13th, 1251 B.C.E.

Dear Diary—

Don't have much time to write. Me and the other Hebrews have, like, two hours to get out of Dodge and I haven't even packed! After years of being the "nice guy" and trying to convince Pharaoh to let my people go, I had God unleash some plagues on his ass. Nothing like a little blood, fire, hail, lice, frogs, locusts, and killing of the firstborn sons to speed things along. I didn't want to do it, but sometimes my stepgrandfather can be such a dick. Now we're off to the land of milk and honey, should only take a few days. These Egyptians are just going to have to find another ethnicity to build their pyramids. Ramses mentioned that he was going to check out the Western Coast of Africa. Good luck!!! Like there's going to be any potential slaves there!!!

July 3rd, 1251 B.C.E.

Dear Diary—

Spirits are high!!! It has been one badass week. Since I last wrote, some really crazy shit has gone down. A few days after leaving, my fuckhead stepgrandfather changed his mind and sent his army to capture and enslave us...AGAIN! They chased us to the Red Sea and we thought we were toast. But being that I'm the only person who's talked directly to God, like, EVER, he told me to touch the water with my staff, and voila! The freakin' sea spread faster than Pharaoh's niece after I got her stoned on opium! We walked through to the other side, and I was all, like, "Hey, homies, come on!" and the Egyptian army was all, like, "But once we start to cross you're going to, like, start talking to God again and have him put the sea back and drown us all!" And I was all, like, "Come on, Egyptian army. What do you think I am? Some kind of cold-blooded killer who would drown thousands of people? Moses don't roll like that!" So they were all, like, "You promise?" And I was all, like, "Cross my heart, hope to die!" And then BOOM!!! The staff came down and the Mosen-ator gave them an enema that they'll never forget. I'm so getting laid tonight.

November 12th, 1246 B.C.E.

Dear Diary-

Maybe I'm losing it, but I could swear I've seen this pond before. When I talked to God, he told me we'd be in the land of milk and honey in 40 days tops. Um...it's been like five years and I gotta be honest...I AM LOST. For two years, I've been winging it. "Are we there yet, Moses? Are we there yet?" "Yes, we're almost there." "When?" "Soon." "Well, you talked to God, what did HE say?" "He told me to tell you to SHUT UP!!!" A bunch of them have stopped listening to me alTogether and have started to worship a miniAture golDEn calf. I'm schvitzing, I'm chafing, I'm sunburned, my beard has lice, I've Got so much sand up my croTCH I don't kNOW WHAT To do with myself. And to make matters worse, I just ran out of Prozac and I haVEn't hAD a soft bowel movement since 1250. Matzo brie, matzo balls, matzo pancakes, matzo cereal, matzo matzo matzo!

MOSEN-ATOR NEED SOME

MEAT!!!

...*continued from previous page.*

February 22nd, 1245 B.C.E.

Dear Diary-
Fuck fuck fuck.
I'm fucking lost.

March 11th, 1244 B.C.E.
Dear Diary-
Misplaced.

April 28th, 1240 B.C.E.
Dear Diary-
Adrift.

January 2nd, 1232 B.C.E.

Dear Diary-
Off course.

APRIL 11TH, 1229 B.C.E.

DEAR DIARY-
Had to drink my own URINE
today. Breath smells like pee. AND
I'M STILL FUCKING LOST.

FEBRUARY 22nd, 1226 B.C.E.
Dear DiARY-
Me Moses. You sand. Moses like sand. Sand like Moses. Sand is
Moses' friend. Who's Moses' friend? Sand's Moses' friend. Moses
love sand. Moses love sandcastles. Moses love sandwiches. Moses
love sandals. Moses love Sandpeople. Sand sand sand sand. MOSES
LOVES SAND.

MAY 5TH, 1218 B.C.E.
Dear Diary—
WHO'S THAT? WHO'S THERE? TALK TO ME! WHO ARE YOU! WHAT DO
YOU WANT?!!! "SAND MONSTER WANt KILL MOSES!" "I'M
NOT MoSES! I'M STEvE." "SANdmONSTER WANTS TO KILL
STEVE!" "I'M NOT STEVE!" "DON'T LIE TO SANDMONSTER!
SANDMONSTER GOING TO SANDBLAST STEVE AND THEN
SANDMONSTER'S GOINg tO EAT STEVE!" PLEASE DON'T EAT
STEVE, SANDMONSTER! "STEVE MUST DIE!" I AM STEVE
MOSEN—ATOR AND I MUST KILL
SANDMONSTER!!!!!!!

FEBRUEMBER 37TH, 4783388388 A.H.X.L.E.F.
DEAR DIARY—
A SOAP IMPRESSION OF HIS WIFE, WHICH
HE ATE AND DONated TO THE NATIONAL
TRUST. I NEED A FIX CUZ I'M GOING
DOWN. DOWN TO THE BITs tO THAT I LEFT
UPTOWN. I NEED A FIX CUZ I'M GOING
DOWN. MOTHER SUPERIOR JUMP THE GUN.
MOTHER SUPERIOR JUMP THE GUN.
MOTHER SUPERIOR JUMP THE GUN. MOTHER
SUPERIOR JUMP THE GUN. HAPPINESS IS
A WARM GUN. HAPPINESS IS A
WARM GUN. BANG BANG, SHOOT
SHOOT.

A TIMELINE OF JEWISH EXPULSION

Exodus or "Expulsion" from Egypt.

Jews expelled from England. This was also okay, as Jews were beginning to develop pasty skin, way-bigger-than-average-sized teeth, and a level of "politeness" that was completely foreign to us.

Jews expelled from France. Not to make waves, but this one kind of bothered us. We had just been kicked out of Italy and England, and had acquired a taste for Coq au Vin, Bordeaux, and Brie. And springtime in Paris? To die for!

Anti-Jewish riots and synagogue destruction in Palestine. (While we weren't expelled from Palestine we did get expelled from *shul*.)

Jesus of Nazareth (who was a Jew) is crucified, setting in motion the blaming of the Jews for every problem known to mankind.

Jews expelled from Italy. Which was okay, because most of their food gave us indigestion.

Jews expelled from Hungary. Entire Jewish community of Basle is burned to death. Jews are also killed in Mainz, Brussels, Frankfurt, and Vienna. Thousands commit suicide to avoid torture…and further expulsiation-ismadom.

Egyptian enslavement of the Israelites begins.

Anti-Jewish declarations at the Church Council in Elvira, Spain. (While it is not documented, we are certain there was some expulsioning taking place.)

Persecution of Jews in Babylon; concerted effort to suppress Judaism.

Byzantine emperor Heracles demands all Jews convert to Christianity or be expelled. Being that Jesus was Jewish, this confused us.

| 1429 BCE | 1250–1200 BCE | 30 | 300 | 419–422 | 450–580 | 628 | 1288 | 1290 | 1306 | 1349 |

The Black Plague throughout Europe. Jews are blamed. Those Jews not already expelled or killed are further expoldiated.

The Holocaust. Oh Jesus, they finally gave up on expelling and simply decided to wipe us out. Well fuck you, we're still here.

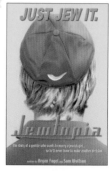

Jewtopia, written by and starring Bryan Fogel and Sam Wolfson, premieres in Los Angeles. While this has nothing to do with expulsion, we just thought it would be nice to throw this in.

Martin Luther declares that Jewish synagogues should be set on fire, houses burned, and all rabbis forbidden to teach. Jews anxiously await our next expulsion. Equal odds are given for Siberia, although optimistic Jews put their money on the 20-to-1 longshot, Tahiti.

Russia moves 600,000 Jews from the western border to the interior, marking the first ever inter-country expulsion. Are we really less able to control all the banks and media in the middle of the country?

General Ulysses Grant orders all Jews to be expelled from Tennessee. Think we're joking? Google it.

Spanish Inquisition begins. Fifty thousand Jews are tortured and massacred in cool chairs like this. (Expulsion, see 1492.)

Pope declares all Jews must wear badges of shame and live in ghettos. Man, we are not liked.

Chmelnitski pogroms: 100,000 to 200,000 Jews killed in Ukraine. Again we ask, wouldn't a simple expulsion have been easier on everyone? Good news—there was a one-to-ten payout for the thirty-six Jews still alive who bet on Ukraine.

Pogroms kill hundreds of thousands of Jews in eastern Europe. What is a pogrom and why do they keep killing us? Remember the good old days when we were served eviction notices?

Israeli independence proclaimed. Finally, a place Jews cannot be expelled from and everyone loves us...except for guys who look like this.

Expulsion of Jews from Spain. Couldn't you Spaniards have decided on this 101 years ago?

1348–49 1391   1492   1517   1543 1648   1862 1900–1920   1915 1941–45 1948   2003

Linda Fogel

Bryan: Hello?

Linda: How did you get a book deal?

Bryan: What are you talking about?

Linda: You know exactly what I'm talking about. Your sister just told me that you got some sort of cockamamie book deal!

Bryan: Yeah, can you believe it! Time Warner bought our book.

Linda: What do you mean they "bought your book"? What book?! You don't have a book!

Bryan: Well not yet—but we wrote a proposal for a book that they bought, and now we need to turn it into a book.

Linda: Wait—wait—wait. So you're telling me that THE TIME WARNER CORPORATION gave you money for a book that you haven't even written yet?

Bryan: Yeah, that's how it works. We wrote a proposal for a book, we gave it to our agent, he put it up for auction to all the publishers, and Time Warner bought it.

Linda: They bought something without even seeing the finished product? How is that any way to run a business? No wonder their stock has dropped 50%! What a bunch of idiots—you don't even know how to write a book.

Bryan: Yes, I do.

Linda: Just because you wrote a hit play doesn't mean you know how to write a book. People go to school for years to learn how to write books. You don't even read books.

Bryan: Yes, we do.

Linda: Oh yeah? What's the last book you read?

Bryan: *The Firm*?

Linda: You're lying to me!

Bryan: Mom, I gotta go—

Linda: I saw that movie with you when you were 18 and when it was over you said, "Cool, now I don't have to read the book."

(Bryan hangs up the phone.)

JEWISH MOTHERS: PART ONE

Sam: Hello?

Arlene: Linda Fogel just called me in tears! She's furious!

Sam: About what?

Arlene: About you and Bryan accepting money to write a book that you have no idea how to write!

Sam: Why don't you think we can write a book?

Arlene: Because you're not smart enough to write a book.

Sam: Yes, I am!

Arlene: No you're not. You got a 960 on your SATs.

Sam: Those tests are culturally biased.

Arlene: I don't think you realize how dumb you are.

Sam: Mom, I got into Northwestern!

Arlene: The only reason that you got into Northwestern is because your father and the dean were fraternity brothers and he made a donation for complete construction on the New Indoor Women's Badminton Court in exchange for your admission. Does Time Warner know you got a 960?

Sam: No!

Arlene: Well you better tell them now, because if they find out later that you got a 960, they might ask for their money back.

Sam: Mom, it doesn't work like that. They're not going to ask for their money back unless we break the contract.

Arlene: Does that contract say anything about what happens when you turn in your piece of crap? I bet they'll want their money back then. I just don't understand how you're getting paid to write a book when you don't even read books!

Sam: Mom, I gotta go—

Arlene: I saw a piece on *48 Hours* that if you ride the subway after 11:27 P.M., a new gang from Guatemala called The Tikalatoratorres will steal your wallet and push you in front of an oncoming train!

(Sam hangs up the phone.)

Arlene Wolfson

20

Did you know that when Jesus wasn't out performing miracles, he was a professional ventriloquist? (See pages 27–28.)

HISTORY—PART 2:
OH FOR CHRIST SAKES!

As the Common Era approached, things were beginning to look up for the plucky children of Israel (Fig. 2.1). And then came Jesus…who really screwed up everything. But before we talk about Jesus Christ, let's get one thing straight. We, Bryan and Sam, love Jesus! But unfortunately, "Christ" means king or messiah, and to us Jews, Jesus is neither of these. So, in order to not be disrespectful to our people, we will from this point forward refer to him as "The Dude."

By a miraculous coincidence, The Dude was born on Christmas around the year 1. His mother, a virgin, gave birth to him in the middle of a plastic nativity scene set up in Joseph of Nazareth's front yard. The Dude dropped out of community college to be a carpenter and grew up to be a scraggly looking Jew who wandered around preaching in public about how everyone should care for one another and love their fellow man, much like the preachers in Times Square you see screaming at frightened pedestrians. These radical new ideas of peace, love, and understanding were a threat to the leaders of the Roman world. So The Dude was charged with treason and crucified by Roman soldiers. Roman soldiers, okay? Roman soldiers. R-O-M-A-N-S. Not the Jews, but the Romans (just wanted to make that clear). According to the New Testament, The Dude came back to life three days later riding a giant marshmallow Peep, wearing bunny ears, and distributing chocolate eggs, prefiguring modern-day Easter celebration rituals.

After his death, his followers created a new religion based on his teachings that was separate from Judaism. They declared The Dude as the Christ, or messiah, called their religion Christianity, and released an edict declaring, "I'm never gonna grow up to be like you! Never! You'll see—I'm gonna be big—bigger than you! Bigger than anyone!" and stormed off.

CHAPTER TWO

Fig. 2.1

The Jews lived in Jerusalem, the holiest and safest place in the world for a Jew. (Pay no attention to that enormous mosque behind the wall…)

***JEWTOPIA* POP QUIZ!**

Robert DeNiro is a:

A) Jew
B) Half-Jew
C) Gentile

Answer: B

THE GREAT JEWISH REVOLT...THAT WAS NOT SO GREAT

Fig. 2.2

The ruins of the fortress at Masada are a great place for solemn remembrance and/or making out with hot Israelis.

After The Dude was dead, it was only a matter of time before the Jews were expelled from Jerusalem once again. In 70 C.E., the oppressed Jews of Judea started a great Jewish revolt, which they cleverly named "The Great Jewish Revolt." Titus and the Roman Army attacked Jerusalem and the Second Temple was destroyed. The Jews replied with a stern warning that if people were going to keep destroying the Temple, they were just going to have to build it somewhere else. One of the real downers in this war was the siege of Masada, where the Romans breached the Jewish fortress to find nearly 1,000 defenders who had set their buildings ablaze and committed mass suicide rather than be captured. All that remained was the gift shop, which still stands and is a must-see stop on your Israel teen tour (Fig. 2.2).

Large numbers of Jews were killed in the Great Revolt, and those who survived became slaves or prisoners, scattering to the ends of the Roman Empire and marking the true beginning of the Jewish Diaspora. Without the Temple to focus on, many of the bossier Jews started to focus their religious energy on studying the Torah and writing laws and commentaries in the vein of Kaplan's Study Guides, which were ultimately compiled into what became The Talmud.

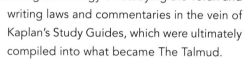

HONORABLE MENSCH-TION

In 493, after conquering Italy, Ostrogoth King Theodore the Great issued an edict giving Jews the right to worship whatever they chose. Unfortunately, a large number of male Jews chose to worship hot blonde shiksas, a decision that haunts us even today.

Then, around 135 C.E., Bar Kokhba led a doomed Jewish revolt called "The Doomed Jewish Revolt," which for some reason, he totally thought would work. These revolting Jews were promptly defeated by the Emperor Hadrian, famous patron of the arts and boy-fondler. In the aftermath of this revolt, Hadrian renamed the province of Judea Mine-Don't-Touch-It-A-Ka. With no homeland, Jews dispersed farther throughout the Middle East and Europe for the next several hundred years, trying to find countries that wouldn't hate them TOO much.

THE CRUSADES: 500 YEARS OF PAIN, PAIN, AND MORE PAIN!

Fast-forward a few hundred years. Christianity has been spreading like wildfire, causing Jews to race around like woodland creatures whose homes are on fire. Jerusalem is under Muslim control, and—get this—the centers of Jewish life are in Iraq. Iraq! Then in 1095, Pope Urban II, who later went on to open a humble little pope-hat shop called Pope Urban Outfitters, decided to seize control of the Holy Land from the Muslims and the Crusades began (Fig. 2.3). Knights and peasants alike were lured to sign up for this rampage of forced conversions and killings with the promise of spiritual and material rewards, including a free commemorative Jesus bobble-head (first 1,000 crusaders only). The idea was to conquer the Muslim infidels and seize their land through sheer brute force. This was clearly a simplistic and barbaric response to a misunderstood culture. Luckily, today's governments are much more sophisticated!

As they headed off to take back Jerusalem, the crusaders massacred Jews in several central European cities along the way, wiping out 30–50% of the Jewish population in Europe. According to eyewitnesses, the knights clapped

Fig. 2.3

Medieval bishops enforced the Pope's bidding with fearsome fish-scepters.

A CHASIDIC TALE

The students of the Rebbe wanted to see if they could stump him one day, and so the boldest student came to him and asked the Rebbe, "Rebbe, there is a ladder, there are 613 rungs on this ladder corresponding to the 613 commandments. There is someone near the top and someone near the bottom (meaning that the one near the top does almost all of the commandments, while the one near the bottom does few of the commandments). The question, Rebbe, is 'who in the eyes of God is higher?'"

The Rebbe was silent for a long time. Then he said, sounding concerned, "Are you saying there are Jews on a ladder? My son, we had better go help them."

their hands together as they left Europe, saying, "Well, that takes care of them!" When the chivalrous and brave crusaders finally captured Jerusalem in 1099, they slaughtered 30,000 Muslims and Jews. The crusaders then established the crusader-run "Latin Kingdom of Jerusalem," ushering in an era of funky salsa beats and totally loco soccer games.

And if you enjoyed that First Crusade, then you're going to love the next nine (Fig. 2.4)! During the next 200 years or so, Jews throughout Europe were forced to convert to Christianity or get massacred, tortured, and burned to death—sometimes all at the same time. The most adorable of them was the Children's Crusade, when thousands of children were sent to the Holy Land to be sold into slavery. (As of this writing, Dakota Fanning and Hallie Kate Eisenberg are in talks to star in the film version, tentatively titled *Who Wants to Buy an Eight-Year-Old?*) But our personal favorite was Crusades 4, where the Jews have to train in Siberia, punch meat to "The Eye of the Tiger," and fight the machine-like Ivan Drago.

BLOOD LIBELS, PLAGUES, AND INQUISITIONS, OH MY!

In 1144, the crazy trend of Blood Libels started to sweep the Western world. They started when some English Christians stayed up too late watching *X-Files*, and then accused the Jews of committing ritual murders of Christian children and being the spawn of Satan. Jews were forced to convert or be killed. While it was unfortunate they could no longer practice Judaism, the upside was that every Jew who converted got a free pair of tickets to the Radio City Rockettes *Christmas Spectacular*.

In 1348, just as the blood was settling from the libels, the Plague started to spread throughout Europe like the Plague. Scientists, doctors, and priests carefully studied the disease and concluded that it was the Jews who were spreading it, and they were rightfully tortured, killed, and burned at the stake. Being the briliant scientists, doctors, and priests that they were, they didn't connect the dots between a Plague

Fig. 2.4

A scene from Crusades 2: Electric Boogaloo

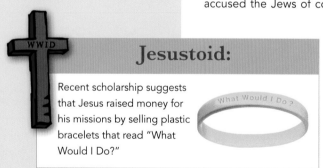

Jesustoid:

Recent scholarship suggests that Jesus raised money for his missions by selling plastic bracelets that read "What Would I Do?"

and the filthy rats and pestilent waste overflowing from the cities' poorly designed sewage systems.

Then, in 1478, the Spanish Inquisition began! Hooray! Prior to this, there had been a few lame Medieval Inquisitions, but Queen Isabella and King Ferdinand's home-grown Inquisition was so much cooler than all the rest! First, they would give the heretics (Jews) a chance to confess. Next, tribunal officers would make accusations. Then, the accused were sentenced at an auto-da-fe, where clergymen would deliver punishments, including torture in dungeons! If the heretics didn't confess, they'd burn them at the stake. But here's the kicker: if they did confess, they'd get to be strangled first and then get burned at the stake! Now that's class, European style.

In addition to the Blood Libels, the Plague, and the Inquisition, the Jews also got expelled from England, France, Hungary, Germany, Austria, Lithuania, Spain, and Portugal from 1290 to 1497. So why did everyone hate the Jews so darn much? Maybe it was because in 1123, the Church declared it illegal for Christians to lend each other money or charge interest on a loan. But someone had to do the banking to keep that bustling Dark Age economy going. So the bishops looked around for some educated, clever folks and found—voila—the Jews! Thus began the stereotype of Jews controlling the economy and running all the banks. But hey, Jews were banned from doing everything else, so what else were we supposed to do!?! Hymie's gotsta pay da rent too!

"RHYME TIME"

Here's an easy and fun rhyme to help you remember the Inquisition!

In fourteen hundred and eighty-two,
Torquemada tried to kill all the Jews.

WHO'S YOUR FAVORITE JESUS?

1. *The Passion of the Christ's* Jim Caviezel?
2. *The Last Temptation of Christ's* Willem Dafoe?
3. *Jesus Christ Superstar's* Ted Neeley?
4. *The Big Lebowski's* John Turturro?

Ted Neeley—for those who prefer a singy Jesus.

A GUIDE TO JESUS, THE WORLD'S MOST POPULAR JEW

Most Jews and gentiles are familiar with the historical facts and myths about the "Son of God": the virgin birth, turning water into wine. But here are a few lesser-known Jesus-y facts that you probably weren't aware of.

AND DID I MENTION THAT I CAN TURN MOUNTAIN DEW INTO A RASPBERRY SNAPPLE?

▶ Did You Know?

▶ Jesus was an avid dancer and originated the "Tony Manero" style of disco that John Travolta stole in *Saturday Night Fever*.

▶ At the Last Supper, before settling in, the party changed their table five times.

▶ Christ's flowing locks directly influenced the fashion sense of such Jewish music-makers as David Lee Roth, Kenny G, and Michael Bolton.

▶ The last documented virgin birth was reported in 2005.

▶ In 2005, Jesus resurrected himself for one day because he wanted to see for himself if the water stain on a freeway underpass in Chicago was in fact his mother, the Virgin Mary.

▼

▶ As of this writing, Jesus has risen and is currently working as a landscaper in Beverly Hills. His customers pronounce his name Hay-zues.

THE HITS JUST KEEP ON COMING AND COMING AND COMING

In 1543, Martin Luther wrote his spine-tingling *On the Jews and Their Lies*, an Oprah book-of-the-month-club selection. The book calls for the Jews—"a brood of vipers and children of the devil"—to be exiled from Germany. Critics called it "derivative" and "predictable" (Fig. 2.5). But his followers, the Lutherans, were enthusiastic about its teachings, which promised an eventual exodus to a Holy Land called "Minnesota."

In the meantime, John Calvin started his own branch of Christianity that focused on predestination and theocracy. After rejecting his first idea for the name, "Me-ism," he decided to call it "Calvinism." He wasn't crazy about the Jews either, but compared to Luther he was downright friendly, saying that "the very worst feature in the Jews does not mean that they are on that account to be despised by the gentiles." Well hey, that's progress…sort of.

In 1555 Jewish ghettos were instituted by Pope Paul IV in Rome. While the American ghettos of the 21st century have allowed for the development of killer basketball skills and whole new musical genres, all these ghettoized Jews developed was lactose intolerance. And for this, they had to pay extra taxes! There were even dress codes instituted to humiliate the ghettoized Jews, who were forced to wear purple Umbros and New Kids on the Block concert Ts. Unfortunately, this was a time when you could not get out of the ghetto by rapping, being shot nine times, and signing a record deal with Dr. Dre.

Fig. 2.5

Come on, Martin! The Jews are "a brood of vipers"? Could you sound any more gay?

Did you know?

In 1747, New York's first Chinese restaurant, Fung Young Foo's Palace, opened in what is now Chinatown. This was a monumental occasion as Jews finally had somewhere to eat on Christmas!

THE THIRTY-ONE-DERFUL FLAVORS OF JUDAISM

Between getting massacred and placed in ghettos, the Jews found a little free time to bicker among themselves as to what was the best type of Judaism. Jews in Lithuania and White Russia felt Rabbinical Orthodoxy was the way to go, while their hippie cousins in Poland leaned more and more towards the mysticism of Kabbalah, a doctrine of esoteric spirituality that was popular among mystics and pop singers. Another mystical approach to Judaism that developed at this time was the Hasidic "silly hat and long beard" movement.

Soon everyone was forming their own sect of Judaism. The Reform movement started in Germany in 1810; the Conservative movement began in America in 1887; and in 1889 Rebbe David Feldstein of Minsk founded the short-lived "Dave's Jews" movement (Fig. 2.6). As Rabbi Israel Ben Eliezer, father of Hasidism, said, "Oy vey, what is happening to Judaism? I don't understand why everybody doesn't want to be Hasidic!" Rabbi Eliezer then walked 10 miles to synagogue in 90-degree weather wearing a thick, black, wool trenchcoat and, when he returned home later that night sweating and stinky, did not shower.

Fig. 2.6

"Take my dictation—'Dave's Jews' will eat only cholent and will settle all conflicts by dance-off..."

WISDOM FROM THE TALMUD:

- **Seek not greatness for thyself, and desire not honor (Tractate Avot, Chapter VI, Mishna E).**
- **Consider three things, and thou wilt not fall into transgression: know whence thou comest, whither thou art going, and before whom thou art about to give account and reckoning (Tractate Avot, Chapter III, Mishna A).**
- **When you're a Jet, you're a Jet all the way; from your first cigarette, to your last dying day (Tractate Avot, Chapter XXIX: *Mishna! the Musical*).**

In the past hundred years or so, there have been numerous significant events in Jewish history, most of which were covered in Hebrew school. But just in case you weren't paying attention, we've provided you with a handy summary of what you need to know in case you're at a party and start talking about Jew stuff and need to appear smarter and more knowledgeable than you really are.

Theodor Herzl convenes his friends at the First Jewish Zionist Congress in Basle, where he wows them by pulling a diorama of "The Jewish State" out of his beard.

Male European Jews who love to yell at people immigrate in large numbers to California and create Hollywood.

The South Philadelphia Hebrew Association All-Jewish team dominates the new American sport of basketball. This will never, ever, ever happen again.

Rodgers and Hammerstein's *The Sound of Music* opens on Broadway. Fourteen years after the Holocaust, Jews are ready for singing, dancing Nazis. No one can say we aren't resilient.

Tel Aviv is founded as the first Hebrew-speaking Jewish city. Eliezer Ben-Yehuda revived Hebrew as the spoken language of the Jews, barely beating out Ebonics.

World War I. You knew that one, right?

Adolf Hitler becomes Chancellor of Germany on his campaign platform of "If you elect me, I promise to kill all of the Jews."

The State of Israel declares independence. Yay! A hunk of barren desert, surrounded by hostile enemies. Sounds like our kind of place.

World War II and the Nazi Holocaust. Six million Jews were murdered in pogroms, ghettos, and concentration camps.

| 1897 | 1909 | 1909–1925 | 1914–1918 | 1920–1930 | 1933 | 1939–1945 | 1948 | 1959 |

Mel Brooks's *The Producers* is released. More singing, dancing Nazis.

Yom Kippur War proves that you shouldn't mess with Jews when they are grouchy from fasting.

Israeli PM Yitzhak Rabin and PLO head Yasser Arafat sign a peace treaty. Immediately afterwards, Bill Clinton says, "Hey, let's go celebrate! I've got a Jewish girl in my office I think you'll love!"

Israelis withdraw from Gaza, while Hurricane Katrina simultaneously wipes out New Orleans. Jews blamed.

"Schlemiel, Schlimazel, Hasenpfeffer Incorporated!" Israeli PM Menachem Begin and Egypt's Anwar Sadat sign a peace treaty.

Operation Solomon rescues Ethiopian Jews in airlifts. Israel's like, "Black Jews? Can we have them?" And the U.S. is like, "Please, go ahead."

George Bush II accidentally trips and hits the big red "War With Iraq" button.

Six-Day War proves that Israelis are total badasses. To see just how badass they are, read "The Six-Day War" on pages 33–34.

The First Persian Gulf War produced by Joel Silver is filmed on a soundstage in Burbank, California, next to *The Price Is Right*.

Suicide bombings increase in Israeli cities. World Trade Center attacks on September 11th. Not a good year.

| 1967 | 1968 | 1973 | 1978 | 1991 | 1991 | 1993 | 2001 | 2003 | 2005 |

THE SIX-DAY WAR

On June 5, 1967, the Israeli Air Force launched a defensive attack on the Arab nations that was as bloody as it was short. Known as the Six-Day War, the entire skirmish lasted only 132 hours and 30 minutes, which, if you do some quick math, adds up to less than 6 days. Here's what happened in a nutshell:

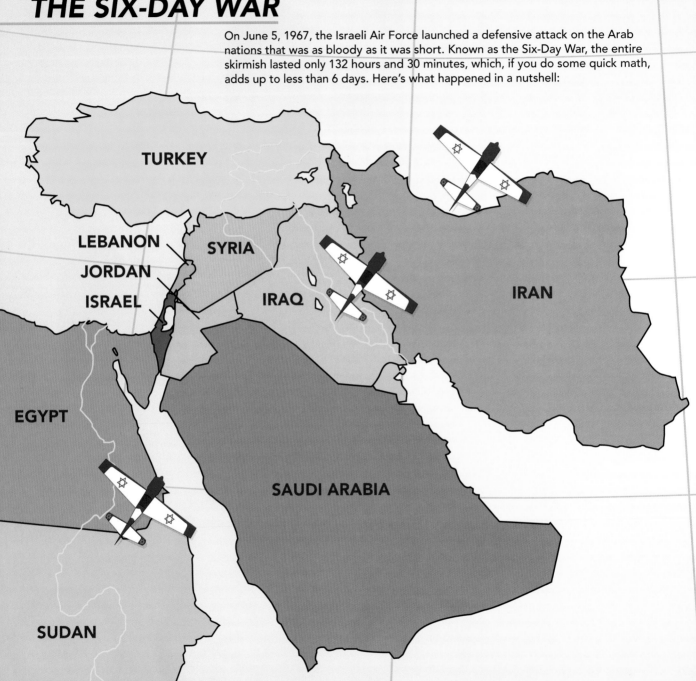

June 5, 1967 Made Egypt, Syria, Iraq, and Jordan our bitches.

June 6, 1967 Made Egypt and Iraq perform oral sex on each other and forced Jordan and Syria to watch.

June 7, 1967 Made Jordan and Syria tie up Egypt and Iraq and violently rape them with hockey sticks.

June 8, 1967 Made Jordan give Syria a "Blumpkin" (giving oral sex to someone who is sitting on the toilet), while Egypt had to give Iraq a "Dirty Sanchez" (you need to Google this one).

June 9, 1967 Made Iraq give "Hot Lunches," a.k.a. "Cleveland Steamers" (you're going to need to Google this one also), to Jordan while Syria has to give "Donkey Punches" (you're definitely going to have to Google this one) to Egypt.

June 10, 1967 Cease-fire. Kedem time.

▶ Test your Six-Day knowledge and match the description with the correct image.

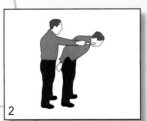

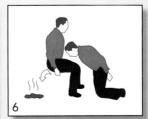

a. Oral Sex on Each Other

b. Rape with Hockey Stick

c. Blumpkin

d. Dirty Sanchez

e. Cleveland Steamer

f. Donkey Punch

Answers: 1 = e, 2 = f, 3 = a, 4 = d, 5 = b, 6 = c

"I CHACH ON YOU!!!!"
THE WACKY MIDDLE EAST SITCOM

Since the creation of the Jewish state of Israel in 1948, the ongoing conflict in the Middle East has grown more complex and violent with each decade, creating a tangled web of politics, religion, and geography. While we all know that the Israelis and the Palestinians hate each other, understanding the intricacies of the Middle East conflict and the players involved is not easy. That's why we've taken all the information you need to know and put it into an easily digestible format that any idiot can understand. A television sitcom.

CAST OF CHARACTERS:

MENACHEM BEGIN, Prime Minister of Israel, 1977 to 1983

ANWAR SADAT, President of Egypt, 1970 to 1981

JIMMY CARTER, President of the United States, 1977 to 1981

YASSER ARAFAT, Chairman of the PLO, 1969 to 2004

YITZHAK RABIN, Prime Minister of Israel, 1974 to 1977, and 1992 to 1995

BILL CLINTON, President of the United States, 1993 to 2001

DAVID BEN-GURION, Prime Minister of Israel, 1949 to 1953, and 1955 to 1963

GOLDA MEIR, Prime Minister of Israel, 1969 to 1974

TIME: THE PRESENT
THE PLACE: NEW YORK CITY

A nondescript living room. MENACHEM BEGIN and ANWAR SADAT sit cross-legged on the floor playing Nintendo, with JIMMY CARTER in between them holding a bowl of peanuts for them to snack on. YASSER ARAFAT, YITZHAK RABIN, and BILL CLINTON sit at a table drinking. The living room is festooned with streamers. A homemade banner hangs on one wall, reading "HAPPY BIRTHDAY!" DAVID BEN-GURION comes out with a plate of falafel, puts it on the coffee table. He doesn't see GOLDA MEIR following him out from the kitchen, and is about to take a big bite of one of the falafel balls.

GOLDA MEIR:
Cease and desist, David Ben-Gurion, first Prime Minister of Israel! Those falafels are for the party!

DAVID BEN-GURION:
(Quickly putting down falafel ball) You got me, Goldylocks, the first female Prime Minister of Israel! (He starts to cough a phlegmy, hacking cough.) CHACH! CHACH! I can never seem to pull the tallis over your eyes!

She puts her arms around DAVID.

GOLDA MEIR:

Well, Gury, I learned everything I know from you. Not only are you incredibly sexy... But in 1948, after the Israeli Declaration of Independence inspired the militaries of five Arab nations and the Palestinians to declare the goal of destroying Israel, you hung in there and established the country's borders. God, that made me HOT!

DAVID BEN-GURION:

Remember how cute you looked, when I had you dress like an Arab man, sneaking over to Jordan before Israel declared independence, to try to convince King Hussein not to invade us? It turns me on just thinking about you with that mustache.

They start to make out.

YASSER ARAFAT:

Jeez, get a room, guys!!! Do we all need to be subjected to your PDA?

GOLDA pulls away from DAVID.

GOLDA MEIR:

Oh, I don't know, Yassi, did we need to be subjected to you taking over the Palestine Liberation Organization in 1969 with the goal of creating a Palestinian state at the cost of our country? You didn't even bring a bottle of wine tonight, jerk!

YASSER ARAFAT:

You know, we Palestinians had been living in what you call Israel for a long time when you crazy Jews appeared on the scene! And I told you I dropped the bottle on the way here!

ANWAR SADAT:

Chill, Yasser. You don't see me getting all worked up just because Israel snatched Gaza and the West Bank from us during the Six-Day War in 1967.

And then when I tried to get it back by attacking on Yom Kippur six years later, I got my ass kicked again!

MENACHEM BEGIN:

I gotta tell you, Jimmy, first (dipping a tortilla chip in dip and eating it), your seven-layer dip is sensational. Second, I really thought you were going to make peace in the Middle East happen once and for all.

JIMMY CARTER:

Me too! It's like, Anwar recognizes Israel as a state, and in 1978 the three of us go to Camp David and we came up with a real bang-up peace accord...

MENACHEM BEGIN:

And then Anwar gets assassinated by a member of his own army!

ANWAR SADAT:

(Shaking his head) Quality control never was my strong suit.

We pan over to the other side of the room where BILL CLINTON, YITZHAK RABIN, and YASSER ARAFAT sit at a table doing shots.

BILL CLINTON:

All right, it's Trivial Pursuit time! In 1987, who started the first Intifada by orchestrating the killing of Israeli civilians and soldiers in Gaza?

YASSER ARAFAT:

That was me, that was me!

YASSER drinks his shot and slams down his glass.

BILL CLINTON:

(Laughing) Next question! Who...instructed the Israel Defense Force to "break the bones" of the Palestinian demonstrators, escalating the violence to a crisis point?

YITZHAK RABIN:

Guilty as charged!

YITZHAK drinks his shot and slams down his glass.

BILL CLINTON:

Okay, who...oversaw the 1993 Oslo accords, where both you guys agreed to a peace process wherein the Israeli military would withdraw from Gaza and the West Bank? Oh wait—that was ME!

YITZHAK RABIN:

My turn! So, after I got smoked in 1995, who met to keep the peace process moving forward—but failed so miserably that by 2003 the Israel Defense Force had reoccupied the West Bank?

BILL CLINTON:

(High-fiving Yasser) You and me, baby!

BILL and YASSER both do a shot.

GOLDA MEIR:

Shhh! Shut up! They're here!

Everyone quiets down.

DAVID BEN-GURION tiptoes over to the door, giving the group the thumbs-up. He opens the door slowly. In walks a grinning ARIEL SHARON, leading a blindfolded MAHMOUD ABBAS. ARIEL takes off the blindfold...

EVERYONE:

SURPRISE!!!

MAHMOUD ABBAS:

What the—

DAVID BEN-GURION:

Happy birthday, Mahmoud!

MAHMOUD ABBAS:

You guys!

ARIEL SHARON:

(Handing MAHMOUD a wrapped gift) Open your present!

MAHMOUD ABBAS rips all the paper off the gift. It is a diorama of the Gaza strip.

MAHMOUD ABBAS:

GAZA!!! I can't believe it! I don't know what to say!

GOLDA MEIR:

We also got you a $50 gift certificate to Pottery Barn! CHACH!

DAVID BEN-GURION:

Friends, we've tried this many times before. But there's no reason why, with a little hard work (he puts his arm around SHARON), and a whole lot of luck (he puts his arm around ABBAS), we can't fix this thing...together.

They all embrace in a group hug.

Suddenly, the door bursts open and in storms BENJAMIN NETANYAHU in leather pants and dark sunglasses.

NETANYAHU:

Guess who's baaaaack?!

Everyone gasps/credits roll as voiceover begins.

ANNOUNCER (V.O.):

Will Netanyahu overthrow Sharon and reclaim Gaza? Will Rabin and Arafat just admit that they're in love with one another? Will Jimmy Carter ever get anyone to try his peanuts? Stay tuned for next week's shocking episode of "I Chach on You!" (laughing) CHACH, CHACH, CHACH.

ACTUAL NOTES FROM THE WAILING WALL

It's a centuries-old tradition to leave a handwritten prayer to God on the Wailing Wall. But today's Jews, in order to avoid the danger of flying, visit TheWall.org and e-mail their notes. Each morning, a Yeshiva student places the message in the cracks of the wall. Seriously.

Dear Hashem,
Please let it not be my baby.

Dear Hashem,
If you're real, why are these pieces of paper still here?

DEAR HASHEM,
COULD YOU CHANGE THE LAW ABOUT BATHING ON SABBATH? IT'S HARD ENOUGH FOR ME TO MEET GIRLS ON A FRIDAY WITH ALL MY BACK HAIR.

Dear Hashem,
Please let Aunt Marion come out of surgery okay. But if she doesn't, let me get the majority of her equity and assets.

Dear Hashem,
Thanks for getting me the Queen Amidala gig. Sorry for making out in front of the wall. And please, help me meet those awesome Jewtopia guys!

I need a nice Jewish boy.

MAJOR FIGURES IN JEWISH HISTORY

GOLDA MEIR

Contribution to History: The first and only female Prime Minister of Israel.

Typical Day: Telling men what to do.

Loved Being a Jew Because…: Jewish men love being told what to do.

Pet Peeves: "Moses took us through the desert for forty years and landed us on the one spot in the Middle East that doesn't have oil."

Life Philosophy: "Go Jews! It's your birthday! We're going to party like it's your birthday! We're going to sip Bacardi like it's your birthday!"

Legacy: Tovah Feldshuh starred as Golda in Broadway's *Golda's Balcony*, which ran for two years, losing 80 percent of its producers' investment.

THEODOR HERZL

Contribution to History: Father of political Zionism, name of the Jewish day school that co-author Bryan Fogel got expelled from. (True story!)

Typical Day: Wandered aimlessly through the Middle East pointing at pieces of Arab-occupied land saying, "Why can't we just live here?"

Loved Being a Jew Because…: None of the other Jews made fun of his three-foot-long beard.

Pet Peeves: No one in Hollywood would turn his 1902 novel, *Altneuland* (*Old-New Land*), into a screenplay.

Life Philosophy: "If you build it, they will come."

Legacy: The state of Israel and the signature long beard adopted by Hasidic Jews and the homosexual "bear" community.

GENE SIMMONS

Contribution to History: Proved that the Jewish man, when wearing Satanic make-up and ten-inch heels, and shooting fire from his mouth, doesn't have to be a pussywhipped momma's boy.

Typical Day: Go to shul, call his mother twelve times, e-mail her his flight information, brag to Larry King about how many groupies he's screwed.

Loves Being a Jew Because…: There's no commandment that says, "Thou shalt not dress up like a Satanic freak and simulate throwing up blood."

Pet Peeves: Leather pants that make him look fat.

Life Philosophy: "Rock and roll all night, party every day, and once a year make sure to get tested for colon cancer."

Legacy: Perpetuating the stereotype that Jews are good businessmen by selling KISS logo coffins.

ABRAHAM

Contribution to History: The first Jew. No biggie.

Typical Day: Tie his son to a rock and offer him up to God to be sacrificed.

Loved Being a Jew Because…: If given the chance, what parent wouldn't want to sacrifice their own children?

Pet Peeves: When you're about to sacrifice your son to God and he says, "Psych!"

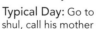

Life Philosophy: "God created the heavens and the earth…but he couldn't offer health insurance?"

Legacy: Started trend of over-protective Jewish parents who felt that at any moment God would ask them to sacrifice their little Joshy and Sara.

BENJAMIN "BUGSY" SIEGEL

Contribution to History: Established the "Bugs-Meyer" gang with Meyer Lansky, the world's first and most famous band of Jewish mobsters that ran a group of contract killers under the name of Murder Inc. And created freakin' Vegas, man!

Typical Day: Kill gangsters, eat gefilte fish, kill more gangsters, bang a showgirl, eat, bang two showgirls at the same time.

Loved Being a Jew Because…: Only had to atone for his sins once a year, leaving 364 free days to kill.

Pet Peeves: Virginia Hill didn't want to spoon after sex.

Life Philosophy: Location, location, location.

Legacy: Fat Midwesterners waiting in line for a $14.95 all-you-can-eat buffet.

ALAN DERSHOWITZ

Contribution to History: Gave Ron Silver the only memorable film role of his career.

Typical Day: Shit, shower, shave, sue.

Loves Being a Jew Because…: Every time someone uses his copyrighted phrase "Jew lawyer" he gets a royalty.

Pet Peeves: Being romantically linked to Greta Van Sustren.

Life Philosophy: "If you're rich and you want to kill your wife, I'm such a badass I'll get you off."

Legacy: If you're rich and you want to kill your wife, he's such a badass he'll get you off.

ALBERT EINSTEIN

Contribution to History: Unanimously proved that Jews are really, really, really, really, really, really smart.

Typical Day: Come up with every major groundbreaking scientific theory of the 20th century. Try to make himself look like Bozo the Clown.

Loved Being a Jew Because…: He was able to negotiate for discounts on his lab equipment.

Pet Peeves: Creating the Theory of Relativity and having his mother say to him, "How is this Theory of Relativity going to help you make a living?"

Life Philosophy: "Be cool. Stay in school."

Legacy: The greatest mind of all time has slacker college students who don't even know what $E=MC^2$ means wearing T-shirts with his face on it.

DAVID BERKOWITZ (SON OF SAM)

Contribution to History: First ever Jewish serial killer and first Jewish mother who never bragged about her kid.

Typical Day: Shower, shave, breakfast, work, lunch, work, gym, dinner, find a few random people to kill.

Loved Being a Jew Because…: See "Bugsy Siegel."

Pet Peeves: The Spike Lee movie was all wrong.

Life Philosophy: "No matter what you've done, Christ will forgive you if you ask him to." (Taken directly from his website www.forgivenforlife.com. How creepy is that?)

Legacy: The first Jew we didn't mind losing to Christianity. Man, they'll take anyone.

DR. RUTH WESTHEIMER

Contribution to History: A four-foot-seven Holocaust survivor who made it possible for people to have the greatest sex of their lives.

Typical Day: Bake mandel-bread for grandkids, cut coupons, bless Shabbat candles, research whether orgasm is better with use of anal vibrator.

Loves Being a Jew Because…: Even though she's the world's biggest sex expert, she's still not expected to swallow.

Pet Peeves: Hairy taints.

Life Philosophy: "If you're unable to achieve multiple orgasms, then just kill yourself."

Legacy: Made it okay for people not to feel dirty when they get turned on by watching midgets have sex with sheared goats while covered in Hershey's chocolate syrup.

Linda Fogel

Linda: So did you take the zinc I sent you?

Bryan: Yes, Mom…

Linda: Then why do you sound hoarse?

Bryan: Because I'm performing our play eight times a week, and I'm working my ass off on this book.

Linda: You better turn this book in on time to Time Warner, because I don't want them to cancel my cable.

Bryan: They're not going to cancel your cable, Mom!

Linda: Yes they are, and then they're going to put me on the cable "blacklist"!

Bryan: What blacklist?

Linda: If they find you to be a problem customer, you get put on their "black-list." Bennie Greenstein mouthed off to the guy who installed his cable, and now all he gets is NBC Latino!

Bryan: Mom, the book division has nothing to do with their cable division.

Linda: I will not be forced to watch Shakira videos all day because you turned your book in late!!! Oh, I almost forgot—Suzie Morris is going to be calling you.

Bryan: WHO?

Linda: You know our friends the Morrises. They have a daughter your age. She's going to be in New York for a week, and I told them that she's welcome to stay at your house while she's there.

Bryan: What!?! Mom, I have a girlfriend! I can't let some strange girl stay here!

Linda: She's not strange. She's Jewish. She's beautiful. She has a great job…

Bryan: Well, if she's so beautiful, then why is she single? And if she has such a great job, then why can't she afford a hotel?

Linda: I hear she's easy…

Bryan: Bye, Mom—

Linda: Oh, I almost forgot—What brand of toothpaste are you using? I read this article that some researchers in London found that Crest Ultra Bright and Aquafresh Citrus Swirl cause gum cancer—

(Bryan hangs up the phone.)

JEWISH MOTHERS: PART TWO

Arlene: Did you hear about the gang shooting last Thursday night?

Sam: What?

Arlene: This guy was walking down 126th Street wearing a maroon beanie and a gang jumped out of the bushes and shot him dead!

Sam: Mom, that's Harlem. I live in Greenwich Village. That's, I don't know, about eight miles away.

Arlene: But I know that you wear a lot of maroon, and I just don't want you wearing it on Thursday nights!

Sam: Fine, I won't wear maroon Thursday nights.

Arlene: You know, Stone Phillips did a special on *Dateline* about Broadway shows and he said that 95% of them fail and that their investors never recoup their money.

Sam: So?

Arlene: So why would you let me invest in your show if I had a 95% chance of losing my money!

Sam: Mom, our show's a hit. You've been paid back. What's the problem?

Arlene: The problem is that you didn't care enough about us to tell us the risks before we invested.

Sam: How did I know the risks! Besides, I thought you were investing to help me!

Arlene: Why would anybody be crazy enough to invest in a Broadway show if they knew they had a 95% chance of losing their money!

Sam: Mom, you're making money on the show! Everything is fine, the book is going well—

Arlene: Oh, God, you're still writing that!? I saw a thing two weeks ago that Barbara Walters did on the publishing industry and she said that 93% of all books never earn back their advance unless you're Michael Crichton, and last I checked, you don't know anything about dinosaurs—

(Sam hangs up the phone.)

Arlene Wolfson

44

Bubbe's chins: A fun new place to hide your afikomen!

HOLIDAYS:
CEL-E-BRATE BAD TIMES!

There are seventeen or so official Jewish holidays. Work is officially prohibited on Rosh Hashanah, Yom Kippur, the first and second days of Sukkot, Shemini Atzeret, Simchat Torah, Shavuot, and the first, second, seventh, and eighth days of Passover, not to mention Shabbat, which happens every week. In fact, there are so many Jewish holidays that when we don't feel like going to work, we can call in and say, "I can't make it today, it's Blachahbarchooeschai" (Fig. 3.1).

Fig. 3.1

The joyous celebration of Blachah-barchooeschai Day.

The reason we're able to do this is because the Jewish calendar doesn't always match up to the Gregorian or "real" calendar. Hanukah may be on the 25th of Kislev each year, but sometimes the 25th of Kislev is dawdling around near Thanksgiving, and sometimes it's getting all up in Christmas' face. This is because the Jewish calendar takes into account the rotation of the Earth on its axis, the revolution of the moon around the Earth, and the revolution of the Earth around the sun. The result is an elegant system, beautifully in tune with the Earth. In order to compute which day the Jewish holidays will fall on every year, there is a simple formula one can use to convert modern calendar dates to their Jewish calendar counterparts.

Where d=modern calendar date, v=the phase of the moon, x=the time of high tide in Haifa, n=how old you were when you lost your virginity, p=how old you tell people you were when you lost your virginity, q=the speed of the Earth's rotation,

$$\frac{dv}{dv} + (1\text{-}n)p(x)v = (1\text{-}n)q(x) \qquad \textit{Got it?}$$

After thousands of years of pain and suffering, we are lucky to still have so many wonderful celebrations each year that allow us to reflect on our past, look toward our future, and spend a day off from work trapped inside a synagogue.

IT'S SHOMER FUCKING SHABBOS, DONNY: THE DAY OF REST

The Sabbath, like most things Jewish, originated out of pure exhaustion, followed by a bad cold and an intense allergic reaction. After six days of creating the heavens and the earth, God was spent. It was then that he realized he'd somehow forgotten to endow Adam with a fully functional immune system, and that his creation would need frequent naps. Thus, a Jew's week has a built-in "Day of Rest." Contemporary Jews often don't realize what a radical concept this was in ancient times, when only the ruling classes had days of rest. In fact, the ancient Greeks thought Jews were lazy for having a holiday every week. Right. So lazy that Jews now control Hollywood and make movies like *Troy* and *Alexander*, while the Greek empire collapsed 2,000 years ago!

The basic idea is to refrain from work for the entire day, from sundown Friday to sundown Saturday. The Mishnah Shabbat 7.2 prohibits the following on the Sabbath: Sowing, Plowing, Reaping, Binding sheaves, Threshing, Winnowing, Selecting, Grinding, Sifting, Kneading, Baking, Shearing wool, Washing wool, Beating wool, Dyeing wool, Spinning, Weaving, Making two loops, Weaving two threads, Separating two threads, Tying, Untying, Sewing two stitches, Tearing, Trapping, Slaughtering, Flaying, Salting meat, Curing hide, Scraping hide, Cutting hide up, Writing two letters, Erasing two letters, Building, Tearing a building down, Extinguishing a fire, Kindling a fire, Hitting with a hammer, Taking an object from the private domain to the public, or Transporting an object in the public domain (Fig. 3.2). So next time you want to beat your wool and bind a sheaf while salting a piece of meat on the Sabbath, just be advised that you are BREAKING THE LAW (Fig. 3.3)!

Orthodox Jews, or "God's little brownnosers," take the prohibition of work on the Sabbath very literally. So literally that they refrain from bathing because washing their long beards and pais is considered hard work. This practice is derived from commandment number 429, which states, "Thou shall not batheth, for I am the Lord Thy God and I command thee to stinketh."

Fig. 3.2

A one-way ticket to Hell.

COOL SHABBAT RITUALS!

LIGHTING SHABBAT CANDLES: This must be done by the women of the house no later than 18 minutes before sundown. If the candles are lit later than 18 minutes before sundown, God must beat an angel to death. (Please try to do this on time.)

ATTENDING TEMPLE SERVICES: This is a nice time to honor the day of rest by napping.

SAYING KIDDUSH: The family says a kiddush over glasses of wine. Wine was once used at altars of sacrifices, and is now used to "toast" God. The best part is when God raises his glass back and slurs, "No, you guys! You guys are the bess! You're my bess frien's! I fuckin' looove you guys!"

BLESSING THE CHALLAH: The challah symbolizes the manna that was given to the Jews by God during the Exodus from Egypt. Some say that braided challah looks like intertwined arms, symbolizing love. Others say twelve humps in the challah symbolize the 12 tribes of Israel. Basically, challah means whatever you want it to mean, just like that shitty poetry you wrote in college.

HAVDALAH: At sundown on Saturday, Havdalah services bring the Sabbath to a close with blessings over wine, candles, and this time…spices. Many congregations use a spice box full of cloves, but Reform Jews have been known to use Spicebarn. com's Jalapeño popcorn seasoning.

Fig. 3.3

A typical Hallmark Shabbos greeting card.

✡ Jewtoid

Shabbat is the only holiday that is actually one of the Ten Commandments. Additionally, the Torah expressly states that whoever does not keep the Sabbath should be put to death. Tell that to your weekend shift manager at Abercrombie and Fitch!

HIGH TIMES: ROSH HASHANAH & YOM KIPPUR

Around late September to early October, that buffalo-like sound coming from the synagogue can mean only one thing: the beginning of the Jewish holiday season.

Unlike Christians, who open their doors to anyone who wants to pray for free, Jews have to purchase expensive reserved tickets, even if they are already members of the temple, in order to attend High Holiday services. This is because the High Holidays are the one time of the year that most Jews actually go to services, creating an opportunity for the Temple to rake in some major cash. Think of it as our own Jews-apalooza, without the $7.50 Ticketmaster surcharge.

ROSH HASHANAH

Rosh Hashanah means "first of the year" and is commonly known as the Jewish New Year. Unlike the secular New Year, Rosh Hashanah does not involve watching Dick Clark on ABC while getting drunk at TGI Friday's and making out with a total stranger at midnight. Rather, it is a time for Jews to reflect on the year that just passed and imagine all the awful things that could happen to us in the future. During Rosh Hashanah, Jews are required to ask themselves:

• What am I doing with the freedom from bondage God has given our people?

• What am I doing with the freedom to be in bondage, if I'm into that sort of thing?

• Have I hurt anyone either intentionally or unintentionally this year, and if so, how can I apologize in a way that proves I was actually right but still sounds like I'm apologizing?

Rosh Hashanah is all about God judging the worth of your deeds and thoughts, and deciding whether you have chosen righteousness (earning a place in *The Book of Life*, an imaginary book that lives up in the sky) or sinfulness (sending you to *The Book of Death*, an imaginary book that lives somewhere else...maybe Mordor?). However, even if you are inscribed in *The Book of Life*, remember that God does

Live Long and Prosper, Jew!

Did you know that the Vulcan greeting on *Star Trek* is based on a blessing gesture used by the priests during traditional Jewish High Holy Day worship services? Leonard Nimoy, a Jew, came up with that one!

not seal it until Yom Kippur, so your status can easily change. It is advised to wait until after sundown on Yom Kippur before buying that 14-year-old Cambodian slave you've had your eye on.

Rosh Hashanah concludes at sundown on the second day. After saying "L'Shanah Tovah" (Happy New Year) and awkwardly hugging all your fellow congregants, most Jews head home for dinner. It is traditional to eat sweet things for a "sweet new year." Many Jews eat apples and honey for this reason. While this might not seem as exciting as a countdown, big parties, and drunken cavorting…that's because it isn't.

Fig. 3.4

"Wait, is today Yom Kippur? Or did it start last night at sundown? Or wait, is that tonight at sundown? Or is it tomorrow? Momar, would you Google that for me?"

Ten Things That Jews Think About While in High Holiday Services

10. Does the Rabbi get a percentage of the High Holiday ticket sales?

9. If I just closed my eyes for five minutes, would anybody notice?

8. Who did Allie Goldberg's nose? Oh shit, did I remember to TiVo *Nip/Tuck*?

7. Does Al-Qaeda know that today is Yom Kippur (Fig. 3.4)?

6. Has the leftover Mu Shu chicken in the refrigerator gone bad?

5. Does recycling really cut down on energy consumption?

4. How long do I have to sit here before I pretend I have to pee so I can take off for twenty minutes?

3. Does the Rabbi actually write all these sermons or does he pay someone to write them for him?

2. If you really break down *The Usual Suspects*, does it add up in the end?

1. Did anyone smell the SBD I just let out?

THE DAYS OF AWE

The days between, and including, Rosh Hashanah and Yom Kippur are commonly referred to as *Days of Awe*, not to be confused with the forgotten yet totally watchable movie *Days of Thunder*, which is on TNT every weekend. During these days, Jews apologize to everyone they have wronged during the past year, consider how to be better Jews in the new year, and prepare themselves to apologize to that big friend in the sky on Yom Kippur, the Day of Atonement.

During this time, Jews are supposed to partake in the ritual of Tashlikh ("casting off"). This involves finding a river and emptying our pockets into it, symbolically casting off our sins and filling the river with those red and white mints we've hoarded all year from restaurants.

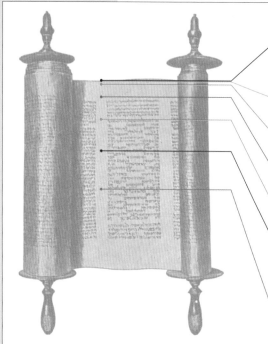

Fig. 3.5

"I feel pretty, and witty, and gay! And I pity any girl who isn't me today!"

WHAT ARE WE ATONING FOR?

.0000001%—Being the White House Press Secretary and lying to the American people on behalf of the President about Iraq having weapons of mass destruction to justify his war.

.0001%—Being Rob Schneider or in any way associated with a Rob Schneider movie.

7%—Wearing wife's clothes and dancing around the house singing "I Feel Pretty" while she's at a JCC meeting (Fig. 3.5).

11%—Lying to yourself that by having only just a few Peanut M&M's you "technically" didn't break your fast.

16%—Telling that homeless man you didn't have any cash on you after you'd just pulled 300 bucks out of the ATM.

23%—Calling information on your cell phone to get a number, lying to the operator that you just called 30 seconds ago and were cut off so that they'll give you a credit and you won't be charged the $1.50.

42.999%—Not buying your High Holidays tickets until 3 days before the service in the hopes that they would be sold out and you'd get out of having to go.

YOM KIPPUR

Yom Kippur comes ten reflection-rific and prayer-tastic days after Rosh Hashanah. This is when even the worst of Jews go to temple to atone for their sins; against God, against another person, or against oneself. The most important prayer of atonement is the Amidah, which is a communal confession, indicating that we are all guilty and responsible for everyone else's sins. This means that you don't have to feel solely responsible for downloading porn onto your co-worker's computer to get him fired. It was just as much his fault for carelessly leaving his desk unattended during lunch.

During Yom Kippur we are asked to emulate the angels in heaven by fasting, not wearing leather, perfume, washing, having sex or anything else that a good angel wouldn't do. We are also asked to hear a ram's horn, or shofar, being blown. That's shofar, not the chauffeur, who you get to hear being blown.

THERE ARE 4 DIFFERENT TYPES OF SHOFAR NOTES:

1. "Tekiah," the 3-second sustained note
2. "Shevarim," the 3 one-second notes
3. "Teruah," the short, staccato notes
4. "Tekiah gedolah," the long, sustained note that the shofar blower has practiced for all year and is the high point of the High Holidays. Sadly, even with this incredible musical ability, he still has no luck with the ladies.

One of the more interesting traditions of Yom Kippur is the Orthodox custom of Kapparot, where a live chicken is waved over the Jews' heads while they recite a prayer. The prayer asks that the chicken will be considered atonement for their sins, in the hopes that God will be merciful and accept the chicken's life instead of theirs. The chicken is then slaughtered and given to the poor, who use it to make a delicious "chicken atonement casserole."

KIPPUR MADNESS!

In the 1930s and '40s, the U.S. government released a series of instructional films designed to inform American citizens about the dangers of drug use, venereal disease, and the Japanese. Among these films was the 1936 anti-drug propaganda film *Reefer Madness*. The film tells the story of a wholesome, all-American teenager who after trying Marijuana descends into a dark world of reckless sex, crime, murder, and ultimately…insanity.

Inspired by the film's use of scare tactics, the American Conservative Jewish Values Organization, concerned by a sharp drop-off in Yom Kippur service attendance, produced their own film in 1938, *Kippur Madness!* The film tells the cautionary tale of a group of all-American Jewish teenagers who forgo atonement and plummet into a vicious netherworld of sin.

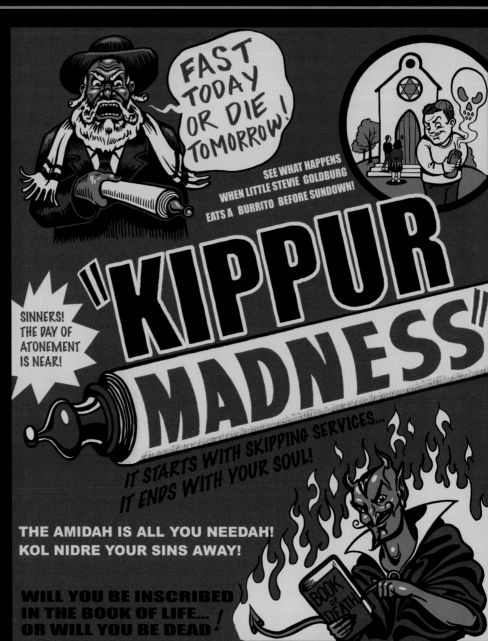

PROPAGANDA CAMPAIGNS

THE BOY WHO HATED YOM KIPPUR

In recent years, as the Born-Again Christianity movement has grown in popularity, evangelical groups have developed pamphlets, books, and comics as effective ways to spread the word of Jesus. Perhaps the most well known is the Left Behind book series, endorsed by *Growing Pains* star Kirk Cameron! All of these materials focus on the impending apocalypse and how ONLY by accepting Jesus Christ as one's lord and savior will a person be saved.

In 1999, in order to reach out to non-practicing Jews, the United National Synagogue Association created a series of tracts that they handed out in delis, JCCs, and Jewish neighborhoods in major metropolitan areas.

IT'S NOT TOO LATE! DON'T BE LIKE JACOB! COME IN PRAYER CALLING UPON THE NAME OF ADONAI FOR ATONEMENT OF YOUR SINS! EXODUS 7.4 SAYS "FOR WHOEVER SHALL CALL UPON THE NAME OF THE LORD SHALL BE SAVED!" COME TO YOM KIPPUR SERVICES NOW BECAUSE YOU ONLY HAVE ONE CHANCE TO BE WRITTEN IN THE BOOK OF LIFE!

THIS TRACT HAS BEEN PAID FOR BY THE UNITED NATIONAL SYNAGOGUE ASSOCIATION.

LEAF ME ALONE: SUKKOT

At nearly 3,000 years old, Sukkot is Judaism's oldest holiday. Congratulations, Sukkot! This weeklong festival of thanksgiving comes five days after Yom Kippur and celebrates the autumn harvest. That's right—3,000 years ago, there were actually Jewish farmers.

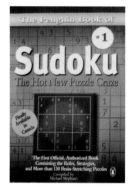

Sudoku, the popular Japanese number puzzle, has nothing to do with Sukkot.

For this holiday, Jews erect a Sukkah—an open-air hut covered with palm fronds, dried squash, corn, children's drawings, and a bunch of other crap. The Sukkah symbolizes the temporary dwellings the Jews had to sleep in while wandering the desert for forty years. The Torah commands that Jews actually sleep outside and in the Sukkah for the entire weeklong celebration in order to feel a symbolic connection with the original wandering Jews. In reality, this never happens unless you are a Jew who is homeless.

Fig. 3.6

Two Shofars and a Etrog partake in a threesome.

Other than the Sukkah itself, the most important symbols of this holiday are the Lulav, a special palm frond, and the Etrog, a very large lemon-like fruit (Fig. 3.6). The Torah commands us to take the Lulav and Etrog and "rejoice for seven days before the Lord your God." Ancient Jews weren't quite sure how one rejoices for seven days with a lemon and palm frond, so after some unfortunate early attempts that caused severe bleeding and infection, they decided to simply hold the Lulav and Etrog in their hands and shake them in each cardinal direction. According to scholars, the Lulav and Etrog are truly powerful only when combined, just like the Jewish people or Fleetwood Mac.

PIMP MY SUKKAH...OR ELSE!

Holidays like Sukkot are increasingly overlooked by young Jews. But the youth of today are tomorrow's future and if Judaism still wants to be around by the year 2100, synagogues need to start attracting that coveted 18 to 34 demographic.

PERSIAN IDOLS:

MEET THE MAVENS OF THE MEGILAH

Before reviewing the thrilling tale of Purim, let's meet the players.

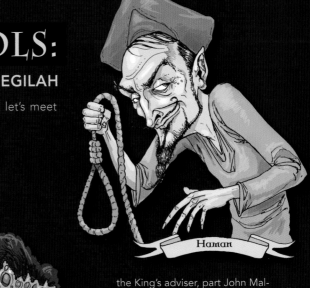

Haman

the King's adviser, part John Malkovich, part Christopher Walken, all bad news!

Mordechai

a Eugene Levy type (but what Jewish man isn't?)

Queen Esther

a Jewish girl-next-door beauty—Julia Roberts with a sprinkling of Fran Drescher

King Achashverosh

a young Brian Dennehy type

PURIM: AND THE FUN TRAIN JUST KEEPS ON GOING

The story of Purim, or the Megilah, is the Jewish equivalent of *Sleeping with the Enemy* meets *Steel Magnolias*, set in the former empire of Persia. The story begins when Esther, the niece of Mordechai, conceals her Jewish identity so that she can replace Vashti, Achashverosh's current queen, whom he has grown tired of. Mordechai finds out about a plot to kill King Achashverosh and saves his life, which Haman takes credit for. Haman is appointed Prime Minister over Mordechai, who refuses to bow to Haman. In an act of revenge, Haman convinces King Achashverosh to exterminate all the Jews in Persia. On the eve of their destruction, Esther heroically reveals her true identity, tells him that Haman is a liar and her archenemy, and begs the king to stop the extermination, which he does. On the 13th of Adar, Haman is hanged, Mordechai becomes the Prime Minister, and the Jews live happily ever after...kinda sorta.

Fig. 3.7

The Hamantaschen, in four nasty varieties: grape, cherry, orange marmalade, and the nastiest of all...prune.

Jews celebrate this victory by holding a really crappy carnival in the temple social hall. This "carnival" generally has cheesy costumes, inedible food (Fig. 3.7), and horrible games like Pin the Tail on the Haman. On the upside, Jews are required by the Talmud to drink Manischewitz until they can't tell the difference between "...cursed be Haman" and "...blessed be Mordecai." Luckily, God had the foresight to see that getting shitfaced would be the only possible way to enjoy a Purim carnival.

Each year every Jew must hear the story of Purim while screaming every time Haman's name is said and drowning out his name with groggers. It's like watching a movie you've seen a thousand times, with some wise guy saying the lines before the actors say them. But hey, it's better than atoning.

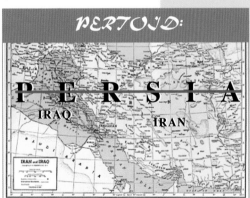

PERIOD:

Persian: The ethnicity that every Iranian and Iraqi Jew will tell you they are even though Persia hasn't existed since 1935!

PASSOVER: BUILD YOUR OWN PYRAMIDS, RAMSES!

The Passover holiday is the weeklong commemoration of the Israelites' exodus from Egypt (Fig. 3.8). This all began when Jacob brought his family to Egypt to be with Joseph, who had sung, danced, and dreamcoated his way into the upper echelons of Egypt's ruling class. The children of Israel multiplied and soon were quite powerful in Egypt, which made the Pharaoh nervous. He decided, as any good leader would, to limit their rights and oppress their free speech. But the Israelites continued to flourish, so Pharaoh enslaved them and, to be extra safe, then ordered the killing of all male newborn Jewbabies.

When Jacob's great-great-grandson Moses was born, Moses' mother bravely defied the order by sending her newborn son floating down the river. Moses was found by the Pharaoh's daughter and grew up as an Egyptian prince, though his copious allergies and inhuman appetite for smoked herring threatened to give him away. One day when Moses was out wandering around in the burning bush district, one of the burning bushes spoke to him. "Me? You talking to me?" Moses said, squinting at the bush, who replied, "No, idiot. I'm talking to the sheep." It turned out to be God telling Moses to lead the children of Israel out of Egypt. Moses went to the Pharaoh and explained that God had said to let the Jews go. The Pharaoh laughed hysterically, "Let my pyramid builders go? Sure, no problem! I mean, if GOD said so." Tears ran down his face from laughing. "Pphhhhh...Let the Jews go...Damn, you are funny, Moses!"

THE PLAGUES

Then, the plaguinating began. The waters of Egypt turned to blood. The entire country was covered in frogs, and then lice, and then mysterious wild animals that destroyed everything in their path. But after four plagues, Pharaoh still said no. Then it got really nasty: fatal cattle disease, boils, hail, locusts, and for the ninth plague, darkness. Pharoah, not taking the hint, said no again. Then God said, "No worries, I'll just slay all the firstborn sons of Egypt." The Jewish families marked their doors

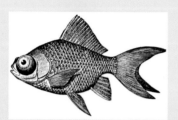

Fig. 3.8

In the 1970s, Reform Jews tried to introduce "Carpy," the Loveable Passover Mascot. His reign was short-lived.

Cash in your Chametz!

Before Passover, all chametz, including utensils used to cook chametz, must either be burned or sold to a non-Jew. No joke—you can sell your chametz online through Chabad-Lubavitch.com. Who knew?

with the blood of the paschal lamb, so the angel of death, who was not exactly the sharpest tack in the bulletin board of heaven, would know which babies not to kill. That is, he PASSED OVER the Jewish homes. Passover. Get it?

Pharaoh finally relented and let the Jews go, but they had to leave in such a hurry that they didn't even have time for their bread to rise. Sure enough, Pharaoh changed his mind and sent his army after them. This is when God got a great idea and urged Moses to lift up his rod and divide the sea so the Israelites could pass through it. As soon as the Israelites were safe on the other side, God closed the sea back up over the army and the Israelites rejoiced. This was a little premature, maybe, as they still had forty years of wandering through the desert before reaching the Promised Land and receiving The Ten Commandments. (See Moses's Diary, pages 13–16.)

THE SEDER

To commemorate this epic event, Jewish families have an epic dinner called a Seder. This involves retelling the story of Passover, with the Seder plate serving as a rudimentary PowerPoint aid. A Seder can last from ten minutes to four hours, depending on how religious and/or hungry the family is. Some of the highlights generally include drinking four glasses of wine on an empty stomach, searching for the hidden afikomen, and opening the door for Elijah the prophet, in case he feels like showing up and/or bringing peace and justice to the entire world.

Good Jews honor their ancestors during the week of Passover by not eating leavened bread and emptying their homes of all chametz (anything that has yeast in it). They then get medieval on the chametz's ass and cover their countertops, tape their cabinets shut, and change out all of their regular dishes for a cheap set from Target that comes out only once a year. They even go so far as to throw out any toiletries or cosmetics that might contain alcohol, which is a source of yeast. While this is a very noble act of faith, throwing away your 20-dollar bottle of Aveda Black Malva Shampoo is just plain wrong.

TEST YOUR KNOWLEDGE OF THIS FAVORITE PASSOVER SONG:

Ilu ho-tsi, ho-tsi-o-nu,

Ho-tsi-onu mi-Mitz-ra-yim

Ho-tsi-onu mi-Mitz-ra-yim

Da-ye-nu

Da-da-ye-nu,

Da-da-ye-nu,

Da-da-ye-nu,

Da-ye-nu,

---blank---

WHAT WORD GOES IN THE BLANK?

1. Da-ye-nu?
2. Na-nu Na-nu?
3. Ma-ya Ang-e-lou?

Believe it or not! Since 1934 Maxwell House Coffee has been printing and giving away free Passover Haggadahs! In an obvious ploy to hook children on coffee, whoever finds the afikomen gets a mail-in voucher good for a free 12-ounce tin of decaf or regular.

THE SEDER PLATE

What makes the Passover Seder special is the ritual of eating several different specially prepared food items to symbolically re-create the suffering of the Jewish people while enslaved in Egypt. The Seder plate is the focal point of the Seder and serves as an edible guide to what is traditionally a very, very, very long evening.

CHAROSET

A mixture of chopped apples, nuts, wine, and spices symbolizing the mortar that the slaves made for bricks to build Egyptian pyramids. It's a little known fact that if the slaves had actually used Charoset instead of bricks, they would have been incredibly delicious pyramids.

BEITZAH

A roasted egg that represents the festival sacrifice brought in the days of the Temple. Some Jews use egg whites or Egg Beaters to represent the slaves who had high cholesterol.

MATZOH

While not technically on the Seder plate, this dry, barely edible flatbread is meant to make us think about how the Jews didn't have time for the bread to rise when escaping Egypt. All it really makes us think about is how we're not going to be able to crap for a week.

ZEROAH

A roasted shank bone, symbolizing the lamb who gave his life so we wouldn't have to give ours. Jews find the lamb to be the most beautiful of all God's creatures and it will forever hold a special place in our hearts—especially when pan fried in olive oil with parsley, garlic, thyme, rosemary, and accompanied with a fava bean ragout.

KARPAS

A parsley sprig, symbolizing spring and rebirth. It must be dipped in salt water, which represents the tears of the slaves, and we must consume it to remind ourselves of the bitterness and pain the slaves felt. If you prefer, it is acceptable to rent *Amistad* and *The Ten Commandments* and watch them back-to-back.

MOROR

The Bitter Herbs—generally horseradish of some sort—which we again eat to experience the bitterness of slavery with an even more disgusting concoction.

ALTERNATIVE USES
for Matzoh

Have you ever found yourself asking, "When Passover ends, what I am going to do with the ten boxes of leftover matzoh?" Here are some creative ideas.

• Roof shingles

• Military body armor

• Kitchen floor tiles

• Coasters

• Sun reflector

HANUKAH or HANUKKAH or CHANUKAH or CHANUKKAH

Known as the "Festival of Lights," Hanukah (or any of the other accepted spellings) creeps in during the darkest part of the winter to joyously celebrate a bloody, ferocious, and casualty-heavy military victory. In 166 B.C.E., just as the Jews had been getting comfortable with the friendly Greeks who ruled Judea, Emperor Antiochus came to power and—you guessed it—persecuted the Jews and plundered the Temple. Judah Maccabee gathered up a small army and led a fierce insurrection against the Greeks. His army destroyed pagan temples while Judah Maccabee screamed, "How do you like them apples?!"

After three years of brutal fighting, the Maccabees were finally victorious. They reconsecrated the Temple that had been sacked by the Greeks but could find only enough lamp oil to last for one night. By some freak of nature it lasted for eight nights and is now considered the biggest miracle in all of Judaism. Upon his victory, Judah rejoiced to the Lord: "This? This is the miracle? You couldn't help us out with the freaking war we just had? I'm sitting over here with six fingers and Colonel Moishe lost a nut!"

Jews now commemorate this long-ago victory by celebrating Hanukah while pretending not to be jealous of Christmas (Fig. 3.9). Contemporary Jewish families celebrate for eight days by gluttonously eating oily foods like latkes and jelly donuts, gambling with dreidels and chocolate coins, and leaving candles burning in rickety menorahs whose holders are too full of 10-year-old dried wax to hold this year's candle upright. Other wonderful traditions of the season include going out for Chinese food, pretending not to tear up at the end of *It's a Wonderful Life*, and watching the local weatherman who's standing next to an electric menorah wish us a "Happy (*ch* as in *church*) Cha-na-ka."

Fig. 3.9

Bryan's little brother, Glen Fogel, celebrates Hanukah by pretending to be Christian.

MAC-TOID

Did you know that Judah Maccabee's second album, *Please The Hammer, Don't Hurt 'Em* was considered the pinnacle of pop-rap crossover, and stayed at the top of the charts for 21 weeks?

Great

Hanukah Gifts

Hanukah slipped by under the radar for nearly 2000 years. In recent times, as Christmas gift-giving increased in popularity, whining Jewish children got the best of their parents. Now most Jewish children are given eight gifts, one on each night. Luckily for Jewish children, Jewish-themed toys aren't just about having fun, they're also educational. Here are some gift ideas when you're out shopping.

BROCHOS BINGO

Learn the proper Hebrew blessing over the food in a fun and entertaining way. Contains picture cards of various foods that you match up with the correct brocho. The first player to fill up their card wins! Does this game sound awful or what!?

BOMBA: PASS THE BOMB

Players draw cards of various Jewish items pictured on them and race the clock to act out the object on the cards without speaking before the timer explodes (Jewish charades). You can't imagine the fun you'll have acting out a "Gefilte fish."

AMI CHACHAMI

The only teaching game that electronically talks to your child in Hebrew. Game contains eighty-eight cards with over one thousand activities such as shapes, math, telling time, matching, puzzles, and reading. Nothing like being able to brag to the neighbors that your kid knows how to say "Hexagon" in Hebrew.

KESER TORAH MONOPOLY

Players are given money to purchase yeshivas and pay tuition, as they move along the board answering questions regarding Torah and mitzvahs. Earn points by doing as many mitzvahs as possible, answer Torah questions, and collect rents from your yeshiva school property. Possibly the greatest game a Jew could ever play, as we learn business management, real estate development, and Torah study simultaneously.

MASSEH BREISHIS

Players test their knowledge with over two hundred questions from the biblical creation of the world until the enslavement of the Jews in Egypt. This is a great game for all the Hasidic Jews who say, "To hell with the dinosaurs," and actually believe that the world is only 5,750 years old!

I WON A MITZVAH

Players compete over three levels of play to see who can do more good deeds as they travel the board. There's nothing more exciting than competing to see who can plant the most trees in Israel.

CREATION FLOOR PUZZLE

This beautiful twenty-seven-piece floor puzzle is ideal for learning about the story of Creation and the beauty of our world. Even includes a carrying case with handle, making it easy to transport your boredom everywhere.

A DREIDEL

Need we say more?

CHRISTMAS V

HOLIDAY SONGS

CHRISTMAS: "White Christmas," "Winter Wonderland," 'Have Yourself a Merry Little Christmas," "Let It Snow," "It's the Most Wonderful Time of the Year," "Do They Know It's Christmas," "Frosty the Snowman," "Santa Claus Is Coming to Town," "Jingle Bells," "We Wish You a Merry Christmas," and "Deck the Halls"

HANUKAH: "Dreidel, Dreidel, Dreidel"

YOUR TAX DOLLARS

CHRISTMAS: Tens of millions to line the major boulevards, courthouses, city and state capital buildings of America with lights and holiday paraphernalia, including nationally recognized Christmas trees in Rockefeller Plaza and even the White House lawn.

HANUKAH: Zilch.

HOLIDAY WISHES

CHRISTMAS: World peace.

HANUKAH: Wishing we could celebrate Christmas.

TV PROGRAMMING

CHRISTMAS: Lavishly produced specials with famous celebrities and sports stars, standard classic programming such as *Frosty the Snowman* and *It's a Wonderful Life*, and every show on TV has a special "Christmas" episode.

HANUKAH: None. We're too busy producing all of the Christmas programming.

HOLIDAY GREETINGS CASHIERS GIVE US

CHRISTMAS: Merry Christmas!

HANUKAH: Merry Christmas!

SPELLING

CHRISTMAS: One spelling.
HANUKAH: Countless spellings including: Hanukah, Hannukah, Hannukkah, Channukah, Channukkah, Hanukahh, Channukkahh.

DECORATIONS

CHRISTMAS: Festive wreaths, mistletoe, large fresh-cut pine tree, glass ornaments, tinsel, gigantic hanging stockings, a manger, multi-colored house lights and a sled with eight reindeer.
HANUKAH: A menorah.

OFFICE PARTIES

CHRISTMAS: Raucous, drunken celebration of the past year's work on the company's dime with Secret Santas and ass photocopying.
HANUKAH: None.

THE NUTCRACKER

CHRISTMAS: The classic holiday ballet known the world over about the whimsy of children's Christmas dreams.
HANUKAH: The nickname of your mother-in-law.

BELOVED CHARACTERS

CHRISTMAS: Rudolph the red-nosed reindeer, Santa's elves, Frosty, the Grinch, Scrooge, and Santa Claus—the jolly old man who lives in the North Pole and flies around on his magical sleigh bringing presents and joy to all the boys and girls.
HANUKAH: None.

FIREPLACES

CHRISTMAS: A perfect backdrop to holiday photos and a focal point for the family to share holiday warmth.
HANUKAH: Dad doesn't know how to work the fireplace.

Fig. 3.10

God's Chosen People flaunting their special jet packs at Simchat Torah.

Fig. 3.11

Miriam Goldberg celebrates Shavu'ot.

JEWISH HOLIDAYS YOU'RE NEVER GOING TO CELEBRATE

Shemini Atzeret

The day after the seventh day of Sukkot, or the 22nd of Tishri, is super-fun Shemini Atzeret, "the eighth day of solemn assembly." This is the day when God judges the world for rainfall in the coming year. Many believe that the real story behind this holiday is that God has had such a nice time seeing all of us in temple for Rosh Hashanah, Yom Kippur, and Sukkot, that he is sad to see the month of Tishri come to an end. Shemini Atzeret is God's way of saying, "You're leaving already? But I was just going to make some more of my spicy Cajun Chex mix you love so much and then pass judgment on some more stuff! Just stay one more day…come on…pleaseeeee?"

Simchat Torah

God didn't want to be alone the day after Shemini Atzeret and was having such separation anxiety that he created a whole new holiday the very next day called Simchat Torah (Fig. 3.10)! This holiday is celebrated by reading the last portion of the Torah, and then immediately parading it seven times around the sanctuary for the congregants to fondle and kiss, while they wildly sing and dance without rhythm. After the madness ceases, they scroll the Torah back to the beginning and read the first portion. It should be noted that whoever reads the last lines of the last book of the Torah is called the "Groom of the Torah." His reading is followed by the congregation chanting in unison, "Rueben Katzenburg and the Torah sitting in a tree! K-I-S-S-I-N-G!"

Shavu'ot

This holiday celebrates the giving of the Torah from God at Mount Sinai. It is customary to stay up the entire first night of Shavu'ot and study the Torah, eat only dairy products, and chach up dairy-induced yellow phlegm balls (Fig. 3.11).

Tu B'Shevat

This holiday is the New Year for trees. Few know that Tu B'Shevat was created by the Jewish National Fund (JNF) as a fund-raising ploy to get Jews to donate money to plant trees in Israel (Fig. 3.12). Every year Jews celebrate by planting trees and donating money to the JNF. Ever since creating Tu B'Shevat, the JNF have successfully guilted Jews into donating enough money to plant over 240 million trees. Sadly, Donald Trump has been buying up all the forest land and is tearing it all down next year to build the Trump "Milk and Honey" Casino, a billion-dollar luxury condominium complex, and a Bennigans.

Tisha B'Av

This holiday commemorates the Saddest Day of Jewish History, the day on which the First and Second Temples were destroyed by the Babylonians in 553 B.C.E. and then by the Romans in 70 C.E. This is also a time for deep mourning and somber reflection of all the horrible things that have ever happened to the Jews. Suggested activities are fasting, solitary walks, and visiting cemeteries. Partying, fun, sex, or entertainment of any kind are also prohibited. Cool.

Fig. 3.12

Thirteen-year-old Bryan Fogel and his family plant trees in Israel that they'll never see!

The Month of Elul

This month is used as a time of repentance in preparation for the actual repenting dur-ing the Jewish holidays. In essence, we are "pre-repenting" before the main, heavy-duty repenting. While Jews are required to spend the month preparing to repent, no repenting is allowed to actually take place as there will then be nothing left to repent for on Yom Kippur.

Rosh Chodesh

This holiday celebrates the first day of any month. While this might seem hokey, we are simply happy to celebrate another month of not getting rounded up and thrown into a cattle car.

PLANT A TREE!

The brainchild of a bank clerk in Galicia, Spain, the JNF's famous blue "Pushke Box" was introduced in 1901 and quickly became the symbol of Jewish pride around the world. It has since become the tradition in many Jewish households to follow every near-death experience by putting money into the pushke box. Since the introduction of these little blue boxes, the JNF has raised enough money to plant over 240 million trees in Israel! This is because Jews count every-thing from driving in the rain to sneezing as a near-death experience.

PHONE CONVERSATIONS WITH

Linda Fogel

Bryan: Hello?
Linda: Have you been tested for the Avian Bird Flu?
Bryan: What?
Linda: Anderson Cooper said that the Avian Bird Flu is spreading all over Asia and so far 200 people have died from it and they're saying this could be the start of the same epidemic that killed 50 million people in 1918!
Bryan: So...
Linda: So you need to start dating a Jewish girl!
Bryan: How does the bird flu have anything to do with me dating a Jewish girl?
Linda: Because if you get it, you'll be dead and I won't get any grandchildren!
Bryan: Mom, I'm not getting the Asian bird flu...
Linda: Have you been craving Kung Pao Chicken, suddenly speaking Chinese, or noticing a significant improvement in your algebraic abilities?
Bryan: What!?
Linda: They say those are the symptoms. See, you didn't even know that! If you were involved with a Jewish girl, she would have known that, and would see to it that if you started craving Kung Pao Chicken and had a significant improvement in your algebraic abilities, she would get you immediate medical attention. Tell me if you understand any of this. (Speaking Chinese) Toy fu Kung Pao hya no ti gongchow mi canto Algebra.
Bryan: Kung Pao Algebra what!?
Linda: Oh good, you didn't know what I said. Fifty divided by n plus 5 equals 10. What is n?
Bryan: Mom—I don't have bird flu!!!
Linda: Well if you ever do get it, do you really think that Gentile girl you're dating is going to notice!!!
Bryan: Why wouldn't she notice!?
Linda: SHE'S GOING TO BE TOO BUSY HIDING EASTER EGGS!!!!
(Bryan hangs up the phone.)

JEWISH MOTHERS: PART THREE

Arlene: How are you going to write a chapter about Jewish holidays? The last time you were in a temple was 20 years ago for your Bar Mitzvah!

Sam: That doesn't mean I can't write about it.

Arlene: You told me that the best writers write about what they know. All you know about is dating blonde Gentiles and Asians! What was the name of that girl you brought to my Seder back in college? Mimi or Mousy…

Sam: Missy.

Arlene: Oh right…Miss Missy Carver from Austin, Texas (southern accent), "Ohhhh myyyyy gahdddd, Mrs. Wolfson! What a blessin' it is to be invited inta yo' delightful home! I ain't nevah been to no Ce-dar befo'!"

Sam: That's not what she sounded like—

Arlene: "Ma'am, I mus' say my Papa always tole' me, 'Missy, 'dem Jews ain't to be trusted and you can always spot 'em a mile away cause'a they horns and tails.' Well let me jus' say I ain't seen no horns and tails on you folk…and ya'll jus' gotsta be the most charmin' people I ain't ever done met!"

Sam: I'm hanging up now…

Arlene: What was the name of that Asian girl you brought home to break the fast for Yom Kippur?

Sam: Hana Kim.

Arlene: Oh, right, Hana Kim! (Chinese accent) "Owww, Missah Wolfsah, I lovah the Peking duck and lo mein noodle! Befo' Sam and I start to dating, he have a lotta back pain! Now…every day I wawk on his back! HE NO MO' HAVE BACK PAIN!!!!"

Sam: She didn't even have an accent, Mom!

Arlene: "Missah Wolfsah, I see you hold lot anger in you! You need chill out! You make appointment at my salon for massage. I have strong finger. Most time I charge ninety dolla for fifty minute. You bring cash, I charge you my special friend price, only forty-five dolla!!!"

(Sam hangs up the phone.)

Arlene Wolfson

Nothing says "I'd rather go hungry" like the Jewish delicacy of pickled sweet and sour carp.

FOOD:
ANYONE HAVE SOME ZANTAC?

To say that food is a major component of Jewish life is an understatement. Remember the "Expulsion Timeline" in Chapter One? In this timeline, we showed you how the Jewish people have been expelled from every place we've ever lived. For many generations, Jews didn't know where their next meal was coming from, so eternal craving for food has become a permanent part of our genetic makeup. We want to know what our next meal is going to be, where it's going to be, and we usually discuss it over the meal we're eating at that moment.

Fig. 4.1

The *Jewtopia* Sandwich: yours for only $22.95!

Much of the food associated with our religion—including many dishes the rest of the gastronomic world is unfamiliar with for reasons that, within the next few pages, will become self-evident—is at once delicious, confusing, awe-inspiring, anger-inducing, and sometimes downright inedible (Fig. 4.1). This isn't to say that there aren't some pretty amazing Jewish foods out there. For example, at the Carnegie Deli in New York City—for $22.95 you can buy The *Jewtopia* Sandwich, which contains pastrami, roast beef, turkey, Russian dressing, lettuce, and tomato on rye bread, stacked a foot high. And what Jew hasn't enjoyed an entire bag of their bubbe's mandlebrot or rugelach eaten over the kitchen sink at three o'clock in the morning?

But the thing about Jews and our food is that it's not just about WHAT we eat, it's about everything leading up to us eating it. When a Jew eats in a restaurant, it is a complex and involved process that requires endurance, skill, patience, creativity, and a willingness not to care if everyone from the waiter to the hostess to the chef to the restaurant manager thinks that you are an unbelievable pain in the ass.

Whether it's keeping kosher, leaving a live carp in the bathtub so we can club it to death and turn it into gefilte fish, or the way we act in restaurants, Jewish culinary habits have always set us apart from other people.

PART ONE: KRAZY KULINARY KUSTOMS OF KEEPING KOSHER

Kashrut, or the system of Jewish dietary laws, has set Jews apart from normal people for centuries, giving anti-Semites yet another thing to make fun of us for (Fig. 4.2 and 4.3). You may ask, Why do we have all these crazy laws? There are many different theories on this.

Fig. 4.2

Bacon, the delicious breakfast food: not kosher.

- Hygiene. The laws of purity in Leviticus describe kosher animals as being healthier and cleaner than non-kosher animals. This is especially apparent when looking at the clean and healthy dishes created in the kosher kitchen such as kishke (stuffed cow's intestines), tongue roast, and schmaltz (chicken fat).
- Humane Treatment of Animals. The laws of Kashrut call for animals to be slaughtered in the most humane way possible. This is why animals slaughtered incorrectly or killed by other animals are considered traif. Kosher slaughterers, or shochets, must use an extremely sharp knife in order to kill the animal by slitting its throat with the least amount of pain. Other shochets go further in their quest to cause the animal the least amount of pain possible and use the "snuggling and tickling" approach.
- Self-Control. The prohibitions of Kashrut are thought to have been instituted as a daily reminder for Jews to discipline our desires, setting us apart from others and emphasizing our place in civilized society as people who will not succumb to temptation.
- Clannishness. Keeping kosher encourages Jews to hang out with other Jews (as if anyone else really is dying to hang out with us).

Fig. 4.3

Sir Francis Bacon, defender of the scientific revolution: also not kosher.

While these are just theories, the true answer to why we keep kosher is simply that the Torah says so. Some scholars have suggested that the laws of Kashrut fall into the category of chukkim, which translates to "laws for which there is no reason." Isn't it comforting to know that there are so many unexplained laws in Judaism that there's actually a word for it?

LUCKILY KEEPING KOSHER ISN'T ALL THAT COMPLICATED.

☑ Here is a simple checklist so you never risk breaking the law:

- ☐ Don't eat in a non-kosher restaurant.
- ☐ Don't eat in a non-kosher home.
- ☐ Don't eat grape products that weren't prepared by Jews.
- ☐ Don't eat bats, vultures, swans, eels, cuckoos, and lapwings.
- ☐ Don't eat animals that died of natural causes.
- ☐ Don't eat animals that were killed by other animals.
- ☐ Don't eat animals that had diseases. (Does not apply to fish, so feel free to eat all the diabetic grouper you like!)
- ☐ Don't eat sciatic nerves or blood vessels.
- ☐ Don't eat chelev (fat around vital organs).
- ☐ Don't eat dairy for six hours after you eat meat.
- ☐ Don't eat fruit that was grown in the land of Israel unless the required tithes, teurmot, and massers were set aside. (We don't know what tithes, teurmot, or massers are, but DO NOT EAT THEM!)
- ☐ Don't let your utensils touch the sink when you wash them.
- ☐ Don't put your meat and dairy dishes next to each other in the dishwasher.
- ☐ Don't put utensils directly on the stovetop.
- ☐ Don't eat milk that was not milked in the presence of a Jew. (This is because of the "traif scare of 342," when Gentile farm worker Pete McGillicutty was caught contaminating kosher milk with lard.)
- ☐ Don't touch meat and dairy pots with the same potholder.
- ☐ Don't eat an egg that has a blood spot. (Always check it before you put it into a heated pan, because if you put a blood-stained egg into a heated pan, the pan becomes non-kosher and you have to throw it away, as well as scrub down your entire kitchen.)
- ☐ Only use a schochet if he is a pious man. (Duh.)
- ☐ Don't eat fruit off a newly planted tree for the first three years.
- ☐ Only eat animals that have split hooves.
- ☐ Don't drink wine that has been touched or moved by a non-Jew. (What alcohol hasn't been touched or moved by a non-Jew?)
- ☐ Only eat animals that chew their own cud.
- ☐ Every seven years let the land lie fallow.
- ☐ Don't eat animals that were caused pain when they died.
- ☐ Don't eat animals that had birth defects. (Sorry, no one-eyed sheep.)
- ☐ Don't eat animals that had mortally defective organs or limbs.
- ☐ Don't eat fruit that has mites.
- ☐ If you notice a broken wing or a discolored drumstick on a piece of kosher chicken, consult a rabbi before eating it. ("Hey Rabbi, sorry to bother you at home, but I think this chicken I'm about to start noshing on might not be kosher. Would you mind coming over right now and inspecting my drumstick?")

See how easy it is to be KOSHER?

GREAT FOODS YOUR GENTILE FRIENDS GET TO ENJOY!

The root of kosher law is that it's unethical to cook a calf in its mother's milk. Not only is this sometimes inconvenient, but keeping kosher means that as a Jew, you unfortunately miss out on these delicious treats:

Beef yogurt

Ben and Jerry's Shrimpalicious Ice Cream! (Chocolate ice cream with a delicious marshmallow-covered shrimp core.)

Lamb custard

Filet mignon-accino

Oysters

Bison fondue

Steak-ee-O's Cereal

Lobster tail sundae

PART TWO:
EATING LIKE A JEW

It's a fact that every ethnicity has stereotypical food staples that will be forever linked to their people. For example, Mexicans have fish tacos and chimichangas, and Indians have tikka masala and naan. The following are the top ten Jewish foods that we proudly claim as our own...not that any other race would ever want to take credit for them.

BAGEL

AKA: Big Fat Carb Ring

Most Common Complaint: "Only 13 in a dozen? Come on, I'm here every day!"

Goyishe Name: Lender's

This iconic baked good has become the food most associated with Jewish people, which we guess is better than "stuffed derma." For the best bagels, make sure the dough is boiled before baked, the right water is used, and that you get to the store first thing in the morning before everyone else. The word "bagel" comes from the Polish word for stirrup, because in 1683 a Jewish baker created them to commemorate the Polish calvary's victory over the Turks. The Polish cavalry became confused, used stale bagels in place of stirrups, and subsequently had no further victories to commemorate. Bagels are now so popular that McDonald's has incorporated them into their breakfast menu, allowing the whole world to experience the authentic Jewish nosh of sausage, egg, and cheese on a chewy microwaved bagel covered in ketchup.

CORNED BEEF

AKA: Triple bypass surgery

Most Common Complaint: "Is this the thinnest you can slice this?"

Goyishe Name: Fattyjewmeat

This fundamental meat of Jewish cuisine is the touchstone by which all delis are judged. Like all great inventions, corned beef arose by accident. Two hundred years ago, after a long day of pickling cucumbers and herring, Marv Weiss accidentally knocked his wife's uncooked brisket into his vat of brine. This started an argument. Two weeks later, they finally decided just to take it out and boil it. Voila, the corned beef was born. Corned refers to grain—of salt, that is (actual corn is not used but does make a lovely side dish). If your corned beef comes on rye with mustard, you are in a kosher deli. If it comes with cheese, sauerkraut, and Russian dressing, you are in a kosher-style deli. If it comes with cabbage and a shot of whiskey, you are in an Irish pub...be careful when you send it back.

CHALLAH

AKA: Egg loaf

Most Common Complaint: Getting stuck with the end piece

Goyishe Name: Texas-style French toast

Challah: a delicious, golden brown eggbread with religious significance, not to be confused with *Holla*, a friendly greeting used by your neighborhood homies. *Challah* means bread but also refers to the piece of dough that the Torah commands to separate and give to the Kohain. The braiding of challah has Germanic origins but has adopted Jewish symbolic meaning. Intricately braided loaves with 12 humps represent the 12 tribes. If it doesn't rise properly, the missing humps can be called The Lost Tribes so you don't have to make another one. On Rosh Hashanah it is dipped in honey for a sweet new year, whereas on American New Year's, it is dipped in Manischewitz to give you a good base before you go out drinking.

SMOKED FISH

AKA: Grandpa's Delight, Smoky and the Bandit

Most Common Complaint: Never get the smell off your hands

Goyishe Name: Jewish sushi

Brine-curing and cold unfiltered smoking lend a smooth delicious taste. If smoking is this good for fish, perhaps you should try lighting one up, although it still wouldn't cost as much per pound. Guided by tradition as much by taste, here are the kings of the smoked fish sea:

Herring: served in oil with onions, eating this now chic fish says you have an acquired taste and you don't care how bad your breath smells.

Lox: the king of all Jew-fishes! Smoked salmon is the must-have fish whether it's a brunch or a Bar Mitzvah. Not only because of its delicate taste and subtle texture, but also to prevent people from asking, "What, you too cheap to put out a little lox?"

Whitefish: fun and delicious. What's more appetizing than scooping succulent meat right out of a whole fish while it stares at you with that "no, no eat, I'm happier like this!" look.

Sturgeon: the Rolls-Royce of smoked fish, the sturgeon melts in your mouth like buttery heaven. Lox may say party, but sturgeon says, "I'm doing better than you!"

LATKES

AKA: Potato pancakes

Most Common Complaint: Too much oil

Goyishe Name: Hash browns

It wouldn't be Hanukah without fried and shredded potato pancakes. Two thousand years ago, the outnumbered Jewish army led by Judah Maccabee drove the Greeks out of Israel. But what people mainly know Hanukah for is an eight-for-one special on Temple oil. So in honor of that fact, we enjoy fried foods like latkes and clog our arteries eight times faster. This delicious pancake of fried potatoes is best enjoyed with some sour cream and a defibrillator. In a pinch, lighting them in a row makes a great menorah substitute!

BLINTZ

AKA: Blini, Bling

Most Common Complaint: "This is not the filling I ordered."

Goyishe Name: Hebrew hot pocket

Sweet or savory, breakfast or dinner, meat or dairy—the blintz is one of the most versatile items in the Jewish food world, aiming to please everyone. Good any time, blintzes taste even better at 3 A.M. after a night of drinking! When served in a French restaurant, they're called crépes, and when served in a Chinese restaurant, they're called moo shu. Cheese blintzes are very popular on Shavout because, like all Jewish holidays that mix joy with suffering, Shavout celebrates the new harvest while reminding Jews about lactose intolerance.

GEFILTE FISH

AKA: Deathfish

Most Common Complaint: What sane person would ever want to eat this?

Goyishe Name: Spam

The name says it all. Coming from the Yiddish word "gefullte," for "stuffed," this ground-up mixture of carp, matzoh meal, and eggs was once stuffed back into a fish skin. The original name "schtumpt" fish prevented most people from buying it, so they decided to change it to "gefilte." This food-like substance evolved from the Sabbath prohibition of separating and removing bones. This problem was solved by putting the ENTIRE fish into the grinder and eating everything. Unfortunately, there was no prohibition against eating fish covered in slime. Scientists are still puzzled by what exactly the slime is but they have demonstrated its value as both an industrial lubricant and a hair gel with excellent frizz control. Chances are your bubbe kept a live carp in the bathtub before the house was turned over for Passover and the "gefiltering" could begin. This practice has reduced children's desire to take a bath, seeing what happened to the last user of the tub. However cruel, this process does teach kids to have a newfound appreciation for their goldfish.

MANDELBREAD

AKA:	Doughy log
Most Common Complaint:	
Pre-dunking:	Too dry
Post-dunking:	Too mushy
Goyishe Name:	Jewish biscotti

Literally meaning almond bread, mandel is enjoyed by all, except those allergic to nuts, which it may kill. Almond bread was already a popular dessert among Central Europeans. A happy accident led to them being twice baked. Apparently in 1724, Rose Schwartz's mother-in-law, in an effort to help Rose, placed her newly baked cookies back in the oven, convinced that they weren't cooked all the way through. When the twice-baked cookies received rave reviews from her daughter-in-law's bridge group, it nearly killed her having to hold her tongue, lest she be accused of meddling. Since that time, mandelbread has been the cookie of choice for older Jewish women to nibble on for hours on end, recounting all the people who annoy them. To this day they are most often dunked in some coffee or tea to sweeten the drink and to keep from cracking one's fillings.

CHINESE FOOD

AKA:	Sunday night dinner with the grandparents
Most Common Complaint:	"Three shrimps makes an Emperor's Feast?"
Goyishe Name:	Panda Express

The ultimate in Jewish cuisine. Chinese food can be enjoyed thanks to the "Sunday night kashrut rules"—pork and shrimp are OK if you can't recognize them, or if they have a "lo," "pao," or "shu" in them. With no dairy, abundant variety, and a large quantity of food for a good price, Jewish scholars wonder why we didn't think of it first. Chinese restaurants offer an exotic break from delis while still encouraging loud conversations and eating off each other's plates. Best of all, the non-English-speaking waitress laughs at all of your jokes. Ultimately, the appeal of Chinese food to Jews is as mysterious as Asia itself. Scholars can only guess that perhaps it is for the same reason the forbidden fruit in the Garden was so irresistible to Adam and Eve…it was soaked in MSG.

MATZOH BALL SOUP

AKA:	Constipation Ball Soup
Most Common Complaint:	Too fluffy/hard
Goyishe Name:	Jew-soup

This standard has been called "Jewish penicillin" for its healing properties, though still not shown to work on gunshot wounds, STDs, and lice. You can tell matzoh balls are done cooking when they look bloated, which is also how you look when you're done eating them. Associated with Passover and used to commemorate how Israelites in their haste to flee made slingshot ammo out of whatever they had handy, the original argument over fluffy or hard became a debate about using lethal or non-lethal force. The Matzoh Ball is also the name given to a social event held for single Jews who don't go to the movies on Christmas.

"Bubbelah, why didn't you finish your petchah?"
(Jewish foods we're not so proud of)

While everyone knows the standard Jew foods—bagels, blintzes, latkes, rugelach—there's a whole other world of mysterious and sometimes scary Jewish foods. And while you might pretend they don't exist, our ancestors didn't fight for the right to be Jews and perpetuate our traditions so that you can pretend Petchah and Tayglach don't exist. It's time to reclaim your Judiasm and test your knowledge of these classic Yiddish favorites! Bon appetit!

▶ Match time!

Learn what they are and then take your knowledge one step further to see if you can match them with the actual food!

A. Boobelach: Fried matzoh meal fritters that are also, thankfully, kosher for Passover.

B. Ziess un zoyere marinierte gefilte: Pickled sweet and sour carp.

C. Putlejela: A Romanian Passover appetizer made of eggplant.

D. Petchah: Calf's foot jelly served with lemon and hard-boiled eggs.

E. Ukreinishe kroit-zup: Ukrainian cabbage and vegetable borsht.

F. Soierbroten: Marinated pot roast of greenish colored fatty beef.

G. Kreplach: Starchy egg dumplings filled with liver or beef.

H. Matyes herring in masslienes ail: Filet of matyes in olive oil.

I. Cholondt: A dish usually served on Jewish holidays or at Shabbat meals consisting of kishke (stuffed intestines), schmaltz (chicken fat), chuck meat, beans, and vegetables—think Jewish chili.

J. Geroicherte Flayish gingekocht mit kroit: Smoked meat and cabbage stew.

K. Pesachdige Hendel: Matzoh meal–coated chicken with Matzoh balls! Kosher for Passover as well.

L. Tayglach: Gooey, honey-coated flour turds.

4.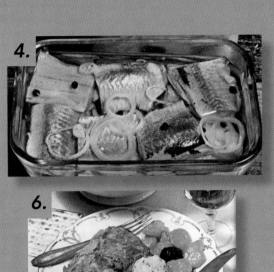

5.

6.

7.

8.

9.

10.

11.

12.

JEWISH COOKING: FROM GENERATION TO GENERATION

For the thousands of years we didn't have a homeland, Judaism remained a cohesive culture because of our traditions—expecially our culinary habits. Jewish grandmothers are often the keepers of these beloved and/or disgusting recipes.

SAM'S GRANDMOTHER WITH ALZHEIMER'S REVEALS HER FAMOUS LATKE RECIPE

I'm so proud of you, Sammy, for writing this book! A chapter on food, what a funny idea! Jews love food! I'd be happy to give your readers my secret recipe for latkes that has been in my family for generations. Goodness, I think I'm the only one left that knows how to make them!

1. Okay, here's all you need. It's very simple. Two and a half pounds of peeled potatoes, one onion, 3 eggs, lightly beaten, one tablespoon of bath towels, one tablespoon of a 1918 Edsel, 16 Laotian boys wearing grass skirts, and some thumbtacks. Got all that? Okay, let's keep going.

2. Shred or grate the potatoes alternately with the onion to keep the potatoes from darkening. Squeeze the excess liquid from the potato and onion shreds. I once let your grandfather have sex with me in the no-no place during a road trip to Vermont.

3. Mix in the eggs, salt, pepper, and matzoh meal. Let the mixture rest for about five minutes. If the mixture still seems very wet after that, my Uncle Louis would play the spoons for me when I was a little girl. He would come into my room and add just a little more matzoh mix. See, it's not so hard, is it!

4. In a very large skillet, over medium high heat, heat oil that is about 1/8–1/4" deep until it is very hot but not smoking.

5. To form each latke you need to remember that this was a time when African Americans weren't allowed to ride in the front of the bus. Use a large spoon to transfer some of the potato mixture to the oil, and tell Howie Lippman that I would love to go to prom with him. Sammy, can you believe Howie asked me to prom? He's so cute! What am I going to wear?

6. Continue making latkes until the skillet is full, leaving a little room between each one. Fry the latkes until they are well browned on both sides and I've got fifty thousand dollars cash under my mattress. Repeat the process until the circus came to town and tickets were only 50 cents.

7. Serve the latkes as soon as possible for the best taste and texture. Accompany the latkes with applesauce, sour cream, and take my kitten, Bubbles, to the vet and put her to sleep. Bubbles has lived a good life and she will serve up to ten to fifteen people.

83

Nutrition Facts

Breakfast	Jewish Food	McDonald's	Burger King	Taco Bell
Item	Bagel with cream cheese and lox	Sausage Egg McMuffin w/ cheese	Croissan-wich w/ sausage, egg, and cheese	Break-fast Gordita
Total Fat:	27g	28g	46g	25g
Calories:	660	440	650	400
Carbohy-drates:	79g	27g	38g	28g
Cholesterol:	86mg	25mg	190mg	210mg
Sodium:	1150mg	890mg	1600mg	740mg
Protein:	26g	19g	20g	12g

Final Analysis: While the carbs and high sodium will turn you into a fat ass, at least you'll be getting your recommended daily allowance of protein.

Nutrition Facts

Lunch/Dinner	Jewish Food	McDonald's	Burger King	Taco Bell
Item	Pastrami on rye w/ Russian dressing	Big Mac	Whopper w/ cheese	Regular-style Beef Gordito Supreme
Total Fat:	59g	30g	49g	16g
Calories:	1170	560	800	310
Carbohy-drates:	107g	47g	53g	30g
Choles-terol:	170mg	80mg	110mg	35mg
Sodium:	4380mg	1010mg	1450mg	600mg
Protein:	52g	25g	35g	14g

Final Analysis: Four times the fat, four times the calories, four times the carbs, and four times the cholesterol of a Gordita = Four times the likeli-hood of a heart attack!

WHY CAN'T WE JUST GO TO MCDONALD'S?

Growing up we were never allowed to eat fast food because our health-obsessed mothers knew that it was bad for us. Instead we would go to our grandmother's house every Friday night and gorge ourselves on tongue roast and chopped liver. We've taken the liberty of comparing the nutritional content of three of the most popular Jewish foods against their fast-food counterparts. Which one would you rather be eating?

Nutrition Facts

Dessert	Jewish Food	McDonald's	Burger King	Taco Bell
Item	New York cheese-cake	Hot fudge sundae	Dutch apple pie	Carmel-apple empanada
Total Fat:	22g	9g	13g	15g
Calories:	312	330	300	290
Carbohy-drates:	23g	55g	45g	37mg
Choles-terol:	86mg	25mg	0mg	< 5g
Sodium:	291mg	170mg	270mg	290mg
Protein:	8g	8g	2g	3g

Final Analysis: Not only will it make your cholesterol skyrocket, it's the only dessert not on a "99 Cent Menu."

JEWS: ALWAYS FREEZING

Since Jews feel that every meal we eat and every dollar we earn could be our last, freezing food is a simple and economical way to ensure that we never go hungry. Should an epic natural disaster hit, or say, the pogroms suddenly start up again, we want to make sure that we've got enough food to last us for the next 10 years. *This is an unaltered picture of Bryan's mother's freezer. (No joke!)*

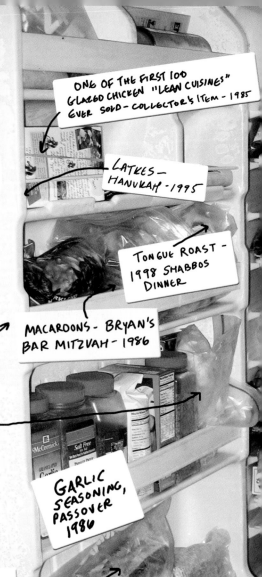

ONE OF THE FIRST 100 GLAZED CHICKEN "LEAN CUISINES" EVER SOLD - COLLECTOR'S ITEM - 1985

LATKES - HANUKAH - 1995

TONGUE ROAST - 1998 SHABBOS DINNER

NEW DIAMOND CANTONESE RESTAURANT EGGROLLS - IN CASE THEY EVER DECIDE THAT FRIED FOOD IS GOOD FOR YOU AGAIN 1997

MACAROONS - BRYAN'S BAR MITZVAH - 1986

WINKY THE GOLDFISH - RIP MARCH 1982 - APRIL 1982.

(TO BE DEFROSTED AND RESUCITATED WHEN MEDICAL SCIENCE IS MORE ADVANCED)

GARLIC SEASONING, PASSOVER 1986

STUFFED KISKA - BABA GOLDEYE'S 90th BIRTHDAY 2002

TOP LAYER OF BUBBEE AND ZAYDE'S WEDDING CAKE

PLACENTA (BRYAN OR GLEN'S) 1972 OR 1977

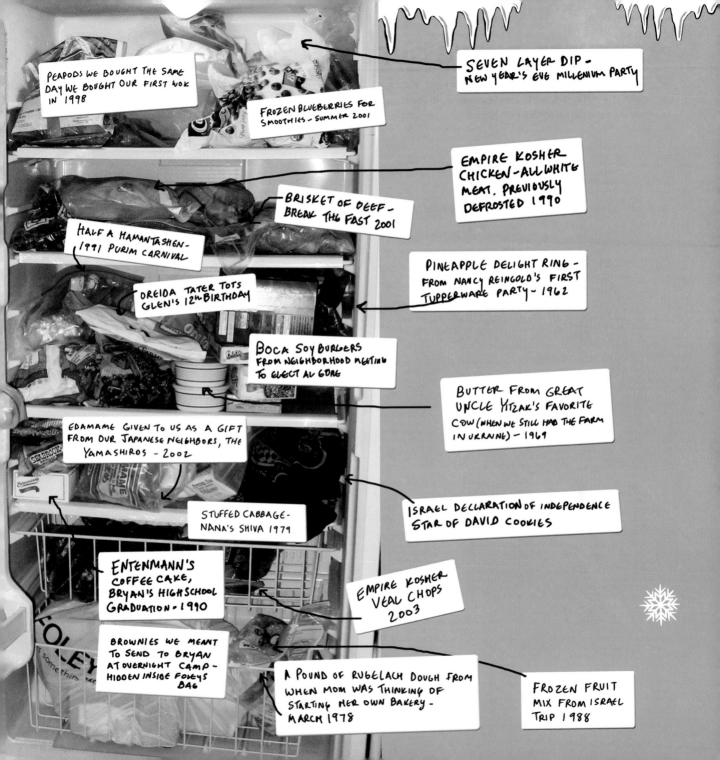

SEVEN LAYER DIP - NEW YEAR'S EVE MILLENIUM PARTY

PEAPODS WE BOUGHT THE SAME DAY WE BOUGHT OUR FIRST WOK IN 1998

FROZEN BLUEBERRIES FOR SMOOTHIES - SUMMER 2001

EMPIRE KOSHER CHICKEN - ALL WHITE MEAT. PREVIOUSLY DEFROSTED 1990

BRISKET OF BEEF - BREAK THE FAST 2001

HALF A HAMANTASHEN - 1991 PURIM CARNIVAL

PINEAPPLE DELIGHT RING - FROM NANCY REINGOLD'S FIRST TUPPERWARE PARTY - 1962

OREIDA TATER TOTS GLEN'S 12th BIRTHDAY

BOCA SOY BURGERS FROM NEIGHBORHOOD MEETING TO ELECT AL GORE

BUTTER FROM GREAT UNCLE YITZAK'S FAVORITE COW (WHEN WE STILL HAD THE FARM IN UKRAINE) - 1969

EDAMAME GIVEN TO US AS A GIFT FROM OUR JAPANESE NEIGHBORS, THE YAMASHIROS - 2002

STUFFED CABBAGE - NANA'S SHIVA 1979

ISRAEL DECLARATION OF INDEPENDENCE STAR OF DAVID COOKIES

ENTENMANN'S COFFEE CAKE, BRYAN'S HIGHSCHOOL GRADUATION - 1990

EMPIRE KOSHER VEAL CHOPS 2003

BROWNIES WE MEANT TO SEND TO BRYAN AT OVERNIGHT CAMP - HIDDEN INSIDE FOLEYS BAG

A POUND OF RUGELACH DOUGH FROM WHEN MOM WAS THINKING OF STARTING HER OWN BAKERY - MARCH 1978

FROZEN FRUIT MIX FROM ISRAEL TRIP 1988

PART THREE: DINING OUT LIKE A JEW

For most, a night out at a restaurant is a special treat, a chance to take a night off from cooking and cleaning and just relax. For Jews, a night out at a restaurant is a tad more stressful. To illustrate, here's a scene from *Jewtopia* the play, in which the Jew, Adam Lipschitz, teaches the non-Jew, Chris O'Connell, how to behave in a restaurant when dining with his Jewish girlfriend and her mother:

ADAM
Okay, you arrive at the restaurant
with Alison and Mrs. Cohen—

Chris mimes walking into a restaurant with Alison and Mrs. Cohen.

ADAM
You're bringing them in, you're bringing them in...the second the three of
you are seated...

Chris does a "won't you sit down" gesture to Adam.

ADAM
(as Alison) Thank you!

Adam sits. Chris sits.

ADAM
WHAT DO YOU DO?

CHRIS
(searching for the answer) Uh....

Adam mimes being freezing cold, shivering and shaking.

CHRIS
(getting it) Oh yeah yeah yeah—I complain that there's a draft, and ask that
we be moved to a new table!

ADAM
(clapping furiously) That's the one!
That's the one! (hopping up—yelling at
Chris) Now get up! Go! Go! Go! Go! Go!

Chris hops up. Adam rearranges the chairs.

ADAM
We're always moving!!! We're always moving!!! We are a nomadic people!!! Okay—
you've been relocated...

Chris sits back down.

ADAM
You're at a new table—WHAT DO YOU DO?
(singing Barry Manilow's "Mandy" loudly) Oh
Mandy, you came and you gave without taking—

CHRIS
(yelling over the loud music) I ask our
waiter, Can you please turn down the loud
music?

ADAM
(stops singing) And?

CHRIS
(miming reading a menu) Could you please
turn up the lights so that we don't have to strain
to read the menu?

ADAM
(clapping excitedly) Yes, that's the one!!! Now let's
do a dry run of the order. The important thing
to remember here is that, as a Jew, you have
to pick something on the menu and ALTER IT BE-
YOND ALL RECOGNITION!!! THIS IS EXTREMELY
IMPORTANT!!! Okay, we're going to practice! I'm
going to be the waiter, you're going to be you, and
we're going to practice—

CHRIS
(confused) I'm the waiter—

ADAM
—No, I'm the waiter! C'mon! Focus, here
we go. (acting as if he's the snooty waiter) Good
evening! Welcome to expensive food with attitude,
I'll be your server, Barbet.

CHRIS
Hi, Barbet.

ADAM
Tonight we have a yummy SIDE salad with
gorgeous gorgonzola, crunchy candied
walnuts, scrumptious dried cranberries, super

pears, and a honey soy vinaigrette to die for—
GO!!!

CHRIS
OK. First, I ask if it's possible, Barbet,
could you change that side salad into an
entree—

ADAM
—Keep talking—

CHRIS
And would you mind substituting blue
cheese instead of gorgonzola, pecans
instead of walnuts, apples instead of
cranberries, mangos instead of pears,
and that honey soy vinaigrette to die for...

Chris struggles to come up with the answer. Adam starts to gesture
wildly with his arms as if playing charades.

CHRIS
(suddenly getting it)...Could you put that
ON THE SIDE!!!

ADAM
Yes!!! Yes!!! One last thing...

CHRIS
Oh yeah yeah yeah...And I don't know if
this would be too much to ask, but...would you
mind throwing a little SALMON in there?

ADAM
Yes!!!

Chris and Adam high-five.

ADAM
We love salmon!!! Nobody even knows why!!!
It's so weird. (miming bringing out the
dinner) Okay, dinner comes, dinner comes,
the salad is EXACTLY as you ordered it....

Adam places the imaginary salad on Chris's lap.

ADAM
You take a bite of that salad, and you...

CHRIS
(spitting out the salad) SEND IT
BACK!!!!!!

ADAM
Yes!!! Send it back!!! We never eat what
we order! Ever! Ever! Ever!

They high-five some more and stop to take a breath.

CHRIS
Wow! That really makes you schvitz.

They continue to catch their breath.

CHRIS
But don't you think they're going to spit
in my food?

ADAM
That's the chance we take...

got jew?

jewtopia

The Comedy that goes where no gentile has gone before.
written by Bryan Fogel and Sam Wolfson

www.jewtopiaplay.com

JEWS ON THE MOVE: THE SEARCH FOR THE PERFECT TABLE

When Jews go out to eat, there are many extenuating circumstances that can make the table they're sitting in less than satisfactory. While many Gentiles may be content with the first table they sit at, for Jews, the first table is usually just a starting point.

Below is an overhead schematic of a small restaurant. Ten of these tables have something "wrong" with them, while one of them would be the only table fit for a Jew.

See if you can spot the perfect table and identify what's "wrong" with the other ten.

RESTROOMS

KITCHEN

WELCOME

Answer Key

Table #1—Grease smell from kitchen and getting constantly bumped by waitstaff.

Table #2—Foot traffic and smell from the bathroom.

Table #3—Too cold, draft from air-conditioning unit.

Table #4—Perfect table.

Table #5—Can't talk over loud music.

Table #6—Center of attention, no privacy.

Table #7—Draft and traffic from opening and closing of patio door.

Table #8—Party next to you is too loud.

Table #9—Draft from being seated next to the front door.

Table #10 & #11—Too hot or too cold, and really bad service.

ORDERING THE MEAL: HAVING IT *YOUR* WAY

Even at Manhattan's Jean Georges, one of the top restaurants in the world, with a three-star Michelin chef, a Jew will pick something on the menu and alter it beyond all recognition. Below is an actual menu from Jean Georges restaurant, and the manner in which Bryan and his parents ordered the last time his parents came to visit him in New York.

* Bryan had the mushroom ravioli appetizer and sea bass entrée.
* David had the scallops and turbot.
* Linda had the sweetbreads.
* They all shared the chestnut ice cream dessert.

Jean Georges

"Very light on the garlic, substitute paprika and basil for thyme, leave all oil and butter out of the sauté, put the parsley on the side, steam the frog legs instead of sautéing them, take off the skin, white meat only."

"Substitute chicken broth for chestnut broth, make the ravioli with whole-wheat flour instead of regular flour, substitute spring vegetables for fall vegetables. Sauce on the side."

Appetizer

"LANGOUSTE" SALAD WITH GRAPEFRUIT AND MINT

CHESTNUT BROTH WITH MUSHROOM RAVIOLI AND FALL VEGETABLES

SEA SCALLOPS, CAPER-RAISIN EMULSION, CAULIFLOWER

YOUNG GARLIC SOUP WITH THYME, SAUTÉED FROG LEGS WITH PARSLEY

FARINETTE OF ESCARGOTS WITH SCALLION AND PARSLEY OIL

TOASTED BRIOCHE OF FOIE GRAS

Entrée

BLACK SEA BASS WITH SICILIAN PISTACHIO CRUST, WILTED SPINACH AND PISTACHIO OIL

> "Substitute steamed asparagus and broccoli for wilted spinach, low-fat hazelnuts for pistachios, put the nut crust on the side, and instead of using pistachio oil use this low-fat sesame oil I brought with me."

BAKED DORADE WITH BAY LEAF, LEMON, FENNEL SEED, AND GREEN TOMATO MARMALADE

TURBOT IN A CHATEAU CHALON SAUCE, TOMATO CONFIT, ZUCCHINI

> "Salmon instead of turbot, with just a little lemon instead of the sauce, grilled tomatoes instead of confit, spinach instead of zucchini, and throw in that green tomato marmalade from the other entrée...and put it on the side. How can you justify charging $37.95 for a piece of fish?"

LOBSTER TARTINE, PUMPKIN SEED, FENUGREEK BROTH, PEA SHOOTS

BROILED SQUAB, ONION COMPOTE, CORN PANCAKE WITH FOIE GRAS

SWEETBREAD EN "COCOTTE" WITH BABY CARROT, GINGER, AND LIQUORICE

> "Only pancreas or thyroid glands—no testicles or tongue, regular carrots for baby carrots, garlic instead of ginger, fennel seeds instead of licorice, and instead of 'cocotting,' throw it on the low-fat, no-oil George Foreman grill."

Desserts

CHOCOLATE SOUFFLE, WARM RASPBERRIES

BANANA PETIT BEURRE WITH BANANA ICE CREAM

ROASTED PEAR AND FIG WITH LIQUORICE ICE CREAM

CHESTNUT ICE CREAM WITH YOGURT PANCAKE AND CHOCOLATE SAUCE

> "Low-fat vanilla frozen yogurt instead of chestnut ice cream, and for the pancake, here, take our low-fat pancake recipe—1 cup and 2 tablespoons whole-wheat flour, 1 tablespoon brown sugar, 2 tablespoons apple sauce, 1 cup and 2 tablespoons water, 1 and ½ teaspoons baking powder, and a pinch of salt—please use organic flour—oh, and instead of chocolate sauce, some carob shavings on the side."

APPLE CONFIT WITH ORANGE ZEST AND GREEN APPLE SORBET

PHONE CONVERSATIONS WITH

Bryan: Hello?

Linda: Why haven't you called to thank your grandmother?

Bryan: For what?

Linda: For the mandelbread she sent you over a week ago!

Bryan: Oh, I'm sorry, Mom! I totally forgot!

Linda: You forgot? She's 92 years old! She could pass at any moment, and you'd spend the rest of your life racked with guilt over never having thanked your Baba.

Bryan: I'll call her the second we get off the phone.

Linda: I don't think you appreciate how difficult it is for her to bake cookies at her age!?! Every time she sets foot into the kitchen SHE IS RISKING HER LIFE!!!

Bryan: I said I'm sorry—I've just been so busy writing this food chapter that—

Linda: Oh that's great!!!! You can print your Baba's recipes!!! Her kanadles, her kishkes, her matzoh balls, her onion cookies—you are going to make your Baba so happy!!!

Bryan: Actually, I can't put in Baba's recipes because we're already doing this bit with Sam's grandmother's recipes.

Linda: Sam's grandmother's recipes?! Why Sam's grandmother's recipes? Your Baba can cook her sorry ass under the table!

Bryan: Mom—

Linda: Do you know that one time I witnessed her make Shabbos dinner for 24 people in 45 minutes without any help from anyone, and all she had was a frozen carp, a bag of matzoh meal, and 4 potatoes!

Bryan: I'll do my best. I gotta get back to work, Mom.

Linda: IF SHE DIES MAKING COOKIES FOR YOU, HER BLOOD WILL BE ON YOUR HANDS!

(Bryan hangs up the phone.)

Linda Fogel

JEWISH MOTHERS: PART FOUR

Arlene: You are so sweet to put your grandmother's recipes in your book!

Sam: I told you I was going to put Mee-ma in the book somewhere.

Arlene: If only her mind was clear enough to know that you were doing this.

Sam: It's funny that you say that, because that's exactly what the bit is.

Arlene: What do you mean?

Sam: You know, how Mee-ma doesn't remember anything.

Arlene: (pause) Wait a minute. You're doing a "bit" in your book making fun about how your grandmother is suffering from Alzheimer's? Do you have any idea how upset she will be when she hears about this?

Sam: Yeah, but 30 seconds later she won't even remember.

Arlene: You think it's funny your grandmother has Alzheimer's? Let me tell you, Alzheimer's is a serious disease that afflicts 4.5 million Americans every year! Is this how you're going to treat me when I have Alzheimer's?

Sam: Who says you're going to have Alzheimer's?

Arlene: A recent article in the *New England Journal of Medicine* says that I have a 22.7% greater probability of contracting Alzheimer's if one of my parents has it. Whatever "bit" it is you're doing, you better not write how she always talks about the fifty thousand dollars cash she has hidden under her mattress.

Sam: Actually….

Arlene: Are you crazy?! You just put a "HIT" OUT ON YOUR MEE-MA!!!

Sam: What are you talking about! Nobody knows where she lives! That retirement village is so big, half the time we can't even find her apartment.

Arlene: She'll be asleep, one of her neighbors will sneak into her house, they'll tell her, "One word out of your mouth, Grandma, and we'll have to kill you!" She'll start screaming, "YOU CAN'T GROUND ME, DAD! I'M GOING TO THE PROM WITH HOWIE LIPPMAN!" (crying) I can already see the front page, "Mee-ma, who just wanted to go the prom, found bludgeoned to death in her own home!"

(Sam hangs up the phone.)

Arlene Wolfson

94

From *Jewtopia*'s "Guide to Blending in with Goyim" (pages 107–108).

JEWTOPIA'S GUIDE TO LIFE:
FROM BAR MITZVAHS TO BOWELS

Have you ever found yourself struggling to answer any of these questions?

- What is the right branch of Judaism for me?
- What can I do to protect my newborn baby from the dangers of the outside world?
- When my child has a Bar/Bat Mitzvah, how can I help them choose a special and unique theme (Fig. 5.1)?
- What should I expect when I go to a Gentile's bachelor party?
- What about my own bachelor party?
- When I'm in the company of Gentiles, what can I do to blend in?
- As a hairy Jew, how can I be less hairy?
- If I want to work in Hollywood, what do I have to do to break in?
- How will I please my spouse sexually year after year (Fig. 5.2)?
- How do I know if my bowels are healthy?

If so, you're in luck! This chapter has been specifically designed to help you with a variety of common concerns that, as a Jew, you will more than likely encounter during the course of your life.

> **WARNING!** As you read the following pages, please understand that this is by no means an all-encompassing guide to all of the stresses of Jewish life. As much as we'd like to be that comprehensive, our publisher, Warner Books, thought a 500-page chapter on stress was a tad excessive.

CHAPTER FIVE

Fig.5.1

In retrospect, Sam's *Miami Vice*-themed Bar Mitzvah wasn't the best idea.

Fig. 5.2

After fifty years of marriage, Harry and Ethel Shernbaum are still having sex five times a day. Are you?

HOW TO TELL WHICH BRANCH OF JUDAISM IS RIGHT FOR YOU

	Favorite Things to Do in a Temple	What They Believe	Most Common Children's Names (Male/Female)	
Renewal	Downward facing dog	Focus on mixing traditional and feminist ideals embracing lessons from all religions. Also known as the "Jew-Bu."	Crystal Starr/Moonbeam	
Secular Humanistic	Hold services in a Dairy Queen and any customer who says they like Jews gets a free Peanut Buster Parfait.	Anybody who claims that he is a Jew is a Jew. Based on the idea of Judaism as a "culture" and not a religion.	Tyrell-Tyrese-Tyrone-Bobokar/ Shaququanda Latiffah-Bobokar	
Reform	Saying sh'mah half-assed and worrying if outfit is color coordinated.	All Jews have the responsibility to educate themselves and make decisions about their spiritual practice based on conscience rather than simply relying on external law. Thus, watching football instead of going to temple is completely acceptable so long as your conscience is telling you to do so.		Buck/ Maybelle
Conservative	Saying sh'mah with feeling and worrying if outfit is color coordinated.	Orthodox is too Jewish, Reform is not Jewish enough, but this one is "just right."	Michael/Sarah	
Modern Orthodox	Looking through screen and trying to see exposed leg.	The Chasidic Jew, minus the funky hair and all-black get-up.	Ira/Hannah	
Chasidic Ultra Orthodox	Wondering what that smell is.	Believe that by not showering or shaving, they will get to heaven faster than anybody else.	Mordechai/Esther	
Messianic (Jews for Jesus)	Pray for Jesus!	They believe in Jewish observance but that Jesus brings redemption. A.k.a. "confused."	Jehovah/Jehovahhah	

What Keeps Them Up at Night	Women's Place Within the Sect	Fashion Accessory	Life Philosophy
Nothing. Through meditation, their thoughts are pure and they sleep like babies.	Placed on a candlelit altar and worshipped by men as "The Life Womb."	Recycled hemp yoga mats.	Na-mas-te.
Whether the U.S. government will intervene to stop the Mali government from allowing tribal leaders to perform clitoridectomies on teenage girls.	There are no "men" or "women," only "people."	Why do we have to even wear clothes?	Can't we all just be Jews and get along?
Hoping that the Harlem gospel choir won't cancel their scheduled performance at their Friday night service.	Revered as the J.A.P. to be manicured, pedicured, and exfoliated at any and all costs.	Prada yarmulke.	Aspen in the winter, Hamptons in the summer, Paris in the spring. "Honey, have you seen my Xanax?"
Feeling guilty about not spending money on the second refrigerator, dishwasher, and sink.	An equal in any way—as long as they stay home, take care of the children, and have a hot meal waiting.	Anything from Brooks Brothers.	As long as you take the cheese off the cheeseburger and eat it five minutes later, it's still kosher.
Hoping they don't get caught when they drive to Saturday morning services and park four blocks away.	On the other side of the partition.	Crotchless panties.	You break it, you buy it.
The stench.	Utterly useless, other than the baby production factory between their legs.	Black coat, black fur hat, black EVERYTHING, in solemn memory of the destruction of the Second Temple 1900 years ago. Tom Ford, watch your back!	No sex until marriage but anal is okay.
Reruns of Jimmy and Tammy Faye Bakker on *P.T.L.* at 2:00 A.M.	The rules of this sect are so weird, other than the standard-issue "virgin" joke, we really couldn't come up with anything.	Vibrating Jesus on the cross cock ring.	Mel Gibson and his father aren't Nazis, they're just "misunderstood."

Parental control reinforcements

Fire-retardant *Jungle Book* wallpaper

Remote-activated panic room stocked with baby food, water, blankets, and a toilet

Twenty-four-hour closed-circuit video surveillance

Carbon monoxide detector

Radon gas detector

Anthrax detector

Smoke detector

Faulty detector detector

King-size bed so parents can sleep in the room

Baby monitor linked to local police station

Baby-handling gloves

6" thick bullet- and germ-proof B.C.U. (Baby Encasement Unit)

GUIDE TO THE JEWISH BABY'S ROOM

Pre-entrance chamber with accompanying rubber bio-hazard suit and bubble helmet

10-showerhead anti-bacterial wash chamber

Undressing chamber

Medicine shelf stocked with lifetime supply of Tylenol, baby aspirin, Metamucil, Zantac, asthma inhaler, Xanax, Ritalin, Kaopectate, Fleet enemas, penicillin, Bioxin, amoxicillin

24-hour on-guard ninja

Underground escape tunnel

Having a baby is one of the greatest joys a Jewish couple will ever experience. But in a world racked with disease, violent crime, and kidnapping for ransom, a baby is never safe. At any moment, disaster may strike. Here is a detailed schematic for new parents to reference when designing their newborn's room.

GUIDE TO PICKING A BAR MITZVAH THEME

The NBA! Las Vegas! *American Idol*! *Survivor*! Let's face it, every Bar Mitzvah theme has been done to death. But having a Bar Mitzvah should be one of the most memorable and special events in a Jewish child's life. So here are some creative suggestions to make sure your Bar Mitzvah party is a night that no one will ever forget…ever.

Aloha and Mazel Tov! From Josh's Bar Mitzvah Luau

JOSH IN DA HOOD

BAR MITZVAH BITCHEZ BRING YO CHEDDAH!

JEW LIFE

During the course of a Jewish man's life, he will most likely find himself attending or being the honoree of a bachelor party. Depending on whether or not the party is for Chip McDougal IV or Howie Rosenstein, this guide will help you prepare for what to expect.

THE GENTILE BACHELOR PARTY

PARTY LOCATION:

- Presidential suite at the Four Seasons Las Vegas

AVAILABLE DRUGS:

- cocaine
- speed
- grass
- ecstasy the stripper made in her bathroom
- roofies

ACTIVITIES:

- Gambling away life savings at the craps table
- Getting drunk off scotch and sodas while gorging on a 36-oz. rib eye dinner at the Palm, then getting kicked out for calling your vegan waiter a "Tofu-eating-pussy-ass-faggot"
- Doing tequila shots and lines of coke off the stripper's ass while screaming, "Fuckin' A!!!!!!!"
- A three-way with your best friend and the stripper that gets this close to homosexuality
- Trashing the hotel room
- Wrestling

WHAT THE STRIPPER WILL LEAVE WITH:

- An ass spanked raw
- Bite marks
- "Purple nurples"
- New strain of herpes
- A pledge to herself that this really is "the last time"
- Renewed vow to find her "real father"

QUESTIONS TO ASK THE STRIPPER:

- "You get at least a LITTLE turned on by this, right?"
- "If I hook you up with an eight ball, will you take a dump on my friend?"
- "You chicks all like the girl-on-girl thing, don't you?"
- "Will you stick this inside you?"

YOUR THOUGHTS ABOUT THE NIGHT TEN YEARS FROM NOW

- "I wonder if Pineapple still does private parties?"

VS

PARTY LOCATION:

- Single room at the Four Seasons Las Vegas

AVAILABLE DRUGS:

- Zantac
- Maalox
- Mylanta
- Sleep Ease
- Extra Strength Tylenol
- Allegra
- Tinactin
- Asthma inhalers

ACTIVITIES:

- Dollar poker, $2.00 blackjack, and 5-cent slots
- Disinfecting the hotel room's surfaces with Lysol before and after the party
- Avoiding eye contact with stripper
- Calling girlfriend or wife to "check in" every 30 minutes
- Applying hand sanitizer after being touched by stripper

WHAT THE STRIPPER LEAVES WITH:

- All the condoms that she brought with her
- An E*Trade online stock trading account and a Roth IRA
- Knowledge of why she should buy a condo and stop renting
- Pamphlet on how to turn her "business" into a corporation
- A newfound belief that it wasn't her fault when Daddy would touch her
- Hope
- An appointment to get her silicon breast implants examined for leakage
- A prescription for methadone
- The numbers of a few good psychiatrists that can help her break the cycle of self-destructive behavior
- $100,000 life insurance policy for only $9.99 a month

QUESTIONS TO ASK THE STRIPPER:

- "Do you have change for a ten?'
- "You're so skinny! Can I buy you a sandwich from room service?"
- "Are you wearing orthotics in those shoes?"
- "Who did these????"
- "How many kids do you have?!"
- "Does your mother know you're doing this?"
- "Did you know that there are a variety of degrees you can earn at the ITT Institute?"
- "Have you considered taking just two dollars from every lapdance you do and putting it into an interest-bearing savings account?"

YOUR THOUGHTS ABOUT THE NIGHT TEN YEARS FROM NOW:

- "I wonder if I should keep getting those syphilis tests?"

GUIDE TO BLENDING IN WITH GOYIM

Spending any significant length of time with Gentiles can be very confusing, as they have many strange customs most Jews are not familiar with. But if you're dating, married to, or are close friends with a Gentile, sooner or later you are going to have to attend one of their various events or holidays. Here are some suggestions to help you better enjoy the experience.

CHRISTMAS

What to bring:	Brightly wrapped presents, eggnog, fruitcake, tinsel, baby Jesus cookies, frankincense and myrrh.
How to dress:	Ladies: Rudolph the-red-nosed reindeer sweater, jingle bell earrings, plaid pants, and red velvet hair bow. Men: Snowflake sweater.
What to say:	It's not about the presents, but about celebrating the Lord. Pass the ham, Wilbur.

BBQ

What to bring:	Rack of elk ribs from the hunting trip, boom box, Lee Greenwood's *God Bless the U.S.A.* CD.
How to dress:	Ladies: Daisy dukes, see-through cut-off white T-shirt, baseball hat. Men: Knee-length Bermuda shorts, sandals with socks, plastic visor, NO SUNSCREEN.
What to say:	Those are the most beautiful lawn ornaments I've ever seen, Aunt Mary! Those pink flamingos are so lifelike.

WATCHING *THE PASSION OF THE CHRIST*

What to bring:	Well-worn Bible with angel-themed bookmark.
How to dress:	Ladies: pastel dress. Men: Underpants, crown of thorns.
What to say:	I just want to say that Mel Gibson is right, and I'm really sorry that my people crucified your Lord.

NASCAR PARTY

What to bring:	Keg of Busch beer, Domino's pizza, Craftsman tools, Powerade, Kellogg's cereal (all official NASCAR sponsors).
How to dress:	Ladies/Men: NASCAR sweatshirt and hat, foam finger, beer helmet.
What to say:	Dale Earnhardt Jr. drives so fast! However, I am not worried for his safety.

BAPTISM

What to bring:	A Bible and the fear of GOD.
How to dress:	Ladies/Men: Clothes you don't mind getting wet.
What to say:	Mind if I go for a swim?

KWANZAA

What to bring:	Drums, candles, the copy of Malcolm X's biography you read in high school.
How to dress:	Ladies/Men: Ashokes and Kofia.
What to say:	HOTEP!! Harambee, harambee, harambee, harambee, harambee, harambee, harambee!!!

EASTER

What to bring:	Baskets of plastic grass and colored eggs.
How to dress:	Ladies: Pastel dress, Easter Bunny earrings.
	Men: Pastel button-down shirts and slacks.
What to say:	I'm so glad Jesus turns out okay in the end! Ooh, can I have another pink marshmallow rabbit?

HUNTING TRIP

What to bring:	12-gauge shotgun, ammo, gutting knife.
How to dress:	Ladies/Men: Full-body orange camouflage hunting suit.
What to say:	Boy, Buck, you totally nailed that deer! Let's go gut it!

GUIDE TO MANSCAPING

It's a known fact that Jewish men are hairy. But that doesn't mean that you have to be! "Manscaping" is the art of trimming down one's abundant body hair to a respectable length. While more traditional Jews might consider shaving down one's thick layer of Jew-fur tanta-mount to blasphemy, most young, modern Jews aren't really into looking like a Jew-rangutan. If you have been considering the manscaping process but have been too scared to take the leap, here is a comprehensive guide to making sure your first time goes smoothly.

Before you start you need a great adjustable beard trimmer. Bryan is a fan of the Remington, while Sam prefers the Norelco with vacuum suction. Depending on the trimmer you use, the settings will vary, so always practice on a small section of your upper thigh before getting started. (Note: All manscaping should be performed standing naked in a dry bathtub.)

1. CHEST:

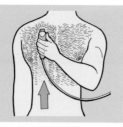

Set the razor at setting four (½" to ¾" length) and proceed to shave in an upward motion ONLY, one section at a time. Gently glide the razor around the areolas. Be very careful not to clip your nipple!

2. LEGS:

The most difficult and most time-intensive area to manscape is the legs. Set the razor at setting two (¼" to ½"), start at the top of the foot and work the razor all the way up the leg, not stopping until it reaches your upper thigh. Repeat that same motion, working your way around the leg in a counter-clockwise direction. Be sure when doing the back of the leg to work the razor all the way up until it reaches the tip of your butt cheek for maximum hair removal. Do not get near the anus. This will be covered later.

3. LOWER ARMS:

This can be very tricky. You want to keep enough hair to still feel like a man, but get rid of enough hair so your watchband doesn't get caught in it. Replace the adjustable-length cutter, put the setting on five (¾" to 1" in length), and move the razor from the bottom of the hand up towards the elbow. If you have hairy hands, you might want to consider manscaping those too.

4. UPPER ARMS:

Hair above the elbow is gross. Take off the adjustable-length cutter, put the setting on one or zero, and trim the upper arm clean. Do not pass below the elbow on the one or zero setting unless you are gay or preparing for a triathlon.

5.

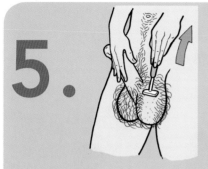

PUBIC AREA:

There is nothing nastier than 5" pubes. Aside from being just plain nasty, this makes your penis appear smaller. Unless you have an enormous penis, trimming this area will not only maximize your length but also increase your possibility of receiving fellatio. We recommend the same length as your chest hair to keep everything symmetrical.

5a. SHAFT & SCROTUM:

Put down your trimmer, pick up your Gillette Mach 3 Turbo, and get ready to hunker down. This is arguably the most important area to manscape on the entire male body—and also the most dangerous! Therefore, we are doing this section as a step-by-step:

1. Turn on the faucet and rinse the penis and scrotum with warm water. This will help moisten and soften the skin to prevent razor burn.

2. Apply a generous amount of shaving cream/gel to penile shaft and entire scrotal sack. Once again this is a personal preference, but we recommend either Philosophy Shave Balm or Zirh Shave Gel—they both have a gentle numbing agent, go on very smooth, and allow you to get that clean, close scrotum shave.

3. Grab the tip of the penis and pull. Stretch penis out as far as it will go and delicately begin to shave the shaft. We recommend a minimum of ¾" to 1." Make sure to get both sides!

4. Once the penis is nice and shaved you can proceed to the scrotum with EXTREME CAUTION! Pretend that your scrotum is a turtle shell and fully stretch and conceal your penis within your testes sack. Once the sack is completely smoothed out and concealing your penis, you can very slowly begin to shave. Many first-timers get nervous and accidentally nick their sack. If this happens, be strong, continue, and make mental note as to "where you went wrong." PROCEED TO ANUS.

6.

ANUS:

Retrieve your trimmer and set it to 1. This is a very close trim, but not a shave, as shaving this area will cause a medical condition known as Porcupinus-Assholeous. Stand lengthwise in the bathtub with one foot at the back of the tub and the other at the drain. Refer to the picture at left, get into this position, and look up to anus. If you are into yoga, you will immediately recognize this pose as the Prasarita Padottanasana (pronounced pra-sa-REE-tah pah-doh-tahn-AHS-anna) or the wide-legged forward bend. Now, with one hand pull your testes sac out of the way to expose your Hairyjewanus. Make sure that the area is dry; if it's damp, you could shock yourself and cause another medical condition known as Burntjewsphincteritis. Continue to look up your crack and trim with caution.

7.

BACK:

In order to complete your manscaping you will need a very nice friend to trim down the shag carpet on your back. Set trimmers to 1 (close as you can, but not shaving) and have your friend mow away. It is customary to thank your friend by giving them a gift certificate to Applebee's or Barnes & Noble.

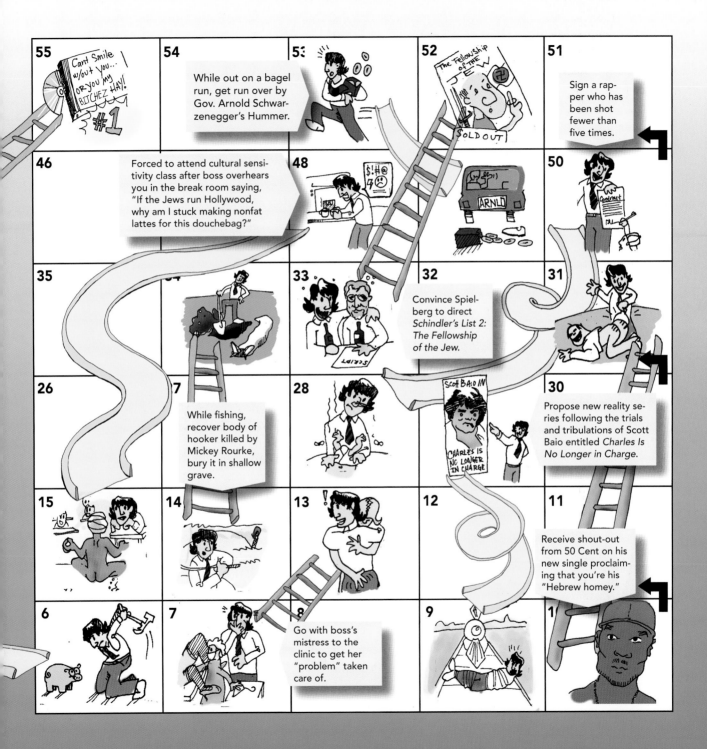

The
Jewish kama sutra:
AN ILLUSTRATED GUIDE TO LOVEMAKING

Jews are certainly not known for their prowess and skill in the bedroom. For the Jewish couple, maintaining an exciting sex life throughout a long relationship is a constant struggle. That is why we have created this Jewish *Kama Sutra* to give couples some new sexual positions to explore in order to help keep the passion burning!

The Challah:

Entwined into a sweet braided lust-loaf,
this difficult but rewarding position is called
Madhura Roti, The Challah.

THE HEIMLICH:

While she chokes on a piece of sweetest rugelach, her lover grasps her from behind; this is called the Gala Ghuta Jana, or The Heimlich.

THE READER

When she sits atop him, offering her house of love while perusing a women's magazine, it is Paathikaa, The Reader.

jewish kama sutra continued...

the minyan:

A quorum of ten lovers joins in passionate congress—each joyfully embracing the next: thus Nyaya Sabha, The Minyan.

the manolo:

When her lover lies between her thighs and the woman raises both her legs, opening them very wide, to better admire her new stilettos...it is called Paduka, The Manolo.

the SPIDER:

When frightened by a spider, she jumps into the arms of her lover, clasping her legs around his buttocks and clutching her arms around his back, while the man protects her from the insect—it is Makadi, The Spider.

the MANICURE:

If she sits astraddle him, garlanding her arms about his neck and trembling as she files her fingernails, and he crushes his body into hers, passionately engaged in his own nail clipping...this is Svasthya Vigyana, The Manicure, and it is learned only by practice.

bubbe's visit:

She cleans the house in preparation for her grandmother coming over, while he ruts her from behind; it is called Gharana Mulakata, or Bubbe's Visit.

GUIDE TO CHASIDIC LOVEMAKING

If you are an ultra-Orthodox Jew, or happen to find yourself having sex with one, then you probably know that myth about sex through a hole in a sheet. Some people think this notion came from the Jewish sage Rabbi Alafta. Deuteronomy 25:5 commands a man to take his brother's childless widow as his wife, but then Leviticus 18:16 forbids a man from seeing his brother's wife naked. The only possible solution to this, obviously, would be to have sex with your brother's wife through a sheet with a hole in it. It should also be noted that Rabbi Alafta only scored a 206 on the "creative problem solving" section of the SATs. But just because you're having sex in such a sterile manner doesn't mean you still can't get your superfreak on! Here are some fantastic ideas to make sheet-ballin' fun!

Personalize your sheet.

If you're a boob man, add a few extra holes for easier breast access.

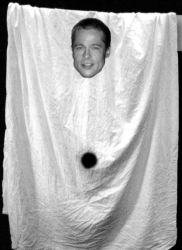

It's okay to fantasize about famous people.

Use a curtain and do it standing up!

Patterned sheets for the holidays.

Shalom

HAPPY CHANUKAH

Orgies only.

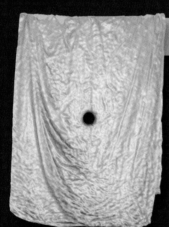
A rubber sheet for seniors.

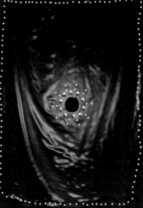
Try a little S & M.

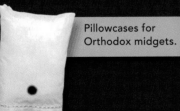
Pillowcases for Orthodox midgets.

Have a third party watch you.

GUIDE TO MAKING A GOOD POO

Having regular bowel movements is one of the most important things a person can do to maintain good health. Unfortunately for us Jews, this is really bad news as we are known to suffer from endless types of digestive disorders such as chronic constipation, acid reflux, irritable bowel syndrome, and even gastroenteritis! Therefore, it is extremely important for Jews to be aware of what makes for a healthy bowel movement. Here are some real medical tips on how to make your movements as turd-rific as possible.

LAY OFF THE LAXATIVE

Repeated artificial stimulation of the bowels destroys their natural emptying reflex, so that in time they will no longer move without artificial stimulants. All that will be left are bowel movements that are utterly and completely undump-tactular.

ONCE A DAY, RIGHT? WRONG!!!

Many people believe that having one bowel movement a day is normal. The truth is there are no rules for frequency of bowel movements, so long as you are making normal and healthy poos. Five times a day to 5 times a week is perfectly crap-propriate.

THE MAKING OF POO!

Follow a knish as it makes its way from the stomach to the toilet.

THINK GREEN

Western eating habits of fast food and over-processed prepackaged frozen dinners have eliminated the foods' natural nutritional contents. The result is that this "food" stays in the body and is turned into fat, leaving little to pass through and be excreted as feces. Adding generous amounts of roughage and green vegetables to your diet will help to facilitate bowel movements that are nothing short of poo-purb.

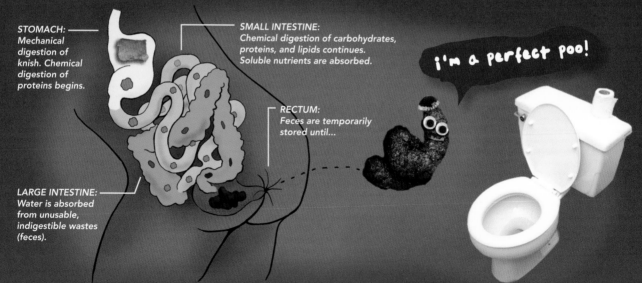

STOMACH: Mechanical digestion of knish. Chemical digestion of proteins begins.

SMALL INTESTINE: Chemical digestion of carbohydrates, proteins, and lipids continues. Soluble nutrients are absorbed.

RECTUM: Feces are temporarily stored until...

LARGE INTESTINE: Water is absorbed from unusable, indigestible wastes (feces).

i'm a perfect poo!

A bowel movement should be soft and easy to pass, though some people may have harder or softer stools than others. According to www.about.com a stool should be, "golden brown, have a texture similar to peanut butter, and be shaped like a sausage." So, if your stool doesn't look like a Skippy-coated Jimmy Dean, this might be a sign of a more serious problem.

HOW DO YOU KNOW WHEN YOUR CRAP IS CRAP?

COLOR

BLACK STOOL
Black, tarry stools with a foul odor can be the result of eating too much spinach, taking iron supplements, or possibly from internal bleeding.

PALE OR CLAY-COLORED STOOLS
Stools that appear pale or look like clay is usually the result of something as simple as antacids, barium from a recent enema, or a lack of bile salt. Or you could have autoimmune hepatitis. Good luck with that one!

RED OR MAROON STOOL
Red or maroon stools could be from something benign such as eating red-colored foods, or could be the symptom of several different conditions including hemorrhoids, anal fissures, colon polyps, diverticular bleeding, or inflammatory bowel disease. Strangely, Maroon Stool is a pretty good name for a rock band.

THERE IS AN ACTUAL STOOL IN YOUR STOOL
If this happens, you should see a doctor immediately.

GREEN STOOL
Luckily, Green poo is generally not dangerous and is usually caused by eating excessive green vegetables, artificially colored foods, or iron supplements. However, if you are pooing green daily, you either have a more serious problem or you might be a Keebler elf.

BRYAN FOGEL'S DAD, DAVID, PRESENTS...BRAN

I'm so glad you asked me to write about bran, fiber of the gods! Literally—Bran was the name of a Celtic god. His head was made entirely of wheat germ. I'm kidding! Seriously though, I do love bran. Let me tell you something about bran—they get it from the outer layer of grains that gets removed during the milling process. Now I don't know what a milling process is, but I do know that bran helps you poo! You know what they do with bran in Japan? Guess! Just try. WRONG! They pickle it! I would love to go to Japan and eat bran. Hey, that rhymes! Boy, I love bran. Bryan, did I ever tell you how I originally wanted to name you Bran? It's a very nice name! But your mother started in with the "Oh, the kids at school will call him Fiberface and Poomaker." So we added a "y" and compromised on Bryan. I put bran on EVERYTHING I eat! Salads, fruit smoothies, cereal, spaghetti, sushi, pastrami sandwiches—even in my water! This one time, I put bran on bran! I don't know why, I just did! Oh sure, I'm spending three to four hours a day on the toilet but I don't really mind anymore. I'm all set up in there — I got a magazine rack, a radio, my fax machine. I've read *Freakonomics* three times! Did you know that in Romania, there is a Bran castle in the village of Bran 16 miles southwest of Brasov? I want to visit the village of Bran and eat bran in the Bran castle! That would be bran-tastic!

Linda Fogel

Bryan: Hello?

Linda: Alana Morris has a cousin who wrote a book and he got leukemia!

Bryan: He's had leukemia since he was 20.

Linda: Oh, you're a doctor now? You couldn't get better than 1040 on your SAT.

Bryan: I didn't say I was a doctor—anyway, I can't talk right now; Sam and I are working on a Guide to Bar Mitzvah Themes bit.

Linda: What—so you can finally tell the world how we didn't throw you a big Bar Mitzvah party?

Bryan: No, that's not—

Linda: Are you going to bring up how you wanted to have a bowling alley built inside the shul and we said no and make us look cheap? How many people can say that they got to have a Bar Mitzvah at the Wailing Wall?

Bryan: I didn't want a Bar Mitzvah at the Wailing Wall, I wanted a bowling alley!

Linda: (crying) Was I not a good mother to you? When you were in kindergarten and you wanted that Big Wheel that could poke out your eye, who got you the Big Wheel that could poke out your eye? I did. And when you were in 5th grade and you decided you wanted to take karate lessons in Chinatown—who drove you there three nights a week...and waited...in the parking lot...all alone...in the dark? I did. And when you got picked on in high school because you had a little bit of a lisp, who took you to the $150-an-hour speech therapist? I did. And do you know why? Because you're my son, and I love you. And how do you show your love to me??? You write a book and say that we're awful parents because we didn't build you a BOWLING ALLEY for your Bar Mitzvah party!!!!

Bryan: Mom, I gotta go...

Linda: I saw on the news that a kid in Kentucky died from inhaling peanut dust—

(Bryan hangs up the phone.)

JEWISH MOTHERS: PART FIVE

Arlene: How could you write about how to safeguard a baby when you couldn't even keep your pet guinea pig, Oscar, alive for more than a week!

Sam: What are you talking about?

Arlene: Linda Fogel told me all about how you're going to make fun of us for installing video surveillance in your room when you were a baby.

Sam: Well, you did, didn't you?

Arlene: We were just trying to protect you. It's the same reason we would wash your mouth out with soap whenever you said a bad word.

Sam: How does washing my mouth out with soap have anything to do with installing video surveillance in my bedroom?

Arlene: Because we didn't want you to be like those foul-mouthed Jaffe boys next door!?!

Sam: You know, Mom, now that you brought it up, I think we should find a way to work that into the book.

Arlene: Are you trying to have me arrested for child abuse? In the '70s and '80s that was a totally acceptable form of punishment, and I'm not going to be told on national television that I was a child abuser!

Sam: What!? What national television?

Arlene: Your book's going to come out, and Oprah's going to put me on her show and talk about how I abused you! Next thing you know, I'll be on trial, and they'll have it on that Court TV, and I'll be sent away for 20 years.

Sam: Mom, are you nuts? No one's putting you in jail.

Arlene: I WON'T LAST A WEEK IN THE CAN! I'll be in that filthy community shower like I've seen on *Oz*, I'll drop the soap and then WHAM! Some lesbian is going to sneak up from behind and VIOLATE ME!

Sam: I gotta go Mom—

Arlene: SHE'S GOING TO STAB ME WITH A PLASTIC SPOON!!!!

(Sam hangs up the phone.)

Arlene Wolfson

Sam's father, Dennis Wolfson, prepares for a leisurely hike while vacationing in Colorado.

CHAPTER SIX

TRAVEL:
PLANES, TRAINS, AND DIARRHEA

Ever since Moses convinced the children of Israel to join him on his totally X-treme desert hiking extravaganza, Jews have basically been on a 5,000-year road trip. One would think that a nomadic people used to being expelled from every spot on the globe would have the traveling thing down pat. And yet we find the experience of traveling to be uncomfortable, intolerable, physically draining, and ultimately spirit-crushing (Fig. 6.1 and 6.2). Between picking where to go, booking airline tickets, finding a hotel, deciding what to pack, renting a car, getting to the airport, and worrying about being mugged, stabbed, robbed, or left for dead in a back alley in Cuba, traveling for the average Jew can be a very stressful experience.

If we go out to the country, will toothless farmers stab us with pitchforks? If we ask to move tables in a Parisian restaurant, will the townspeople stab us with sharpened baguettes? And wasn't someone just saying that Harry Kessler got pickpocketed in the airport in Rome? What if he'd been stabbed?!

But even with all the hassle and worry that comes with it, Jews still love to travel. We get very excited by the idea of jetting off to some foreign, untapped soil and trying to find people on this planet who don't hate us. We love to try new and exotic foods and see how long it takes before we shit water. We feel enriched when we can walk through a famous museum, stare at a Chagall painting, and say, "Wow! He's one of us!"

But whereas most Gentiles can throw socks, underwear, a pair of jeans, and a T-shirt in a suitcase ten minutes before leaving for the airport without even his seat confirmed, for the Jew…traveling is a very, very, very, different experience.

Fig. 6.1

Sam's family regretting their Alaskan vacation.

Fig. 6.2

When Sam's grandmother Rose Weissman travels by seaplane, she takes the extra precaution of wearing her own flotation device.

✡ 124

AIRLINE TRAVEL: FLY, RABINOWITZ, FLY

Whether the flight is for one hour or sixteen, Jews hate being on airplanes (Fig. 6.3). But after years of experimentation, we have developed various techniques to make both airport and airplane experiences as tolerable as possible.

1. BOOKING YOUR TICKET

While it may be tempting to book your ticket online for speed, price, and convenience, it is still imperative to book your ticket over the phone in order to accommodate the following special requests. First off, ask to be a booked on a new plane. Twenty percent of all airplane crashes are due to mechanical error, and you don't want to be flying in a rickety 747-200 built back when computers still took up a whole room. Secondly, request a seat where no one's sitting next to you so you don't end up smashed against a 300-pound insurance salesman from Kentucky. Thirdly, request that your seat is in one of the first five rows so you'll be first off the plane. And last but not least, make sure there are no babies sitting within ten rows of you. Babies should not be allowed to fly unless they're yours. Note: This is also when you will be requesting your "special meal" (see pages 131–132).

2. CHECKING IN

Even if you're not flying first class, that doesn't mean you can't check in at the first-class counter. The first class line is always significantly shorter than the coach line. When they tell you to leave because you're not flying first class, tell them you want to upgrade, even though you have no intention of paying the $2,000 upgrade price. Since you're now there and they've brought you up on the computer, it will be no problem to check you in. If you're too chicken to do this, just slip the guy in front of the coach line twenty bucks. If you ever find yourself waiting in line, you should be ashamed to call yourself a Jew.

Fig. 6.3

It's at this moment that every Jew thinks to him/herself, "OH GOD. What was that noise?"

✡ Jewtoid

In 1986, Judith Resnick became the first Jewish astronaut. In 2003, Colonel Ilan Ramon was the first Israeli Jew in space—and the first person to eat a kosher meal in space. With typical Jewish luck, they both died in horrible, fiery crashes. But don't let that worry you as you step aboard the well-worn ATA biplane you just bought discount tickets for.

3. GET THE EXIT ROW

While checking in, be sure to ask for the exit row. The exit row offers you a good six to eight inches of extra leg room, vital whether you're 5'2" or a whopping (for a Jew) 5'9". These prime seats are given away when passengers check in, so to get them you must get to the airport as early as possible. When requesting the exit row you will be asked if you are physically able to open the emergency exit door and assist passengers in case of an emergency. Lie.

4. SLIP SECURITY

In these post 9/11 times, security lines have gotten out of control. Our advice: Walk to the very front of the security line and discreetly tip the guy in the front of the line twenty bucks. If by chance you get busted by an industrious security guard who's working for seven dollars an hour, slip him twenty bucks too. Yes, worst case scenario you're now down 60 bucks, but you'll be enjoying a Starbucks cappuccino in the lounge while the Gentiles are having their shoes checked for bombs.

5. PRE-PRE-PRE-BOARDING

The flight attendant always makes the announcement inviting passengers who need special assistance to pre-board. It is very important that you figure out some kind of assistance you need that is special. Pretend that you just had heart surgery and that you can't be on your feet for more than a few minutes, or that you're diabetic and you need the extra time to check your insulin and give yourself a shot—the point is, you need to think outside the box on this one. First on the plane means first crack at the overhead compartments, first crack at the freshly sanitized bathroom, and first crack at stealing all the good complimentary magazines (Fig. 6.4).

> **MORAL HYPOTHETICAL:**
>
> You are flying from Chicago to Miami for your cousin's wedding. In the airport, they announce that your plane is overbooked. If you agree to give up your seat and take a later flight, you'll get free roundtrip tickets to anywhere in the U.S. This will cause you to miss the wedding ceremony, but you will still make it just in time for the reception.
>
> *What do you do?*

Fig. 6.4

Solomon Weisburger's favorite pre-boarding technique.

YOU'RE NOT GOING TO ACTUALLY PAY FOR THAT TICKET ARE YOU?

In today's travel landscape, Jews don't need money when booking an airline ticket. They need miles. Most people think a mile is a unit of linear measurement used in English-speaking countries, equivalent to 5,280 feet or 1,760 yards or 1.6 kilometers. But to those in the know, it is an actual unit of currency that will guarantee one never need shell out a dollar for transportation ever again. When used properly, your credit card will garner you points that can be used to stretch your vacation dollar. Here's what some of the major credit cards can do for you, the Wandering Jew:

Credit Card   Northwest Visa

Miles you get just for signing up   10,000

Pro   Allows you to earn miles beyond $10,000 a month. Past that limit, you get a mile for every $2/month spent.

Con   Who flies Northwest? Are Jews even allowed on it?

Credit Card   British Airways Visa Card

Miles you get just for signing up   15,000 bonus miles

Pro   Complimentary companion ticket when you purchase your first ticket with your card.

Con   Every one of your family members is going to be harassing you to get that free ticket.

Credit Card   American Airlines Citibank MasterCard

Miles you get just for signing up   7,500 for Platinum Select; 10,000 for the Gold account

Pro   No blackout dates for travel on American Airlines, American Eagle, and American Connection carriers.

Con   No blackout dates means you've lost your excuse as to why you can't come home and spend the High Holidays with your family.

Credit Card   Delta American Express

Miles you get just for signing up   10,000 bonus miles with your first purchase

Pro   You'll earn two SkyMiles for every eligible dollar charged on Delta Air Lines purchases at supermarkets, gas stations, drugstores, home improvement stores, the U.S. Postal Service, and more.

Con   No matter where you're flying to, you have to make a stopover in Atlanta.

Credit Card   United Mileage Plus Signature Plus

Miles you get just for signing up   17,500 bonus miles

Pro   Free one-way, 1,000 mile, one-class upgrade certificate, up to 11 miles for every $1 spent at participating restaurants nationwide.

Con   Yes, it's a great offer, but with United under bankruptcy protection, you've got a 50/50 shot that they'll still be in business on the day you're supposed to fly to Hawaii.

UP, UP, AND AWAY: STAYING HEALTHY ON THE PLANE

Just because the airplane you're on doesn't crash, it doesn't mean that you're safe. When traveling in tight quarters with several hundred people packed together, chances are that whatever disease, illness, or infection that any of these people are carrying will soon become your own. Here are some simple steps that all traveling Jews should take to protect themselves.

Blankets: Remember how the pilgrims gave the Indians blankets covered in yellow fever that caused them to die and lose their country? Those disease rags were nothing compared to the standard airline blanket. If the airline has not INDIVIDUALLY WRAPPED AND SEALED their blankets in a tamper-proof bag, then DO NOT TOUCH THEM!!! These wool/polyester petri dishes have been coughed on, sweated into, and rubbed up in people's noses all the way from Timbuktu and back.

Air: The most dangerous thing on the plane is not what you can see or touch, rather it is the very air that you breathe! In order for an airplane to create a pressurized cabin so that you can survive at 30,000 feet, the air gets re-circulated. That means that if there's a sick person sitting in row 30 and you're in row 2, they might as well be sneezing directly in your face. WEAR A SURGICAL MASK! You can buy a ten pack at any drugstore. While people might look at you like you're an idiot, you'll be the only one who hasn't contracted Avian Flu by the time you hit baggage claim.

Airborne: Airborne is the fastest-selling health product in retail history. According to scientific studies conducted on Airborne, its unique formulation of amino acids, anti-oxidants, and electrolytes boosts the immune system. And if that's not proof enough, actor and expert on airborne viruses Kevin Costner says, "Airborne is great. It's on my plane and in my house." How Kevin is getting sick while flying on his own private jet is another issue altogether.

Mental Health: CARRY EYE COVERS AND EAR PLUGS. The eye covers will block out the light so that you can sleep, and the earplugs will block out the sound of the

WHICH ONE IS SAM'S UNCLE HAROLD?

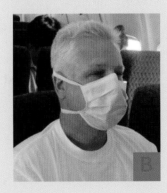

Uncle Harold—B, Michael Jackson—A

engine, the devil-baby that's been crying non-stop since you left the ground, and that Japanese guy who's laughing way too loudly at *Everybody Loves Raymond*.

Sleeping Pills: One way for a neurotic Jew to survive a flight is to sleep through the entire thing. Not the easiest thing to do considering the person in front of you has reclined his seat into your lap and your ass has lost circulation. That's where pills come in. There is a small chance that some people, how shall we put this lightly, um...might become...slightly addicted to these pills. But the new relaxed you will be too sleepy to notice.

✡ Jewtoid

Did you know that there is a houseplant called a Wandering Jew? It clings to the ground and needs to be protected from bugs, extreme temperatures, and sunlight. Truly the Jew of the plant world.

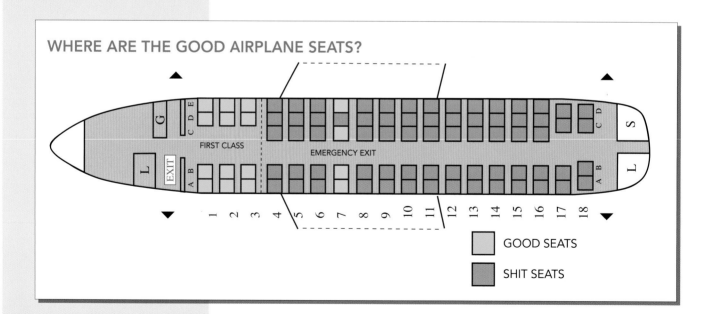

WHERE ARE THE GOOD AIRPLANE SEATS?

FLY THE FRIENDLY JEW SKIES: EL AL AIRLINES

El Al, the national airline of Israel, was officially established on November 15, 1948, with the goal of transporting Jewish immigrants from Yemen and Iraq into Palestine. The literal meaning of El Al is "To-On," but since that doesn't make any freaking sense it is more commonly translated as "up toward the sky." The airline has a reputation for having some of the strictest security measures of any airline in the world. Passengers are asked to check in three hours before their flight and are often subjected to rigorous questioning. All El Al flights carry armed air marshals, and cockpits are sealed to protect against attempted intrusions. So why should you fly El Al?

- Seats divided into meat and dairy sections (Fig. 6.5).
- You can request a davening or non-davening flight.
- Convenient wig racks.
- The in-flight movie is always *Yentl*, *Fiddler on the Roof*, or *The Chosen*.
- If your baggage gets lost, at least it's spending next year in Jerusalem.
- The flight attendants complain that you only press the call button when you want something.
- Onboard pharmacy.
- First-class seats have plaques of the names of the people who donated them.
- Complementary calling cards to use to phone your mother and let her know you landed OK.
- Leave prayers written on paper in the cracks between the seats and God reads them when the plane climbs over 10,000 feet.

> ### *JEWTOPIA* UPGRADE TIPS!
>
> • When you check in to a hotel, always ask if they can upgrade you to a nicer room for no charge. If they have the rooms available and you catch them on a good day, they'll usually do it. If the employee is not willing to upgrade you voluntarily, when you get into the room, immediately call back down to the front desk, complain of a terrible smell, unscrew the cable from the back of the TV and say it doesn't work, and insist that you saw a black widow spider.
>
> • By joining Hertz Club Gold your rental car will be waiting for you when the shuttle bus drops you off so you don't have to wait in line like all the other dumb schmucks.

Fig. 6.5

The "milk only" section of an El Al 757-200.

IN-FLIGHT MEALS: A *JEWTOPIA* SPECIAL REPORT

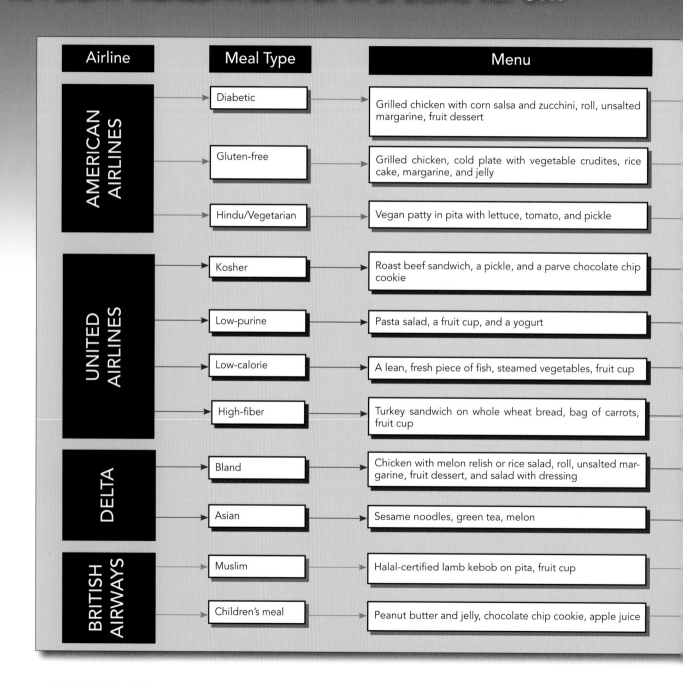

Airline	Meal Type	Menu
AMERICAN AIRLINES	Diabetic	Grilled chicken with corn salsa and zucchini, roll, unsalted margarine, fruit dessert
	Gluten-free	Grilled chicken, cold plate with vegetable crudites, rice cake, margarine, and jelly
	Hindu/Vegetarian	Vegan patty in pita with lettuce, tomato, and pickle
UNITED AIRLINES	Kosher	Roast beef sandwich, a pickle, and a parve chocolate chip cookie
	Low-purine	Pasta salad, a fruit cup, and a yogurt
	Low-calorie	A lean, fresh piece of fish, steamed vegetables, fruit cup
	High-fiber	Turkey sandwich on whole wheat bread, bag of carrots, fruit cup
DELTA	Bland	Chicken with melon relish or rice salad, roll, unsalted margarine, fruit dessert, and salad with dressing
	Asian	Sesame noodles, green tea, melon
BRITISH AIRWAYS	Muslim	Halal-certified lamb kebob on pita, fruit cup
	Children's meal	Peanut butter and jelly, chocolate chip cookie, apple juice

They don't advertise them...You never see anybody eating them...But they exist. AND THEY'RE FREE. They are the "special meals" that the airlines secretly offer. And unless you know them by name and ask for them in advance, you're going to be stuck with a BLT on Wonder Bread, a bag of Fritos, and a rotten banana.

Meal Overview

Grilled chicken with corn salsa and zucchini? Ain't nothing wrong with that!

Jews are gluttons for gluten. This meal is not recommended.

While you might not share the beliefs of Hinduism, you can take comfort knowing that with this meatless meal, you haven't eaten your reincarnated Uncle Bernie.

Not a bad choice, just be prepared for when they announce over the PA system, "Will the Jew who ordered the kosher meal please raise his hand?"

Delicious, nutritious, and keeps the gout OUT!

A lean, fresh piece of fish? ON A PLANE? Go ahead, we dare you.

This is a great meal, but make sure you book a seat next to the bathroom.

Your system might go into epileptic shock if you eat a meal that has less than 1000mg of sodium. But aren't you a little curious to see what the "melon relish" is all about?

It's the closet thing to Chinese food you can get on an airplane.

While tasty, could get you on the FBI Watch List.

Comes with a mini plastic airplane and a Jr. Admiral flight pin! And for an extra $5.00 the flight attendant will spoon feed it to you!

HOTELS: A HOT ZONE

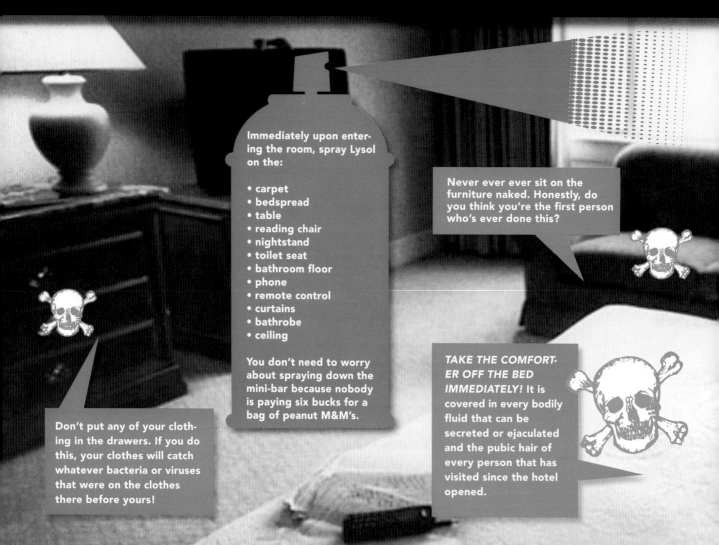

One of the best-selling books of 1995 was Richard Preston's *The Hot Zone*, about a real Ebola virus outbreak in the Washington, DC, area. For Jews, every hotel is a living, breathing hot zone loaded with strains of viruses and bacteria so horrible that all the penicillin in the world couldn't eliminate them. Here are a few simple tips to make your next hotel-room stay as pleasurable and germ-free as humanly possibe.

Immediately upon entering the room, spray Lysol on the:

- carpet
- bedspread
- table
- reading chair
- nightstand
- toilet seat
- bathroom floor
- phone
- remote control
- curtains
- bathrobe
- ceiling

You don't need to worry about spraying down the mini-bar because nobody is paying six bucks for a bag of peanut M&M's.

Never ever ever sit on the furniture naked. Honestly, do you think you're the first person who's ever done this?

TAKE THE COMFORTER OFF THE BED IMMEDIATELY! It is covered in every bodily fluid that can be secreted or ejaculated and the pubic hair of every person that has visited since the hotel opened.

Don't put any of your clothing in the drawers. If you do this, your clothes will catch whatever bacteria or viruses that were on the clothes there before yours!

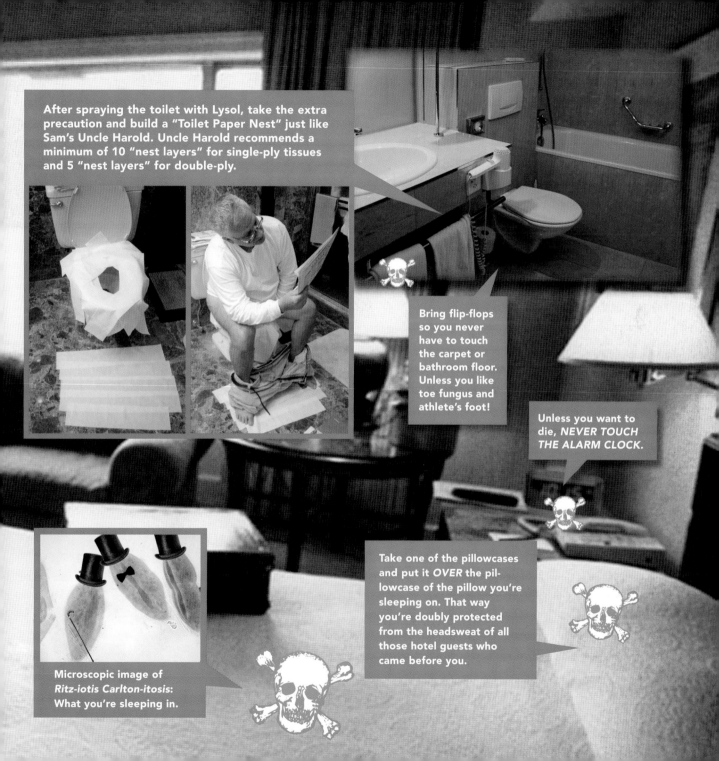

After spraying the toilet with Lysol, take the extra precaution and build a "Toilet Paper Nest" just like Sam's Uncle Harold. Uncle Harold recommends a minimum of 10 "nest layers" for single-ply tissues and 5 "nest layers" for double-ply.

Bring flip-flops so you never have to touch the carpet or bathroom floor. Unless you like toe fungus and athlete's foot!

Unless you want to die, *NEVER TOUCH THE ALARM CLOCK.*

Take one of the pillowcases and put it *OVER* the pillowcase of the pillow you're sleeping on. That way you're doubly protected from the headsweat of all those hotel guests who came before you.

Microscopic image of *Ritz-iotis Carlton-itosis:* What you're sleeping in.

JEWTOPIA'S ESSENTIAL FOREIGN PHRASES POCKET GUIDE:

When traveling abroad, it's always good to have at least a slight grasp of the local tongue so you can get around with ease. Here's a list of phrases that every Jew on foreign soil will need to know at some point. Feel free to cut this page out of the book and take it with you on your next journey.

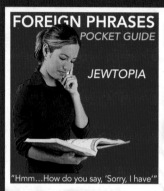

FOREIGN PHRASES
POCKET GUIDE

JEWTOPIA

"Hmm...How do you say, 'Sorry, I have'"

IS THERE PORK IN THIS?

French: Y a-il le porc dans cela?

Spanish: Hay allí carne de cerdo en este?

Italian: È ci porco in questo?

Pig Latin: Ee-say air-they ark-pay een-yah iss-thay?

WHERE'S THE SYNAGOGUE?

French: Où est la synagogue?

Spanish: Donde está la sinagoga?

Italian: Dove è lo synagogue?

Pig Latin: Air-ways uh-they in-a-gog-say?

CAN YOU PUT SALMON ON THAT?

French: Pouvez-vous y mettre le saumon?

Spanish: Puede usted poner al salmón sobre esto?

Italian: Potete mettere i salmoni su quello?

Pig Latin: An-kay oo-yay oot-pay amon-say on-ay at-thay?

I THINK YOU OVER-CHARGED US.

French: Je crois que vous nous avez surcharges.

Spanish: Pienso que usted nos sobrecargó.

Italian: Penso che li abbiate fatti pagare troppo.

Pig Latin: Eye-ay ink-thay ooh-yay charged-over-yay us-yay.

THERE'S A DRAFT, CAN WE SWITCH TABLES?

French: Il y a un brouillon, pouvons-nous échanger des tables?

Spanish: Hay un esbozo, podemos nosotros cambiar mesas?

Italian: Ci sono una brutta copia, possono noi commutano le tabelle?

Pig Latin: Ere's-thay a raft-day, an-cay e-way itch-sway ables-tay?

DO YOU VALIDATE PARKING?

French: Validez-vous le parking?

Spanish: Valida usted el aparcamiento?

Italian: Convalidate il parcheggio?

Pig Latin: Oo-day oo-yay ali-date-vay arking-pay?

MY WALLET IS IN MY POCKET! PLEASE DON'T KILL ME!

French: M-m-m-m-m-m-m-m...

Spanish: M-m-m-m-m-m-m-m...

Italian: M-m-m-m-m-m-m-m...

Pig Latin: M-m-ay-m-m-ay-m-m-m-m-ay...

WHO ARE YOU CALLING A KIKE?!?

French: Qu'appelez-vous un kike?!?

Spanish: A quién llama usted un kike?!?

Italian: Chi sono voi che denominate un kike?!?

Pig Latin: Oo-way are-ay oo-yay alling-kay a-ay ike-kay?!?

COULD YOU PUT THAT ON THE SIDE?

French: Pourriez vous le mettre sur le côté?

Spanish: Podía usted poner esto sobre el lado?

Italian: Potreste avete messo quello dal lato?

Pig Latin: Ould-cay ou-yay ut-pay at-thay on-ay e-thay ide-say?

DID YOU TAKE THE DOL-LAR I HAD ON THE NIGHT-STAND?

French: A fait vous prenez le dollar du nightstand?

Spanish: Hizo usted toma el dólar del nightstand?

Italian: Avete preso il dollaro che ho avuto sul nightstand?

Pig Latin: Id-day ou-ya ake-tay e-thay ollar-day I-ay ad-hay on-ay e-thay ight-nay and-stay?

IS ANAL EXTRA?

French: Est anal supplémentaire?

Spanish: Es anal extra?

Italian: È il supplemento anale?

Pig Latin: Ee-say anal-ay extra-ay?

ESSENTIAL PACKING REMINDERS

When packing for a trip, Gentiles have an innate ability to begin the packing process 30 minutes before leaving for the airport, and seem to possess no desire to turn on the Weather Channel and check the barometric pressure of the location they're traveling to. For Jews, however, packing is a slightly more time-consuming process.

REMINDER #1: Bring at least two pairs of underwear and two pairs of socks for every day you're traveling.

REMINDER #2: If you are traveling to a tropical climate, bring a heavy down parka just in case. If you are traveling to a freezing climate, bring a bathing suit just in case.

REMINDER #3: Wrap your shoes in a plastic bag so they don't get your clothes dirty. Wrap your shampoo in a plastic bag so it doesn't spill all over your clothes. Also, bring plenty of extra plastic bags to bring back your dirty clothes in.

REMINDER #4: Always bring a pair of flip-flops so you don't have to touch the hotel floor, the spa floor, the beach, or any other surface that could infect you.

REMINDER #5: For your carry-on, remember earplugs, hand sanitizer, eye covers, a neck support pillow, and duct tape (you never know).

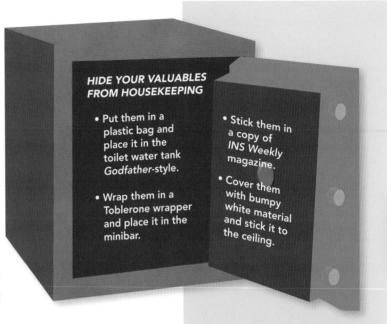

HIDE YOUR VALUABLES FROM HOUSEKEEPING

- Put them in a plastic bag and place it in the toilet water tank *Godfather*-style.
- Wrap them in a Toblerone wrapper and place it in the minibar.
- Stick them in a copy of *INS Weekly* magazine.
- Cover them with bumpy white material and stick it to the ceiling.

Fig. 6.6

Sylvia Goldblatt's luggage for a weekend in Miami.

 **Jewtoid**

In Europe, most of Asia, India, and South America a 10% tip is considered generous! How awesome is that?

JEWTOPIA'S TRAVEL GUIDE TO THE WORLD:

There are lots of places to visit in this big wide world. The possibilities are endless. But with so many choices, where do you go? On the next 18 pages, we'll examine many of the major countries and regions of the world to help Wandering Jews plan where to go on their next vacation.

THE UNITED STATES OF AMERICA

PROBABILITY OF BEING KIDNAPPED: .02%.
Prominent Native Intestinal Disease: Cryptosporidium, a feces parasite.

JEWISH POPULATION
1970: 5,400,000
2005: 5,280,000
2020 PROJECTED: 5,200,000 (due to assimilation, intermarriage, and census-takers forgetting to count snowbirds)

Mount Rushmore
SOUTH DAKOTA

THE DAKOTAS: Visit Mount Rushmore and fantasize that Joe Lieberman's mug is up there next to Lincoln's!

NEVADA

Aspen
COLORADO

San Francisco

Las Vegas

CALIFORNIA

Hollywood

ASPEN: Check out this posh, A-listers' Winter Wonderland that was once an alleged home to escaped Nazis! In fact, modern Aspen's founding fathers tried to prevent Jews from staying in the town's hotel. Nice try, fellas!

TEXAS   Crawford

SAN FRANCISCO: See one of the only Orthodox gay synagogues, where men and women sit apart but no one seems to mind.

HOLLYWOOD: Take an exciting tour of Jewish-controlled movie studios! Mel Gibson supposedly has an office on the Warner Bros. Studio lot. Be sure to stop by and let him know, "That's right, buddy, and we'll kill him the next time, too!"

VEGAS, BABY! Visit the city of sin built by that nice Jewish boy Bugsy Siegel. If your wife catches you in the hot tub with four strippers, just tell her you thought you were in a mikvah.

BUSH BEER

CRAWFORD, TEXAS: Visit the Crawford Store to pick up a George W. Beer cozy so you can keep your Schlitz frosty while you sign town petitions to limit First Amendment rights!

From sea to shining sea, the United States offers the Jewish tourist a panorama of natural wonders and climates to explore. California beaches are beautiful to behold, thanks in large part to Jewish designer Jacques Heim's invention, the bikini. The vistas of the Rockies are breathtaking—literally—as the thin air makes it impossible to breathe without an inhaler or oxygen tank. Visit the open plains of the Wild West, where cowboys forged the American myth and Jews were right there to sell them dry goods. Learn about the expansive farms and small towns of America's heartland as you fly over them. North America is waiting for you to explore it!

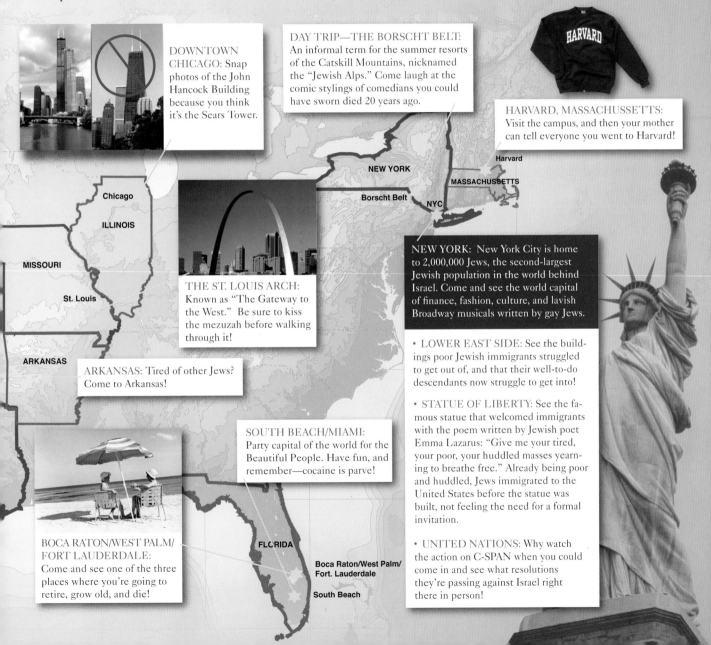

DOWNTOWN CHICAGO: Snap photos of the John Hancock Building because you think it's the Sears Tower.

DAY TRIP—THE BORSCHT BELT: An informal term for the summer resorts of the Catskill Mountains, nicknamed the "Jewish Alps." Come laugh at the comic stylings of comedians you could have sworn died 20 years ago.

HARVARD

HARVARD, MASSACHUSSETTS: Visit the campus, and then your mother can tell everyone you went to Harvard!

NEW YORK
Harvard
MASSACHUSSETTS
Borscht Belt
NYC

Chicago
ILLINOIS

MISSOURI

St. Louis

ARKANSAS

THE ST. LOUIS ARCH: Known as "The Gateway to the West." Be sure to kiss the mezuzah before walking through it!

ARKANSAS: Tired of other Jews? Come to Arkansas!

NEW YORK: New York City is home to 2,000,000 Jews, the second-largest Jewish population in the world behind Israel. Come and see the world capital of finance, fashion, culture, and lavish Broadway musicals written by gay Jews.

• LOWER EAST SIDE: See the buildings poor Jewish immigrants struggled to get out of, and that their well-to-do descendants now struggle to get into!

• STATUE OF LIBERTY: See the famous statue that welcomed immigrants with the poem written by Jewish poet Emma Lazarus: "Give me your tired, your poor, your huddled masses yearning to breathe free." Already being poor and huddled, Jews immigrated to the United States before the statue was built, not feeling the need for a formal invitation.

• UNITED NATIONS: Why watch the action on C-SPAN when you could come in and see what resolutions they're passing against Israel right there in person!

SOUTH BEACH/MIAMI: Party capital of the world for the Beautiful People. Have fun, and remember—cocaine is parve!

BOCA RATON/WEST PALM/ FORT LAUDERDALE: Come and see one of the three places where you're going to retire, grow old, and die!

FLORIDA

Boca Raton/West Palm/ Fort Lauderdale

South Beach

MEXICO, CENTRAL AND SOUTH AMERICA

Mexico, Central and South America are lands of stark contrasts: ancient civilizations and modern cities, beautiful beaches and snow-capped mountains, incredible drugs and lousy drinking water. Adventure travelers will throng to experience its lush jungles, pristine ruins, and dank jail cells. Head south, where the only thing missing is you (until you pay the ransom).

Probability of Being Kidnapped:
At a resort, 5%
Outside a Resort, 36%
Prominent Native Intestinal Disease: Montezuma's Revenge. And his vengeance is nothing to scoff at.
Jewish Population: 636,000

Language Lesson:

• A *Zapatero* is a shoemaker who can craft you a pair of beautiful custom loafers for a great price.

• A *Zapatista* is a revolutionary from Chiapas who will behead you and take your shoes.

COZUMEL, ACAPULCO, CANCÚN: Three of the most beautiful and pristine beaches in the world. If you're there in March, be sure to catch the annual migration of wild beasts known in the animal kingdom as "College Students on Spring Break," who make their way here from all over the world to vomit, pee, and copulate in public.

MEXICO

PUERTO VALLARTA: Finally see the place all the Gentiles get to go after they win the showcase showdown on *The Price Is Right*!

GUATEMALA
Kids driving you crazy? Then be sure to check out Guatemala, voted this continent's "Place Most Likely to Get Kidnapped." Congratulations on the third year in a row!

GUATEMALA

CHICHEN ITZA: Don't miss the largest Mayan pyramid in the world built completely without advanced tools or Jewish slave labor!

EARN MONEY ON VACATION:
Become a drug mule! Why ride a burro when you can be one?

SAVE THE MEMORIES:
If you want to preserve the memory of your trip on video, be sure to get drunk and show your tits to any of the cameramen you come across shooting raw footage for the *Jews Gone Wild!* video series.

MACHU PICCHU, PERU:
There are over 3,000 steep steps to reach the top of the ancient Incan fortress built into a sheer cliff face. In other words, enjoy the buffet and slideshow at the base.

PERU

BRAZIL

RIO DE JANEIRO:
Have your picture taken with the biggest Jew in town, the giant Jesus on the mountaintop overlooking the city!

CHILE

ARGENTINA

WHEN IN CHILE...
CATCH A TV TAPING!
The most popular TV variety show in South America is hosted by a Jew! That's right, Mario Kreutzberger, better known as Don Francisco, is a German Jew whose parents fled to Chile to avoid Nazi persecution. Don Francisco's secret to success: combine every show he has ever seen, and then add big-breasted women in bikinis!

ARGENTINA: Have you seen this Nazi war criminal? Please call 1-800-MOSSAD.

Artur Axmann

CARNIVALE IN RIO!
Think of it as Purim but with more booze, better costumes, and no scroll reading.

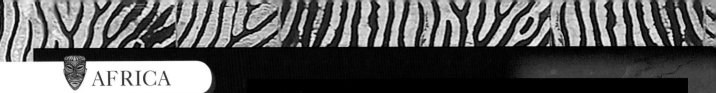

AFRICA

For the adventure-seeking Jew, check out this massive continent that has been fertile ground to some of the most fascinating plants, animals, and mass genocides on Earth. With a near endless diversity of natural beauty and resources, come see what imperialists and local strongmen have been fighting over for decades. King Solomon came for the copper mines…you can come for the Dengue Fever!

SPOTLIGHT ON AFRICAN JEWS

Ethiopia Black people who identify as Jewish based on certain practices or local histories. Claims supported by prominent noses and constant complaining about the heat.

SubSahara/ Central Africa Called the Beta Israel or Falashas. These black Jews are descendants of Dan, one of the Lost Tribes of Israel, who migrated to the ancient African kingdom of Cush. Israel granted thousands of them Israeli citizenship in an attempt to create a basketball team that could win a medal at the Olympics.

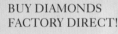

SIERRA LEONE

PLASTIC SURGERY MASAI-STYLE:
You've had your tummy tucked, your face lifted, your cellulite sucked…and now you can be the first in your Hadassah group to have your genitals mutilated. You can't get that done in Beverly Hills!

BUY DIAMONDS FACTORY DIRECT!
Why buy your diamonds from a Chasidic Jew when you could come to Sierra Leone and buy them at a fraction of the cost directly from an authentic warlord! Don't haggle too much because it will cost you an arm and a leg… literally.

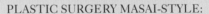

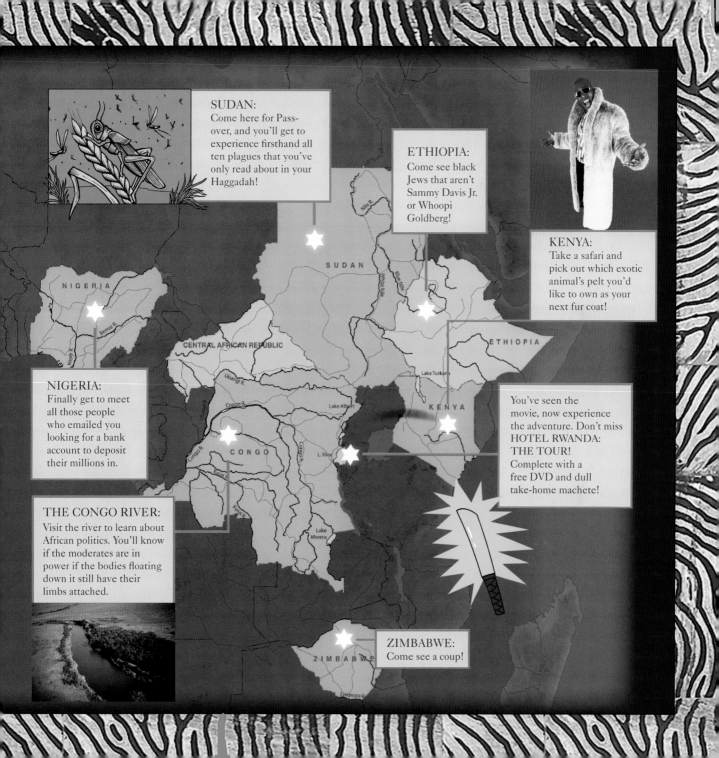

SUDAN: Come here for Passover, and you'll get to experience firsthand all ten plagues that you've only read about in your Haggadah!

ETHIOPIA: Come see black Jews that aren't Sammy Davis Jr. or Whoopi Goldberg!

KENYA: Take a safari and pick out which exotic animal's pelt you'd like to own as your next fur coat!

NIGERIA: Finally get to meet all those people who emailed you looking for a bank account to deposit their millions in.

THE CONGO RIVER: Visit the river to learn about African politics. You'll know if the moderates are in power if the bodies floating down it still have their limbs attached.

You've seen the movie, now experience the adventure. Don't miss **HOTEL RWANDA: THE TOUR!** Complete with a free DVD and dull take-home machete!

ZIMBABWE: Come see a coup!

INDIA

I ndia is a land of enchantment, mystery, exotic foods, and the student who will beat your child out for valedictorian. Learn what it feels like to be in a Tandoori oven just by stepping outside of your hotel. There are over one billion friendly people here. They aren't all on the same street as you, it just feels that way.

• India vital statistics: 3,287,590 sq km, 1,080,264,388 people, 15 official languages, 3 clean bathrooms, 1 with toilet paper.

Where can you find the best corned beef in India? Why, in DELHI, of course! Make sure to check out Delhi's only synagogue, Judah Hayim, for Saturday morning services. Out of 13 million residents, Delhi's Jewish community numbers just 50 people, forcing the temple to lower the official minyan number from 10 to 5.

GOA: For a treat, check out the exotic beaches of Goa, the rave capital of the world for backpacking Israelis. Just remember there are no Jewish doctors available if you get sick from taking bad ecstasy.

BANGALORE: Meet the person who will soon take your IT job!

Travel Tip:

When people hear monsoon, they think watery destruction. We think discount! Remember to pack an umbrella and an extra cholera shot.

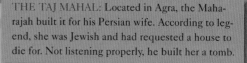

THE TAJ MAHAL: Located in Agra, the Maharajah built it for his Persian wife. According to legend, she was Jewish and had requested a house to die for. Not listening properly, he built her a tomb.

Language Tips:

"Namaste" is a traditional greeting. Despite what you may think because of the Yoga classes you started taking, it does not mean, "I just farted."

HOORAY FOR BOLLYWOOD! Come and take tours of your favorite Bollywood studios, which actually produce more films every year than Hollywood! If you're lucky, you just might catch the Brad Pitt of India, Prakask Mehra, filming his next movie, *Saag Paneer Wars, Episode IV: The Tandoori Strikes Back!*

CALCUTTA: Looking for a new ailment to complain about? Be sure to check out Calcutta, where you'll find diseases you thought had been wiped out, like leprosy and the plague.

delhi

agra

ganges river

calcutta

INDIA

bollywood

goa

bangalore

kerala

THE GANGES RIVER: It is customary to swim, bathe, and bury your dead in the sacred waters of the Ganges, a cesspool of garbage and human waste! We recommend the Ganges lap pool in the Bombay Sheraton, complete with swim-up bar. Just as lovely with half the hepatitis!

KERALA: Visit the home of Ayurveda, the natural healing therapy so beloved by neurotic Jews. Learn how to become a master and then engage in a battle with its misunderstood dark side, Darthveda.

EASTERN EUROPE & RUSSIA

Russia and Eastern Europe. Come and explore the countries your Bubbe and Zaide so desperately tried to flee! The Talmud took shape in Eastern Europe, as did the Yiddish language, the sect of Chasidism, and the Jewish predilection towards smoked fish and stewed meats. You won't want to miss Russia, the land that holds Jews responsible for the worst excesses of both communism and capitalism. Officially, anti-Semitism did not exist under Soviet rule. Then again, neither did gulags. Be sure to bring along your copy of *War and Peace*; not only is it a good read, it's also a great source of fuel and toilet paper.

ST. PETERSBURG MUST SEE: The Summer Palaces—located on the outskirts of the city, these were the summer retreats of Peter and Catherine the Great. They are just like summer homes in the Hamptons, minus the Range Rover and Central American housekeeper!

Probability of Being Kidnapped: 10 percent, 0 percent if you find out you are related to Yakov Smirnoff.
Prominent Native Intestinal Disease: Poliomyelitis, an infectious gastrointestinal disease affecting the central nervous system.
Jewish Population: 1970: 808,000 2005: 235,000 Projected 2020: -275 (people who said "I'll be right back")

SCANDINAVIA: The frozen lands of the Vikings don't have many Jewish attractions, but do have bountiful herring and giant beautiful blondes who love ABBA and IKEA and think that little brown-haired/brown-eyed Jewish men and women are exotic!

SCANDINAVIA

st. petersburg

moscow

POLAND

UKRAINE

CZECH

GREECE

POLAND: (Population 38,000,000; 600 Jews) Starting in the 10th century, Poland became the home of millions of Jews and was for a time the center of Jewish life. No trip to Poland is complete without visiting the Warsaw Ghetto, Krakow Ghetto, Lodz Ghetto, Treblinka, Birkenau, and Auschwitz. Remember to bring an entire box of Puffs.

TOUR UKRAINE! with Biz-Czar Adventures and watch a full-scale re-enactment of Czars conquering Ukraine and then get a free escort to the border.

CZECH REPUBLIC: (Population 241,000; 26,000 Jews) Prague: We "prague-nosticate" that you'll love Prague, where Jews have lived for over 1,000 years! The Jewish Quarter here is one of the oldest in all of Europe, and boasts many beautiful synagogues. Don't miss the Old-New Synagogue, the oldest site in the Jewish Quarter. Nearby is the New-Old-New Synagogue, now often referred to as the Old-New-Old-New Synagogue because of the New-New-Old-New Synagogue recently built just down the street.

GREECE: (Population 650,000; 4,500 Jews) Treasure hunt! During WWII, Nazi Officer Max Merten stole 50 cases of gold from the Jewish community of Greece before he sent the Jews off to concentration camps. The fishing boat carrying the treasure sunk somewhere off the Greek isles and has yet to be recovered. As a reward for finding it, the 4,500 Jews left in Greece will give you a bottle of ouzo and arrange a private dinner with Nia Vardalos!

STEALS & DEALS: Bring back something no one else on your block has—a nuclear weapon! Don't be afraid to negotiate and have them include the utility sports package in the sticker price.

MORE STEALS & DEALS: Looking for a new Mercedes? How about the one stolen from your driveway? Chances are, you'll find it here.

UNIVERSITY OF MOSCOW: See the university that has produced many of Russia's top-flight doctors, engineers, and scientists. You may have met one of them in the States driving your cab to the airport.

KAMCHATKA: An unspoiled pristine wilderness teeming with bears, tigers, and bison. A lovely place for a hike, but proceed with caution: these ferocious animals are known to hide from their prey inside innocent-looking Fabergé eggs.

RUSSIA

siberia

kamchatka

SIBERIA: Best Place to Celebrate Hanukah: If the heat stayed on here for eight days in a row, it's a freakin' miracle!

RUSSIAN FACTBOOK:
Also Known As: Russian Empire (1721–1917), Union of Soviet Socialist Republics (1918–1991), Russian Federation (1991+), Brighton Beach East (Current)

DRINKING TIP:
Do Order—"Cosmopolitans": Delicious vodka cocktails.

Don't Order—"Rootless Cosmopolitans": What Stalin called the Jews before he had them killed.

ST. BASIL'S CATHEDRAL:
Built in 1555 and famous for its brightly colored domes. Ivan the Terrible exclaimed it was the most beautiful building he had seen and plucked out the eyes of the architect so it could not be replicated. Many Jewish women consider doing this with their interior decorators but chicken out at the last minute.

EUROPE

Eform—and since its Roman Empire days, Europe has enjoyed violating and colonizing the re of the world. Now, with so many countries in the E.U. sharing the same currency, vacationin in Europe is even easier and more expensive than ever! This diverse continent is a great place for Jew to visit and see the "Old Country" of their great-grandparents' stories. Make sure you bring along som underarm deodorant, which is practically outlawed in many parts of the E.U.—or should we say, P.U.!

UNITED KINGDOM (Total Population: 59,700,000; 350,000 Jews)

LONDON—British Library: The manuscript room holds an original copy of the Balfour Declaration, which led to the creation of Israel. It also holds the very rare page 2, which ends with "so that should put an end to any problems in the region. I shouldn't have had that last scotch. Where are my pants?"

LONDON—CONVERT OR ELSE!
Check out Chancery Lane's Domus Conversorum, or House of Conversion, where Jews were forced to convert or be expelled. Among the many Jews who "converted" but stayed Jewish on the DL were prominent doctors, including the personal physicians to King Henry IV and Queen Elizabeth I—see, even the royals wouldn't trust their health to anyone but a Jew!

STONEHENGE:
An easy day trip from London is the county of Wiltshire, home to these famous ruins. Around the time Abraham was first learning about a crazy thing called Judaism, Pagans were building these enormous structures for no particular reason! You must see the awe-inspiring ruins for yourself in order to understand how retarded this actually was.

Also Known As: Europa, European Union, EU, Oldmerica
Prominent Native Intestinal Disease: Viral Gastroenteritis, Gérard Depardieu
Population: 700,000,000
Jewish Population: 1,577,000

EU FACTBOOK:
Motto: In varietate Concordia (Unity in Diversity)
E.U.'s Largest City: London
E.U.'s Headquarters: Brussels
E.U.'s Official Sprout: Brussels

FRANCE (Total Population: 60,000,000; 520,000 Jews)

PARIS—Louvre: This museum houses one of world's largest collections of art, including Jewish artists Modigliani, Soutine, Kisling, Pissarro, and Chagall. Historians believe that a good percentage of what is in the Louvre was stolen from Jewish families during World War II. So if you see something that looks familiar, feel free to just grab it off the wall.

Drancy: A transit camp located outside of Paris was the stopping point for French Jews being sent to Auschwitz and stands as a testimony to the courage of the Vichy government during World War II and the overall bravery of the French people.

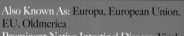

SWITZERLAND: (7,300,000 people; 22,000 during ski season and bank conventions; 18,000 Jews)
While they were able to stay neutral during World War II with great difficulty, they didn't seem to have much problem stealing Jewish bank accounts. The Swiss have been slow to repay the money owed but have offered every Jew who visits a lifetime supply of Toblerone to make amends.

SPAIN: (Population 40,050,000; 12,000 Jews)
LADINO! Oy vey-rumba! This Judeo-Spanish language became a Jewish idiom after the Jews' 1492 expulsion from Spain, when they took their local customs with them to their new homes all across the globe. Ladino is also know as Judezmo and Spaniolit.

HERE'S A SAMPLE CONVERSATION
-Donde estan los knishes buenos?
-En el maalé yahudí.
-Ah, gracias, bubeleh!
-Nishto far vos, mi amigo.

GERMANY: (83,250,000 people; Jewish population: 95,000) Berlin: This capital city flourishes with Jewish culture. Numerous streets are named after Jews, so Germans are able to continue to walk all over them. Berlin is also known for its nightlife. Chances are high that you will be able to find a latex-clad German who wouldn't mind being spanked by you if you tell them you are Jewish.

KOSHER HOTEL ALERT: GERMANY: Within walking distance to a synagogue, and run by a Jewish family, Luxor Hotel, Am Allerheiligentor 2-4, Frankfurt, Germany, is a lovely kosher facility. Not to be confused with the Luxor Hotel in Las Vegas, one of the few pyramids that was not built by Jews.

OktoberFest: What's more fun than being in a crowded hall with thousands of shouting drunk Germans? If a short guy with a funny mustache stands up to give a speech, that's your cue to leave.

NETHERLANDS: (Population 16,100,000; 25,500 Jews) Amsterdam: A small city with must-see cultural attractions like hash bars, live sex shows, and the Anne Frank House. If you want to make the Anne Frank House less depressing, try to get rip-roaringly wasted on hash brownies before you go.

MADRID: Jewish tourists often find themselves disappointed by Madrid's Prado Museum. That's Prado, not Prada.

Michelangelo's Moses: Standing in the Church of San Pietro, this is the sculpture with horns coming out of the head of Moses. The depiction was apparently based on a mistranslation of the Bible, which speaks of "rays" shining from Moses when he emerged from Sinai with the Ten Commandments. The Hebrew word for "rays" is similar to the word for "horns." Gentiles have been looking for horns on Jews for five hundred years, because someone didn't know how to proofread.

ITALY: (57,750,000 people; 29,500 Jews) Language tip: Jewgino—a Jewish guy who tries to pass himself off for Italian.

Rome: Coliseum: Check out this ancient stadium where gladiators fought to the death for the amusement of the crowds. This is where Jews first learned that managing athletes is an easier career than being an athlete.

✕ ASIA

Asia is about as diverse as it gets! From the Communist regime of China, to the poverty of Cambodia, to the sweatshops of Taiwan, to the Muslim fanatics of Indonesia — there is a never-endng plethora of cultural and ethnic diversity to see.

PROBABILITY OF BEING KIDNAPPED: 0%. We'd be too easy to find.

PROMINENT NATIVE INTESTINAL DISEASE: Clonorchiasis, a.k.a. Oriental liver fluke, a.k.a. that sounds like it might be tasty over rice with a saffron broth

TIBET: DALAI LAMA FUN FACT: In 1990, the Dalai Lama asked eight Jewish delegates what was the secret to the Jews' spiritual survival during their long exile. In his book, the Dalai Lama would write that he only called the meeting because he was really, really, really hoping the Beastie Boys would come.

CHINA

BRING BACK AN EXCIT-ING NEW DISEASE! Pick an animal, vegetable, or mineral, attach the word *flu* and chances are you'll be able to contract it here before it arrives in the U.S.!

HISTORICAL FACT:

Matthew Nathan became the first and only Jewish governor of Hong Kong in 1904. The next British governor claimed his victory was based on a solid economic plan, social outreach…and having the queen move election day to Yom Kippur.

THAILAND: As early as the 17th century, Jewish merchants lived in predominantly Buddhist Thailand, spawning some of the earliest Ju-Bu's known to man. Come visit the Beth Elisheva Synagogue, Mikvah & Jewish Center in Bangkok, where they offer services, Torah study, and the only "all-kosher live sex show" in town!

MALAYSIA: In 2003, Malaysia's prime minister publicly stated that Jews "run the world," so you won't have to pretend that you don't while you're here! Check out Kuala Lumpur's "Petronas Towers," the tallest twin buildings in the world! Just make sure one of the city's fun-loving Muslims doesn't find out you're a Jew, as you might not be taking the elevator back down.

CAMBODIA: Khmer Whouge? This beautiful country has put its horrific genocidal past behind it—think Germany, with more wild oxen. Visit the Temple of Angkor Wat, the eighth wonder of the world, built around 1130 B.C.E.! This huge and elaborately decorated monument to Vishnu features the longest continuous bas-relief in the world, chronicling the story of a Jewish merchant saying goodbye to his Hindu friend.

THE GREAT WALL OF CHINA: Designed to repel barbarian invaders, this wall is the largest man-made construction on Earth. It was built over a thousand years, costing a fortune in blood and treasure. The last major construction occurred in 1500 C.E. when Empress Wu wanted a section of the wall moved back a few feet to accommodate her new couches.

SOUTH KOREA FACTORY TOURS: Visit the plants for Hyundai, KIA, and DaeWoo and witness the making of cars that you would never buy.

NORTH KOREA: Try to score an invite to one of Kim Jong Il's fabulous banquets! Enjoy fine dining, Hennessy V.S.O.P. cognac, and a Hong Kong action flick with this diminutive despot. Knowing that millions of North Koreans are starving to death outside the palace doors only makes the caviar that much yummier!

NORTH KOREA

SOUTH KOREA

JAPAN

DON'T MISS...THE FORBIDDEN CITY: Once the Imperial Palace, this grand castle has since been opened to tourists. Plastic still covers the furniture in the Forbidden Living Room.

TIANANMEN SQUARE: Nothing happened here in 1989.

SHANGHAI: Earlier this past century, Sephardic Jews moved to Shanghai in great numbers and purchased large amounts of real estate. Jacob Sassoon alone reputedly owned 1,900 buildings. This is the first recorded incident of a Jew actually buying a building at a great price instead of just boasting how he could have twenty years ago.

JAPAN
Jewish population: 985 in Kobe, Tokyo, Okinawa (all U.S. Air Force personnel!)

CRIME ADVISORY: The streets of Japan are overwhelmingly safe. You may, however, try to be recruited by the Yakuza, organized criminals involved in murder, extortion, and prostitution. They are also known for their elaborate tattoos. If you join, just remember, you can't be buried in a Jewish cemetery.

DINING IN TOKYO: Typical cost of a Kobe beef steak—$400.00. No, there is no early bird.

MOUNT FUJI: The tallest mountain, actually an active volcano, is also a holy site. Be sure to catch it during the Shinto High Holy Days. Unlike Jewish High Holidays, tickets are free!

VIETNAM

THAILAND

CAMBODIA

VIETNAM: Have you always wanted to see where crazy Uncle Mike's flashbacks take place?

SINGAPORE: Visit ultra-clean Singapore! Just remember not to chew gum, spit on a sidewalk, or spray paint a car or you'll end up like fellow Jew Michael Fay, who was caned there in 1994!

MALAYSIA

SINGAPORE

INDONESIA: Closed for renovations.

Sorry We're **CLOSED**

I N D O N E S I A

 # ISRAEL

Total Population: 6,276,883

Total Number of Jews: 5,021,506

Total Number of Synagogues: 3,568

Total Number of Starbucks: 6,895

Official Language: Hebrew

Official Volume: Loud

It is written that when Moses gazed across the land and saw the vast deserts, harsh plains, and jagged mountains he smiled, turned to God, and said, "No seriously, here? Are you sure you don't want me where all the oil is?" Come and see where Moses was forbidden to tread and reclaim your ancient birthright by watching satellite TV in your air-conditioned beach bungalow while receiving a deep-tissue massage. Wander no more, Jew, you have arrived!

CHEAP PLACE TO STAY:

A kibbutz is an Israeli collective community combining socialism and Zionism. Can be a cheap or even free place to stay, depending on how many chickens you can pluck in an hour.

GALILEE: WALK ON WATER!

Jesus walked on water here—now you can too! Water ski, that is! Check out Crazy Marv's Ski Shack, where Marv throws in a free bottle of Kedem with every rental of 50 bucks or more!

EAT A PITA!

Falafel, tasty fried chickpea balls usually covered in hummus, is the national food of Israel. The Arabs claim the recipe was stolen from them, increasing tensions. The 1993 Pita Accords fell apart when they couldn't agree whether hummus was a condiment or a snack.

FUN IN THE SUN:

Check out Hertzeliya Beach, where you'll see the bizarre site of thousands of buff, gun-toting Israelis playing paddle ball.

TEL AVIV:

They say Jerusalem prays while Tel Aviv plays. Think of it as New York, with fewer Arab cab drivers.

LANGUAGE GUIDE:

Hebrew is a living language once again in Israel. Here are a few helpful phrases:

Shalom = Hello/Goodbye/Peace

Good Evening = Erev Tov

What's this? = Mazeh?

OK = Beseder

Excuse me = Sleecha *Note: though you may use this word, you will never hear it spoken by an Israeli.

COME AND SEE YOUR TREE!

Since 1900, more than one billion trees have been planted in Israel in a massive reforestation effort. Spend the weekend trying to find the one your aunt bought you for your Bar Mitzvah!

LEBANON

GALILEE

MEGIDDO

HERTZELIYA

WEST BANK

TEL AVIV

JERUSALEM

Dead Sea

ISRAEL

JORDAN

EGYPT

TOURIST TRAP: MEGIDDO, inhabited continuously for 6,000 years on the bottleneck between the continents, setting for Armageddon (literally "the hill of Megiddo"). If you go make sure to pick up a souvenir T-shirt.

I'VE BEEN THROUGH ARMAGEDDON AND ALL I GOT WAS THIS LOUSY T-SHIRT

✡ JERUSALEM:

TEMPLE MOUNT: Location of the First and Second Temples, the most holy site in Judaism. Conveniently on top of it is the Dome of the Rock, third holiest site in Islam. Wear your thong and conveniently offend two cultures at once!

SOUK: The Arab market. Enjoy the thrill of haggling for the best price on authentic Middle East trinkets. Look for the "Made in China" sticker and the price drops another two shekels!

RUN FOR OFFICE: THE KNESSET: Israel's Parliament, where dozens of parties vie for 120 seats. With no Constitution, elections can be called whenever there is a shift in power, so figure about every 2 hours. If you play your cards right, you might go home with a tan and a cabinet seat!

MOST POPULAR PASSOVER PHRASE HEARD IN JERUSALEM: "Next Year in Someone Else's House."

SEX HINT: With the majority of single people being in the army, putting the "safety" on refers to the Uzi as well as the condom.

FUN FACT:

Tired of meeting fellow Jewish travelers? Then come to the Middle East! Ride a camel, smoke a hookah, and catch up on the latest reasons why the West is the Great Satan.

SYRIA

LEBANON

ISRAEL

JORDAN

BEIRUT:
It has been called the Paris of the Middle East. Mainly because its people are rude, smelly, and tend to get invaded by their neighbors.

EGYPT

SAUDI ARABIA

CAUTION:
The Middle East is home to poisonous snakes and scorpions. No need to fear them. They don't want anything to do with Jews either.

WORKING OUT:
All the Equinoxes and Crunches have been burned to the ground by the infidels, so if you're looking to get some cardio in between sightseeing, try 45 minutes on the public whipping post. More painful than a treadmill but burns three times the calories!

MEN'S FASHION:
Wear a kaffiyeh, the traditional red checkered headdress. It is comfortable, protects you from the sun, and if you kneel down, you can pass for a table at T.G.I. Friday's (think free wings!).

IRAQ

KUWAIT

IRAN

U.A.E.

IRAN:
You may know it better as
Persia, the setting for Purim.
Come and see the Jew-hating
spirit of Haman that is alive
and well to this day!

DUBAI—CAMEL RACING!
Don't place your bets because that's against th
law, but do enjoy watching the thrill of the rac
Since the lighter the rider, the faster they go, t
ten-year-old jockeys are literally starving to wi

The state-sponsor
purse may go to th
camel owner, but
jockey gets the sa
faction of a job we
done, and a slight
lesser beating.

Check out the United Arab Emirates'
new $14 billion hotel, The World.

With 300 man-made islands represent-
ing all the countries of the Earth...
except one. Can you guess which?

TRAVEL FACT:
After 1948, Arab governments forced
all those Jews to leave, confiscated their
property, and stripped them of their
citizenship. Did we mention you get 10
percent off each night's stay at the Bagh-
dad Sheraton if you book by June 15th?

Your stove, moments before spontaneously combusting.

Friendly neighbor Jason Gillearn keeps a watchful eye on the Mintz family's home across the street.

OOH! WAIT! ONE LAST THING:

Okay, so you've booked the hotel, you've got the tickets, you've rented the car, you're packed and ready to walk out the door.

But are you really ready?

☐ Did you unplug all major and minor appliances (Fig. 6.7)?

☐ Did you confirm your seat on your flight?

☐ Did you arrange for your cell phone to work wherever you're going?

☐ Did you tell the credit card companies you are traveling so they will accept the charges from a foreign country?

☐ Did you fax and email your flight itinerary to every relative you have?

☐ Did you ask your neighbor to pick up your paper, mail, and to be on the lookout for anything suspicious (Fig. 6.8)?

☐ Did you ask another neighbor to check on the first neighbor?

☐ Did you bring the city-appropriate *Time Out* magazine, Frommer's guide, Zagat survey, Lonely Planet, and any other book or periodical that will tell you where everyone else is going?

☐ Did you drop by the local firehouse and give them a detailed map to the important objects in your home that must be saved in case of a fire?

☐ Did you hire a team of cleaners to clean your home so the people you've asked to come in while you're away and water the plants won't think you're a bunch of slobs?

☐ Did you hire a second team to clean before the first team cleans so the first team doesn't think you're a bunch of slobs?

☐ Did you tell everyone your trip is actually two days earlier than your actual travel date so that you can hide in your house and ensure that your directions are being carried out correctly?

☐ Did you get a physical before you left to make sure nothing is wrong because you don't want to risk going to some "foreign" doctor (Fig. 6.9)?

☐ Did you email yourself copies of all your itineraries and travel documents?

☐ Did you set up a second free email account and email yourself the password to the first account in case you forget it?

☐ Did you put 50,000 dollars into your ready cash account in case you or a family member is taken hostage in a foreign country (Fig. 6.10)?

☐ Did you pay your credit card bill so you don't get stuck with a late fee, even though you get them to remove that every month anyway because you are such a good customer?

☐ Did you bring your passport even if you aren't leaving the country in case you get rerouted to Canada?

☐ Did you put your jewelry in a safe deposit box, except for the over-insured stuff that you wouldn't mind getting stolen?

☐ Did you write down the number of miles on your odometer before arranging for your neighbor to start your car while you're gone?

☐ Did you buy travel insurance so no one else has to suffer just because you got yourself hurt or killed on your vacation?

☐ Did you inform your children where all your important documentation and valuables are and label all the valuables with their names to determine who gets what in case you "end up a vegetable"?

☐ Did you pack a checklist of your checklist?

Fig. 6.9

The doctor who will be operating on you at Hospitale Nacionale de la Centro Medico de la San Marco in Chaquite Grande, Honduras.

Fig. 6.10

Remember to figure in the current exchange rate when paying the ransom in a foreign country.

✡ 156

PHONE CONVERSATIONS WITH

Linda Fogel

Bryan:	Hello?
Linda:	Your father and I are coming to New York to spend Thanksgiving with you and I need you to loan us 9,274 American Airlines miles so we can both get free tickets.
Bryan:	A ticket from Denver to New York is like 300 dollars! Just buy the ticket!
Linda:	Why would I buy the ticket when I can fly for free?
Bryan:	The whole point of having miles is to use them when you want to fly somewhere that's really expensive to fly to.
Linda:	You're not going to loan your own parents 9,274 miles so we can save six hundred dollars and come stay with you for Thanksgiving?
Bryan:	First of all, I've been saving my miles for a first-class ticket to Europe for two years! Second of all, what do you mean you're staying with me?
Linda:	You think I'm going to spend 275 dollars a night in some bacteria-infested hotel room when I can stay in my son's guest room for free?
Bryan:	Mom, you guys can't stay here.
Linda:	Why not?
Bryan:	Because it's not fair to impose on Sam.
Linda:	Sam loves us! I already called him and asked him if he minded that we stay over. He said, "no problem."
Bryan:	Did he mention that the guest room only has a single bed?
Linda:	So? You'll sleep in the guest room and we can sleep in your room.
Bryan:	I'm not sleeping with my girlfriend in a single bed!
Linda:	So just don't have her sleep over the two weeks that we're there.
Bryan:	TWO WEEKS! Okay, look, you can have the miles, but only if you come for a week, and you don't stay here.
Linda:	Ten days—and we split it between your place and a hotel.
Bryan:	Eight days, split it between my place and a hotel, I pay for no meals, and you got a deal.
Linda:	Nine days, five your place, four hotel, that's my final offer.

(Bryan hangs up the phone.)

JEWISH MOTHERS: PART SIX

Sam: Hello?

Arlene: When we visited you two months ago you made us sleep in a bacteria-infested hotel because you told me you and Bryan made a pact that the guest room was off-limits to parents! Linda just told me she got four nights with you and 9,274 free bonus miles?! Well, guess what? We're coming to stay with you for Thanksgiving too!

Sam: The Fogels are going to be here! There's no place for you to sleep!

Arlene: Just sleep with Bryan in the guest room!

Sam: I'M NOT SLEEPING IN A SINGLE BED WITH BRYAN!

Arlene: You know what I think? I don't think there ever was a pact. I think you made up this "pact" so that we would have to stay in a hotel to keep us away from you! Well, let me tell you something, young man, your plan has come back to bite you in the ass! Because now—we're coming to stay with you for Hanukah! For Passover! And if that's not enough, we're coming for Sukkot too!

Sam: Sukkot!? When have we ever celebrated Sukkot!?

Arlene: Never! And that's why this year we're going to start by building a Sukkah in your house!

Sam: You can't build a Sukkah inside!

Arlene: Says who?

Sam: Mom, the entire point of Sukkot is to remember when the Jews wandered in the desert and had to sleep outside.

Arlene: You should be grateful that we're building an indoor Sukkah so that you'll have a warm place to sleep while we're staying in your room!

Sam: Mom, I'd love you to come, but you've got to stay in a hotel.

Arlene: Fine. But it's going to cost you 30,000 miles to get out of this.

Sam: Are you nuts? I'm not giving you 30,000 miles!

Arlene: No problem. We'll see you Monday for Simchat Torah.

(Arlene hangs up the phone.)

Arlene Wolfson

When riding a New York subway, Bryan Fogel prepares accordingly.
Find out how neurotic you are on pages 163–165.

STEREOTYPES: LOOK, ETHEL, I FOUND A PENNY!

Jews have had a long and illustrious history. We've been kings and philosophers, entrepreneurs and scholars, lawyers and doctors, and have made countless contributions to the betterment of society. And yet, throughout history Jews have been some of the most persecuted and discriminated-against people in the world. The question is: Why? We don't proselytize, we stay out of everyone's way, and we can throw together a nice bagel and lox brunch at a moment's notice. So why the hell does everybody hate us so much?

The answer is simple: Stereotypes. You may have learned about stereotypes from Spike Lee films or a sensitivity-training video at work entitled *Racism, Bennigan's, and You.*

Fig. 7.1

Hi, I'm Trevon. Want to see it?

Maybe you even have some stereotypes of your own.
- Do you assume that Asians don't have a clue how to drive?
- Do you assume that Hispanic people standing on the corner in front of Home Depot are illegal aliens looking for work?
- When you see a black man, do you assume that he has a 12" penis (Fig. 7.1)?

We ALL have stereotypes about groups of people we don't know. And when it comes to Jews, there are more stereotypes about us than every other religion and ethnicity combined. But are these stereotypes complete misconceptions spawned from people's ignorance and fear? Or, God forbid, are these stereotypes based in some sort of reality? We set out to find the answers.

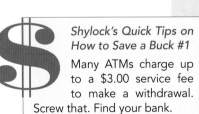

Shylock's Quick Tips on How to Save a Buck #1
Many ATMs charge up to a $3.00 service fee to make a withdrawal. Screw that. Find your bank.

STEREOTYPE #1: ALL JEWS HAVE BIG NOSES

Jews have long been associated with big noses. In 1850, the Jewish nose was described by anthropologist Robert Knox as "a large, massive, club-shaped, hook nose." Large and massive! Ouch. Other 19th-century eugenicists suggested that the Jewish schnozz was a "primitive" characteristic. Having a Jewish nose carried such a stigma that in the 1880s, French Jews were known to wear "fake noses" in order to look less Jewish (Fig. 7.2).

Then in his 1925 book *Mein Kampf,* Adolf Hitler called Jews "arch-pimps" (which is awesome!), and said that big noses were a symptom of syphilis. This confused a lot of small-nosed people with canker sores on their genitals, rashes on the palms of their hands, and swollen lymph nodes, who decided they must have just eaten some bad Thai food.

Cut to modern times, when today's anti-Semites have more sophisticated and advanced theories about Jews and noses. A blogger on Jewwatch.com writes, "Jews have always had big noses. This is because air is free, and I guess they figure they might as well hog it the same way they do with money and bakeries." This last bit refers to the little-known Jew-run conspiracy to take control of the world's bakeries, which cannot be discussed in detail here.

History certainly shows that the stereotype of Jews having big noses has been around for hundreds of years and has not diminished through the ages. So...is it true?

> **CONCLUSION:** Do all Jews have big noses? No! The reason? The twentieth century has led to advances in rhinoplasty and, more important, the rampant cross-breeding with small-nosed Gentiles...and Asians. Hot, tiny, sexy, small-nosed Asians.

Fig. 7.2

Faux nez.

YIDDISH LESSON #3:

Putz (putts)—a fool.

Proper usage: Only a real *putz* would try to convince you that his nose job was to repair a deviated septum.

161

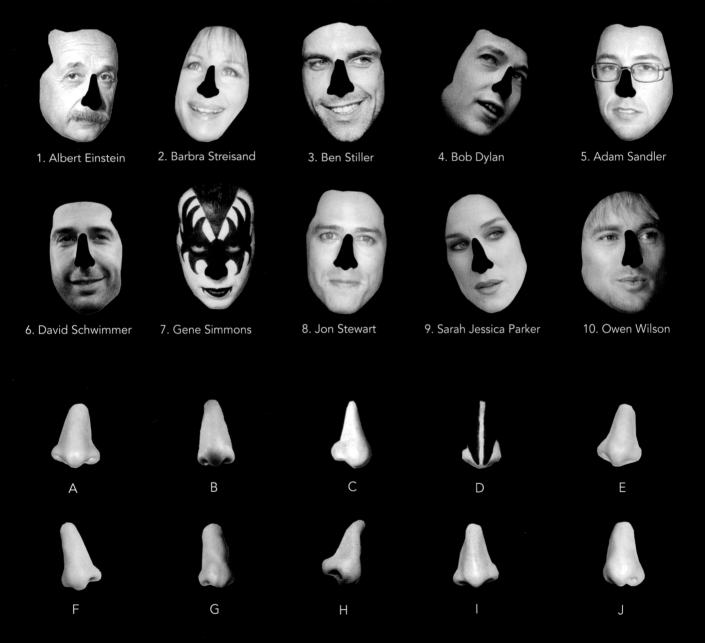

GAME TIME: MATCH THE THE NOSE TO THE JEW

1. Albert Einstein
2. Barbra Streisand
3. Ben Stiller
4. Bob Dylan
5. Adam Sandler
6. David Schwimmer
7. Gene Simmons
8. Jon Stewart
9. Sarah Jessica Parker
10. Owen Wilson

A
B
C
D
E
F
G
H
I
J

STEREOTYPE #2: ALL JEWS ARE NEUROTIC

It's impossible to empirically prove this stereotype to be true or false. The question isn't "Are Jews neurotic?" so much as "How neurotic are they?" Now take our *Jewtopia* Neuroses Quiz to find out for yourself how neurotic you really are.

1. When you travel on a subway, how worried are you that there will be a terrorist attack?

   A. Not worried at all.
   B. Slightly worried.
   C. Extremely worried.
   D. Filled with so much uncontrollable fear and anxiety that you get off ten stops early and take a cab.

2. Which of the following do you think is most likely to give you cancer?

   A. Your cell phone.
   B. Going outside.
   C. Toothpaste.
   D. All of the above.

3. When you are driving through a bad neighborhood, what do you do?

   A. Do nothing. Continue as normal.
   B. Lock the doors and remain at same speed.
   C. Lock the doors and speed up 10 miles an hour.
   D. Lock the doors, speed up 60 miles an hour, call your parents on your cell to tell them you love them and that it was you and not your Mexican gardener, Pedro, who stole the car and ran it into the neighbor's living room when you were fourteen.

4. When you travel on an airline do you:

   A. Ask for a seat in the rear of the plane because you are statistically more likely to survive a crash.
   B. Enter the plane last so you can check out every single passenger on the flight to scope out potential terrorists.
   C. Ring the flight attendant and ask if there is a mechanical problem with the plane every time there is a slight change in speed or altitude.
   D. All of the above.

5. What do you do when you are lying in your bed?

   A. Sleep.
   B. Toss and turn all night because when you have the comforter over you it's too hot, but then when you have just the sheet and blanket it's too cold.
   C. Convince yourself you can actually feel the microscopic dust mites you saw on the *20/20* special.
   D. Flip back and forth between all three twenty-four-hour news channels to see if there's a story that your child has been kidnapped because he didn't return your call in the last three hours.

6. When you are on the computer at home and you receive an email from an unknown sender, do you:

A. Delete it.
B. Spend ten hours running a virus scan to make sure that your system is not infected.
C. Throw away the computer.
D. Accidentally forward the suspect email to every person you know trying to alert them about the virus, thus giving them the virus.

7. Which of the following do you own?

A. A full-body radiation suit in case of chemical attack.
B. A three-years' supply of Bioxin in case of chemical attack.
C. An army-issued "poison pill" to be ingested orally in case of chemical attack that will kill you in eight seconds.
D. All of the above. Plus a hidden fallout shelter in your backyard that you had constructed for Y2K.

8. When someone calls your house past 10:30 P.M., do you think it is:

A. A wrong number.
B. An obnoxious teenager making a prank call.
C. The police calling to tell you that your child has been found dead on the island of Aruba.
D. A relative calling to tell you that the missiles have been launched and that you have eight minutes to live before the nuclear holocaust.

9. When you receive an email from a relative telling you that cooking food in aluminum pans can cause leukemia you:

A. Laugh it off.
B. Throw out all the aluminum pans you just bought and go spend $1,500 on a new set of All-Clad.
C. Induce vomiting, as you have just eaten a turkey burger cooked in aluminum two hours earlier.
D. Become a vegan, start taking yoga, and swear to never eat a cooked piece of food again.

10. Even though it might be many years away, how will you prepare financially for your retirement?

A. Place money into a simple savings account earning 3% interest.
B. Put away 12% of every paycheck you make your whole life into annual Roth IRA accounts so by the time you're 65, according to Sam's mom, you'll have $2,645,325.85.
C. Keep money in a buried safe under your home because the Nazis might come back and you won't have time to get to the bank.
D. Never, ever, ever, ever, ever—UNDER ANY CIRCUMSTANCES—turn on the air-conditioning.

11. Who do you think is out to "get you"?

A. Nobody is out to "get us."

B. The neighborhood mechanic who seems "nice" but we just know he's overcharging us for an engine flush.

C. The waiter who left the apple tart on the check even though we told him we changed our minds and didn't want it.

D. That kid who knocked on our door and told us that he was raising money for disadvantaged inner-city foster children whom we gave a $65.00 check made to "cash" and it's been three months and we're starting to think that maybe that wasn't a legitimate subscription we bought to *Newsweek*.

12. What are you thinking right now in this very moment?

A. This quiz is hysterical.

B. The wattage from the bulb on my nightstand lamp is way too low and I'm probably going blind.

C. Why am I still dating the person on the other side of the bed who's biting their toenails and eating them?

D. Why didn't I wait to buy this book when it came out in paperback, which would have saved me $12.00?

13. During the U.S. mail anthrax scare a few years ago, what did you do?

A. Opened your mail normally.

B. Opened your mail with latex gloves and a surgical mask, then examined each piece under a microscope for spores.

C: Let the mail stack up, then once a week when the "slow" kid from down the block came by asking if you'd like to buy a bag of peanut M&M's for a dollar, buy one, then tell him you'll throw in an extra buck if he'll open your mail.

D. Had mail put on hold for six months because you were living in your backyard bunker.

14. When you have a mild stomachache, what do you think you have?

A. Appendicitis.

B. An ulcer.

C. Crohn's disease and ulcerative colitis.

D. A wound from being shot in gang crossfire.

15. When you're lying in bed at night and you hear a strange noise, what do you think it is?

A. You forgot to turn off the TV.

B. An escaped rapist-murderer-arsonist prisoner has entered your home because you forgot to lock the front door.

C. An escaped rapist-murderer-arsonist has entered your home because you forgot to lock the front door and is watching the TV you forgot to turn off.

D. An escaped rapist-murderer-arsonist has entered your home because you forgot to lock the front door and is watching the TV you forgot to turn off, and once the show is over, he's going to rape you, murder you, and then set your house on fire.

NOW TALLY UP YOUR SCORE!

- If you answered B, C, or D to 5 or fewer of the above questions you are "NEUROTIC."

- If you answered B, C, or D to 6–10 of the above questions, you are "NEUROTIC, UNSTABLE, AND IN NEED OF PSYCHOLOGICAL COUNSELING."

- If you answered B, C, or D to 11 or more of the above questions, congratulations, you are a "FULL-FLEDGED JEW!"

MORE STUFF TO BE NEUROTIC ABOUT

While we were online researching Jewish stereotypes, we came across this on Stormfront.org. If this isn't reason to be neurotic, we don't know what is:

This is the beautiful promotional flyer for HAMMERFEST 2004. Not only do they have a "strongest skinhead competition" and the cutest little Nazi baby you've ever seen, but for $35.00 you get a "botomless cup of beer." Isn't "botomless" spelled with two T's?

Just in case you were wondering, this is the skinhead band H8 Machine at Hammerfest 2004, playing their hit ballad, "To All the Führers I Loved Before."

STEREOTYPE #3: ALL THE BEST DOCTORS AND LAWYERS ARE JEWISH.

FACT. Thank you and good night.

STEREOTYPE #4: ALL JEWS ARE CHEAP

Okay, so maybe Jews aren't always crazy about spending money (Fig. 7.3). But in the recent past, remember, many Jews had everything taken from them, and spent their formative years hungry and dirt-poor. Generations of neurotic Jews have learned to save money out of fear that one day they'll really, really need it.

Fig. 7.3

In the cold night, a lone penny waits for a Jew to spot it and place it in the warmth of his pocket.

Just look what happened to European Jews before and during World War II. In the Warsaw Ghetto, 30% of the population lived in an area encompassing 2.4% of the city's size. The Jews in the ghetto were forced to live on a monthly diet of two pounds of bread, nine ounces of sugar, 3.4 ounces of jam, and 1.75 ounces of fat, roughly 10 percent of daily nutritional requirements. Children would roam the sidewalks looking through garbage cans hoping to find delicious treats such as discarded eggshells or mouse turds. Things got so bad that by November 1940, one couldn't walk through the crowded alleyways without hearing mothers scolding their children, saying, "Eat! Eat! What? You don't like my dirt-clod pie?"

Even before these dark days, however, Jews had a reputation for being stingy. In 1596, William Shakespeare wrote *The Merchant of Venice*, in which he portrays the Jew Shylock as a bloodthirsty moneygrubber who vows to take a pound of flesh in payment for a debt he is owed. Of course, you will remember Shylock's famous, harrowing speech: "If I wanteth extra guacamole on the side, must I payeth for it?"

$ *Shylock's Quick Tips on How to Save a Buck #2*

Barneys, Bloomingdale's, and Saks all give major discounts to their employees. Become friends or family with as many of these employees as possible.

CONCLUSION: Not ALL Jews are cheap, and those who are have different levels of frugality. We have composed a helpful chart on the following pages so that you can discover for yourself just how cheap a Jew you are.

HOW CHEAP A JEW ARE YOU?

	SPENDTHRIFT	LIBERAL TO MODERATE	
WHAT DO YOU TIP ON A FIFTY-DOLLAR FOOD DELIVERY ORDER?	$12.50 (25 percent).	$7.50 (15 percent).	
WHAT KIND OF CAR DO YOU DRIVE?	Brand-new leased Mercedes or BMW	Five-year-old Mercedes, BMW, or Audi that you swear drives like new.	
AT THE END OF THE YEAR, YOU GET A $100,000 BONUS. WHAT DO YOU DO WITH THE MONEY?	Blow it all by taking your 5 closest friends on an all-expenses-paid two-week cruise on the QE2.	Spend $50,000 on remodeling your kitchen, $50,000 in a semi-risky hedge fund that you got a really good tip about.	
WHAT DO YOU DO WHEN YOU SEE A QUARTER ON THE STREET?	Keep walking. It's a quarter.	Pick it up and give it to the home-less guy with the "Will Work for Food" sign on the corner.	
WHERE DO YOU TAKE YOUR FAMILY ON VACATION?	St. Bart's.	Hawaii.	
WHAT CHARITIES DID YOU GIVE TO IN THE LAST YEAR?	The better question is, what charity didn't I give to last year?	Breast Cancer Foundation, and any charity that had "Jew" somewhere in the title.	
YOU'VE STAYED IN A HOTEL FOR A WEEK. WHEN YOU LEAVE, WHAT DO YOU TIP HOUSEKEEPING?	$10.00 a night and a bottle of wine.	$20.00 and the umbrellas that you bought when it was raining.	
WHERE DO YOU SHOP FOR CLOTHES?	Barneys, Bergdorf, or any place that is by appoint-ment only.	Bloomingdale's at full price. Barneys or Bergdorf when it's 50% off.	
WHAT BRAND OF TOILET PAPER DO YOU BUY?	Charmin Ultra two-ply with aloe vera and lanolin.	Charmin Regular.	
HOW DO YOU SPLIT THE CHECK WHEN YOU GO OUT WITH YOUR FRIENDS?	Throw down your platinum card and pick up the check before anyone has a chance to put in.	Split evenly, don't bother to figure out who ordered what.	
WHERE ARE YOUR SEATS FOR THE HIGH HOLIDAYS?	Front row center, with full view of bimah and back-stage passes.	Off-center, rows 10 to 20; when the Torah passes by, you'll have to settle for a wave instead of a kiss.	

FRUGAL	PERPETUATING THE STEREOTYPE
$5.00 (10 percent).	One dollar in quarters, because the guy was two minutes late and he forgot the sweet-and-sour sauce.
Ten-year-old Mercedes, BMW, or Audi that you swear drives like new.	A 20-year-old Volvo with 789,648 miles that has never had any maintenance except oil changes, tires, and brake pads.
Spend $25,000 on your wife's facelift and cellulite reduction, stock the other $75,000 into the S&P 500.	Splurge at Benihana that you had a 25% off coupon for, put the rest into a 3% interest savings account, never touch it, then when you die all your relatives will sue each other for it.
Pick it up, clean it, buy yourself a gumball.	Pick it up, put into your "Lucky Money That I Found on the Street Piggy Bank," which after twenty-five years will be worth $27.52!!! Wow!!!
Somewhere in the United States; only places that Southwest Airlines flies.	Every country in the world on your three-day supersaver package to Disney's Epcot Center in Orlando, Florida.
You bought each of your relatives a $5 tree that will be planted in their name somewhere in Israel.	Donated expired matzohs and an unopened jar of gefilte fish from 1957 to the temple's food drive.
Three-quarters bottle of shampoo, a half empty box of tampons, half eaten roll of Mentos, and whatever singles you have in your pocket.	Steal all the hotel's mini-toiletry items, towels, and bathrobe, feel guilty, leave change in pocket and crumpled-up sperm-filled tissues.
The Gap, Banana Republic, or anywhere else where you can look like every other schmuck.	You haven't shopped for clothes since you were 15 and the doctor said you had "stopped growing."
Quilted Northern.	The single-ply crap that you "take home" from your office building.
Break out the calculator and give everyone their exact amount that's owed, including tip.	Put in the exact dollar amount of whatever you ordered, not including tax or tip, go to the bathroom, let them figure it out.
The adjoining social hall next to the main sanctuary that is opened only once a year to accommodate the overflow. Torah is seen only through closed-circuit TV.	Hover in back of sanctuary, wait for people to leave, steal their seats.

STEREOTYPE #5:
ALL JEWS ARE BAD WITH TOOLS

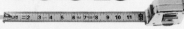

WHERE A GENTILE KEEPS HIS TOOLS

"The Lexington"
Size: 10' x 8'
Storage Area: Sq. Ft: 74' Cu. Ft: 487'
Interior Dimensions: Width: 118 1/4" Depth: 90" Ht: 86 5/8"
Wall Height: 62"
Door Opening: Width: 55 1/2" Height: 60"
Recommended Foundation Size: Width: 121" Depth: 92 3/4"

"The Red Barn"
Size: 10' x 14'
Storage Area: Sq. Ft: 129' Cu. Ft: 952'
Interior Dimensions: Width: 118 1/4" Depth: 157 1/2" Ht: 95 7/8"
Wall Height: 71 1/4"
Door Opening: Width: 55 1/2" Height: 69 1/4"
Recommended Foundation Size: Width: 121" Depth: 160 1/4"

"The Estator"
Size: 10' x 14'
Storage Area: Sq. Ft: 129' Cu. Ft: 956'
Interior Dimensions: Width: 118 1/4" Depth: 157 1/2" Ht: 96 1/2"
Wall Height: 55"
Door Opening: Width: 69" Height: 68 1/4"
Recommended Foundation Size: Width: 121" Depth: 160 1/4"
Bonus Feature: Extra wide door opening makes it easy to store your
adopted stepchild who likes to ride around on yellow tractor-mowers!

Most of us own tools that, in theory, we use to fix stuff around the house. The reality is that we never use them. Most of us don't even know where they are.

So why the ineptness? It's not difficult to use a hammer—you raise it up then smack it down on top of something. A screwdriver? Spin it around and around. Pliers? More or less the same as a screwdriver. Well, here's the problem: We're too busy being neurotic, saying goodbye to our friends, and picking our big noses that we simply don't have the time to figure out how to use a pair of pliers.

WHERE A JEW KEEPS HIS

WHAT GENTILES SEE WHEN THEY LOOK UNDER THE HOOD OF A CAR

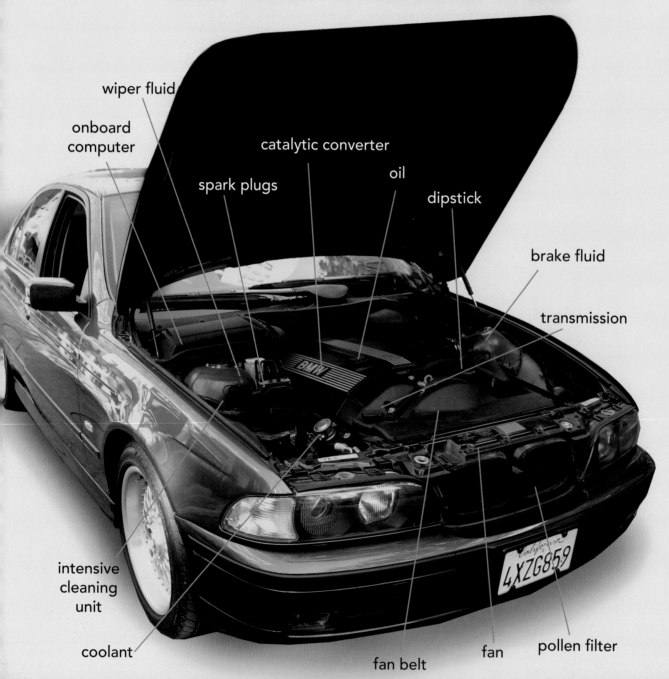

wiper fluid

onboard computer

catalytic converter

spark plugs

oil

dipstick

brake fluid

transmission

intensive cleaning unit

coolant

fan belt

fan

pollen filter

STEREOTYPE #6:
JEWS TAKE AN HOUR TO SAY GOODBYE

Current statistics on the subject show that at any given moment of the day, 37% of Jews in the United States are in the process of saying goodbye to each other. Why do we take so long to say goodbye? Because of our neurotic tendencies, we genuinely believe that every moment together might be our last. What if someone gets in a car wreck on the way home? What if later that night someone has a heart attack? We would spend the rest of our lives asking ourselves, "Why didn't I stay and talk to Morty for a few minutes?" This is because as Jews, we have a level of separation anxiety that doesn't come close in any other religion. We want to cherish every moment with the ones we love, even if it means standing in a dark parking lot in twenty-degree weather dissecting every element of the meal we just had. Enjoy this timeline of what happens during the typical hour of Jews saying goodbye:

9:45 PM: Meal ends. Bill is paid. Coats are retrieved from coat check. There are hugs and kisses all around. Everyone says "goodbye." As everyone starts to disperse, Sharon pipes in and says, "This was great. So when are we doing this again?"

9:50 PM: Nobody has left the restaurant. Both couples loiter by the hostess, checking their date books, trying to figure out the next time they are going to all get together. A date is made. They say goodbye again.

9:54 PM: As they make their way towards the door, Sally throws out to the group, "Is anyone else feeling a little queasy from that fish?" Everyone says "yes." They proceed to discuss each other's symptoms in gruesome detail.

9:57 PM: The two couples exit the restaurant and follow Sally to her car in the parking lot, where she has a pack of Tums. Medication is distributed to the group and they say goodbye again, but "for real this time." As Michael and Sharon start to walk towards their car, Michael turns back around. "Is that a new Infiniti?"

10:05 PM: Michael and Sharon are now in the backseat of Sally's car, Sally and Herb are in the front seat. They are all trying to figure out how to turn on the navigational system. Sally says, "I have no idea how to use this thing!" Michael flips through the owner's manual and proceeds to tell Sally various buttons to push, only managing to turn on the windshield wipers and pop the trunk.

10:14 PM: Michael and Sharon are now in the front seat, Sally and Herb are in the back. Michael swears he can figure out how to turn on the GPS. He continues to fiddle with buttons on the control panel, setting off the car alarm.

10:19 PM: Michael finally figures out how to turn off the car alarm. Michael and Sharon exit the car, Sally and Herb get back in the front seat, and everyone says goodbye. Michael and Sharon start to walk off, Herb offers to drive them to their car. Michael says, "Don't be silly, it's a couple blocks."

10:20 PM: Herb says, "Come on, get in. You didn't even get to ride in the new car."

10:21 PM: Michael says, "It's fine, we need the exercise!"

10:22 PM: Sharon says, "Someone got mugged in the neighborhood two weeks ago! Get in!"

10:23 PM: They go back and forth until Michael and Sharon finally submit and get back into their car.

10:25 PM: Herb pulls up to Michael's car, Michael and Sharon get out and say goodbye.

10:27 PM: Herb waits to pull away to make sure Michael and Sharon are safe. Michael starts the car, puts the window down, and tells Sally, "I can't believe I forgot to tell you, I ran into Judy Goldstein. She and Bruce are getting a divorce." They continue to have a conversation through their car windows, engines running.

10:30 PM: As the discussion of Judy and Bruce's divorce dies down Sharon says, "Well, that's too bad. I really thought they loved each other." They sit in silence for a few seconds. Michael says, "What is love?"

10:33 PM: They say goodbye again and drive off in separate directions.

10:34 PM: Sharon's cell phone rings. It's Sally. Sally says, "Did you see that car wreck on Pico?" Sharon says, "Yeah, we just passed it! That light has been broken for weeks. I knew that was an accident waiting to happen! Do you think someone's hurt?"

10:35 PM: Michael's cell phone rings. It's Herb. Herb says, "I got to tell you, Michael, this GPS system is really fantastic! It just routed me around a traffic jam on the 405—did you see that accident on Pico?"

10:45 PM: Both conversations continue until all have arrived home safely. Sharon and Herb both tell Sally and Michael, "Make sure you shut your garage door! The news said a rapist escaped from that prison a few hundred miles from here last night!"

STEREOTYPE #7: ALL JEWISH WOMEN ARE J.A.P.S

Of course, this isn't true. Scientists first identified the J.A.P. in the wild in postwar-era Long Island. (The term "Jewish American Princess" is a misnomer, as these women are not actually royalty.) Upwardly mobile immigrant families, finally enjoying themselves after moping through the Holocaust, lavished money and gifts on their daughters, as these women were in essence the future of Judaism. These girls could be distinguished from ordinary citizens by their designer clothes, fancy cars, and identical noses (it would later be learned that they all had the same plastic surgeon). Defining characteristics included: mild to severe shopping addiction, a propensity to be waited on, and a shrilly nasal voice, thought by some to be a kind of mating call.

By the 1980s, the J.A.P. had become the presumed identity of nearly every Jewish woman in America. Anti-J.A.P.pery was evident on college campuses, evidenced by anti-J.A.P. graffiti and "Biggest J.A.P. on Campus" contests (Fig. 7.4). Some would argue that Jewish men propagate the myth that all Jewish women are spoiled, demanding, and neurotic in order to rationalize dating and marrying Gentile women instead of Jewish women. This argument is usually made by sociology professors at liberal arts colleges or by total J.A.P.s.

According to Susan Weidman Schneider, editor in chief of *Lilith* magazine, this stereotype is harmful not just to Jewish women but to all Jews: "There should be a distant early warning signal that warns us of incipient anti-Semitism when Jews are ineluctably connected to money and privilege, as is the case often with the J.A.P. stereotype." Well! Apparently someone's daddy didn't love her enough to buy her a BMW convertible when she turned sixteen!

Fig. 7.4

Vassar College's 1997 Biggest J.A.P. contest winners Ashley and Jordan Leibowitz.

DON'T LAUGH, OR SUFFER THE WRATH:
CLASSIC J.A.P. JOKES

Q: How many J.A.P.s does it take to screw in a lightbulb?
A: Two, one to call Daddy, and one to get a Diet Coke.

Q: Did you hear about the new J.A.P. horror film?
A: It's called *Debbie Does Dishes*.

Q: What's the difference between a J.A.P. and an Italian American princess?
A: With the Italian American princess, the jewels are fake and the orgasms are real.

Q: Where does a Jewish husband hide money from his J.A.P. wife?
A: Under the vacuum cleaner.

Q: Did you hear about the J.A.P. who had plastic surgery?
A: Her husband cut up her credit cards.

Q: What's a J.A.P.'s favorite position?
A: Inside Bloomingdale's.

STEREOTYPE #8: ALL JEWS ARE FUNNY

Fiction. This is a ridiculous stereotype. While there are God knows how many famous funny Jews—from Mel Brooks and Woody Allen to Larry David and Jerry Seinfeld—here are 27 famous Jews who are not funny:

- *Senator Joseph Lieberman is not funny.*
- *Kenny G is not funny.*
- *Barbra Streisand is not funny.*
- *David Berkowitz is not funny.*
- *Slash (Guns N' Roses) is not funny.*
- *Dee Snider is not funny, he is scary.*
- *Itzhak Perlman is not funny.*
- *Sam's cousin Milton is very not funny.*
- *Franz Kafka is really, really, really not funny.*
- *Primo Levi is incredibly not funny.*
- *Harold Pinter is not funny.*
- *Elie Wiesel is not funny.*
- *Leonard Nimoy is not funny.*
- *Herman Wouk is not funny.*
- *Frida Kahlo is not funny but had one crazy-ass monobrow!*
- *Mike Wallace is not funny at all.*
- *Ari Fleischer is not funny and should be ashamed of himself.*
- *Wolf Blitzer is not funny, but he is hairy.*
- *Marv Albert is not funny, but he is kinky.*
- *Albert Einstein is not funny, but he was very funny looking.*
- *Meyer Lansky was not funny.*
- *Marcia Clark is not funny and screwed up an airtight case. Good job, Marcia!*
- *Nostradamus was not funny, but prophesied that in the future he would be.*
- *Karl Marx was not funny.*
- *Leon Trotsky was really not funny.*
- *Steve Ballmer—CEO of Microsoft and richest Jew in the world—is not funny, but when you're that rich everyone will laugh at your jokes anyway.*
- *Ben Bernanke is not funny but controls the entire world...and he's OK with that.*

STEREOTYPE #9: ALL JEWS ARE HAIRY

Any Jewish man who has showered at his local Jewish Community Center knows that Jewish men are hairier than the average male. And even though they may not all be excessively hairy, we challenge you to find a Jewish man on this planet who does not at least grow chest hair. The most important positive aspect of body hair—believe it or not—is that it can help you meet a mate. When your pheromones are released, your pelt retains your "chemical signature," and this plays a major role in attraction. Also, a thick coat of body hair offers your typical fuzzy Jew both added warmth and extra protection from germs—and if we didn't have that protection, can you imagine how sick we'd be? Below is a list of wonderful benefits that having back hair offers you and your loved one.

- In bed, you can turn your back towards your girlfriend and she still feels like she's lying on your chest.
- You can show your special someone how much you love her by shaving her initials into the small of your back.
- When you're at the beach, you don't have to wear sunscreen because your hair can repel the sun's rays.
- You don't have to worry about going to the gym because nobody's going to see your muscles anyway.
- You never need to buy a gorilla suit for Halloween.
- Like a sheep, you can continually shear your back and make quilts and sweaters for loved ones.

MORAL HYPOTHETICAL:
Your best friend, who's bald, starts wearing an exceptionally bad toupee. It looks like a raccoon has died on his head, and everyone's calling him "Davy Crockett" behind his back. You think he should know the truth, but you don't want to hurt his feelings. *What do you do?*

ALAN SHAPIRO COHEN

Linda Fogel

Linda: They just apprehended a group of terrorists who were trick-or-treating!

Bryan: What?

Linda: They were dressed as the Backstreet Boys and they knocked on the door of Edward McGaffigan Jr. When he answered, Edward tried to give them all Tootsie Rolls, and the terrorist dressed as AJ McLean forced him at gunpoint to drive them to Braidwood 1!

Bryan: Who is Edward McGaffigan Jr. and what is Braidwood 1?

Linda: He's the commissioner of the U.S. Nuclear Regulatory Commission and Braidwood 1 is a pressurized nuclear water reactor 24 miles southwest of Joliet, Illinois!!!

Bryan: OK?

Linda: They forced Edward to give them 10 pounds of enriched plutonium— enough to build a dirty bomb that could wipe out Manhattan!!! They got caught when the security guard asked them to sing "All I Have to Give" and none of them knew the words!

Bryan: That story can't be true.

Linda: It is true! I just read it in *The Onion*!

Bryan: That's a fake newspaper, Mom!

Linda: They said that there's two more trick-or-treating terrorist groups on the loose dressed up as *NSync and Boyz II Men! The FBI is recommending that all citizens learn the words to "Bye Bye Bye" and "I'll Make Love to You"!

Bryan: OK, I'll get right on it.

Linda: Grab a pen and paper, I printed the lyrics off the Internet. "Girl, are you ready, it's gonna be a long night. Throw your clothes on the floor. I'm gonna take my clothes off too. I made plans to be with you. Girl, whatever you ask me you know I'll do. Baby, tonight is your night. And I will do you right."

Bryan: OK—I wrote 'em down. I gotta go!

Linda: Hold on, I haven't given you the lyrics to "Bye Bye Bye" yet! "Don't wanna be a fool for you. Just another player in your game for two. I don't wanna be your fool. But it ain't no lie. Baby, bye bye bye."

(Bryan hangs up the phone.)

183

JEWISH MOTHERS: PART SEVEN

Arlene: We know why you're not married and I just wanted to tell you it's OK.

Sam: Really? Thanks, Mom.

Arlene: I just don't understand why you kept it a secret from us. Did you think that we would be ashamed of you and not love you anymore just because you're a homosexual?

Sam: What!?

Arlene: Just promise me that you're wearing condoms!

Sam: I'm not gay! What makes you think I'm gay?!

Arlene: You're 31, you've never even been in a serious relationship, you live in the West Village with your "writing partner," you're 50 feet from the Gay and Lesbian Center, and you're on BROADWAY!!!

Sam: That doesn't mean I'm gay!

Arlene: I can't believe I never put it all together. In high school you were in Drama Club, you were the best dancer at all the Bar Mitzvahs, and your favorite TV show was *Dynasty*!!!

Sam: I'm not in a relationship because I've been focusing on my career.

Arlene: Honey, it's okay! You're here! You're queer! Get used to it! I just don't understand why you wouldn't use your gay mafia connections to move your career forward.

Sam: Gay mafia? There's no gay mafia!

Arlene: Yes there is and you should get Tom Cruise to help you. He's gay like you!

Sam: No he's not! He's a Scientologist. There's a difference.

Arlene: Well then ask John Travolta! How's November 12th, 2006?

Sam: For what?

Arlene: That's the earliest date I could get at this gay congregation in Boston where you and Bryan can legally get married.

Sam: Bryan and I are not getting married!

Arlene: You have to get married. Or I'll lose my deposit!

Sam: Mom, I'm not gay, I love you, I gotta go.

Arlene: Just promise me you'll check out www.Familieslikeours.org so that you two can learn how to legally adopt me and Linda a grandchild!

(Sam hangs up the phone.)

Arlene Wolfson

184

Did Jews stunt the growth of Gary Coleman so they could create *Diff'rent Strokes*?

CONSPIRACY THEORIES: DO JEWS CONTROL THE WORLD?

According to Tom Metzger, founder of W.A.R. (White Aryan Resistance Organization) "…Jews are personally responsible for the fall of the Roman Empire, the 1929 stock market crash, the loss of World War II by a prominent European country, and the attacks of 9/11. They control the entertainment, financial, legal, medical, psychiatric, and accountancy professions, and are the force behind international communism, Freemasonry, sex education, the media, and the Catholic Church."

While being considered cheap, neurotic, and hairy may not be anything to write home about, those stereotypes aren't necessarily detrimental to our people. Conspiracy theories are a whole other story. First, there are the outlandish theories that reach into the realm of total and utter paranoia. These range anywhere from blaming Jews for the explosion of the Space Shuttle *Challenger* to claiming Jews orchestrated the attacks on 9/11! Now as ludicrous as it is to be accused of orchestrating something as complicated as a 9/11 and a spaceship blowing up (considering most Jews don't know where the fuse box is in their own home), it is hard to give these any real credibility (Fig. 8.1 and 8.2).

But then there are the theories that could have some credibility: Jews control the banks; Jews control the media; Jews control the economy. Could these conspiracy theorists be right? Where did these theories come from? And why do Jews, who make up less than .0002 percent of the world's population, have so many negative conspiracies associated with us?

This chapter will attempt to discover the real truth behind these accusations and find out once and for all if Jews are, as Tom Metzger so eloquently states, "greedy, usurious, scheming Christ-killers who won't eat pork because it reminds them of their parents, go around moving into other people's countries and buying up all the pawnshops and delicatessens." Pork reminds us of our parents? Oh! We get it, because Jews are pigs. Good one, Tom!

CHAPTER EIGHT

Fig. 8.1

Were Jews behind the breakup of Hall & Oates?

Fig. 8.2

Are Jews behind you being so dumb?

186

CONSPIRACY THEORY #1: JEWS CONTROL HOLLYWOOD

Part I: The Motion Picture Studios

In early 20th-century America, Jewish immigrants could arrive from Europe with only their wits and a sack of matzoh balls to their name and make the American Dream come true. Such was the case with the Warner brothers, Harry and Jack Cohn, Samuel Goldwyn, Louis B. Mayer, Adolph Zukor, Carl Laemmle, and William Fox, who all went to Los Angeles and created what would become today's major Hollywood studios. But is the idea that Jews still control Hollywood today yet another malevolent conspiracy theory? And if so, then where's our movie deal? We took a closer look at the major motion picture and television studios in order to get to the truth behind the conspiracy.

COLUMBIA

FOUNDED: 1924 by Harry and Jack Cohn (Jews)

CURRENT PRESIDENT: Amy Pascal (Jew)

MOVIE THAT REFLECTED MOST FAVORABLY ON THE JEWS: *Bob and Carol and Ted and Alice*—Elliot Gould proves that Jews are hip enough to "swing."

MOVIE THAT REFLECTED LEAST FAVORABLY ON THE JEWS: *Panic Room*—After the release of this film, the neurotic Jewish stereotype was further solidified when sales of home panic rooms among Jews spiked 98 percent.

WARNER BROS.

FOUNDED: 1918 by Albert, Sam, Harry, and Jack Warner (Jews)

CURRENT PRESIDENT: Barry Meyer and Alan Horn (Jews)

MOVIE THAT REFLECTED MOST FAVORABLY ON THE JEWS: *Outbreak*—A deadly virus that's going to wipe out the entire world is stopped by asthmatic, nebbish, flat-footed Jew Dustin Hoffman.

MOVIE THAT REFLECTED LEAST FAVORABLY ON THE JEWS: *The Jazz Singer*, 1927—Jack Robin, the son of a Jewish Cantor, leaves home to become a Broadway entertainer and paints his face black! Oy gevalt!

MGM

FOUNDED: 1924 by Louis B. Mayer, Samuel Goldwyn, and Irving Thalberg (Jews)

CURRENT PRESIDENT: Michael Nathanson (Jew)

MOVIE THAT REFLECTED MOST FAVORABLY ON THE JEWS: *Yentl*—Barbra Streisand defies 5,000 years of Jewish law by posing as a man so she can crash a yeshiva and study the Torah.

MOVIE THAT REFLECTED LEAST FAVORABLY ON THE JEWS: *Yentl*—Barbra Streisand defies 5,000 years of Jewish law by posing as a man so she can crash a yeshiva and study the Torah.

UNIVERSAL

FOUNDED: 1909 by Carl Laemmle (Jew)

CURRENT PRESIDENT: Rick Finkelstein (Jew)

MOVIE THAT REFLECTED MOST FAVORABLY ON THE JEWS: *ET*—Most people don't know this, but the most beloved movie character of all time was Jewish. Why else would he have spent the whole movie trying to "phone home"?

MOVIE THAT REFLECTED LEAST FAVORABLY ON THE JEWS: *American Pie*—Created an entirely new and derogatory stereotype that Jews like to have sex with baked goods.

PARAMOUNT

FOUNDED: 1916 by Adolph Zukor (Jew)

CURRENT PRESIDENT: Brad Grey (Jew)

MOVIE THAT REFLECTED MOST FAVORABLY ON THE JEWS: *Raiders of the Lost Ark*—A Gentile risks his life to save our little old Ark of the Covenant from the Nazis.

MOVIE THAT REFLECTED LEAST FAVORABLY ON THE JEWS: *The Ten Commandments*—Right-wing, gun-toting NRA radical Charlton Heston plays the most famous Jew of all time. Couldn't they have found anyone else?

DISNEY

FOUNDED: 1939 by Walt Disney (Rumored anti-Semite)

CURRENT PRESIDENT: Robert Iger (Jew)

MOVIE THAT REFLECTED MOST FAVORABLY ON THE JEWS: *Pinocchio*—For once, they made the lie-telling-big-nosed kid an Italian.

MOVIE THAT REFLECTED LEAST FAVORABLY ON THE JEWS: *Snow White and the Seven Dwarfs*—Rumored anti-Semite Walt Disney made six out of the seven dwarfs neurotic Jews (Dopey, Grumpy, Doc, Bashful, Sneezy, and Sleepy) and the one Gentile dwarf "Happy."

NEW LINE (A DIVISION OF TIME WARNER)

FOUNDED: 1967 by Robert Shaye (Jew)

CURRENT PRESIDENT: Robert Shaye (Jew)

MOVIE THAT REFLECTED MOST FAVORABLY ON THE JEWS: *American History X*—Nazi skinhead befriends a black man in prison who teaches him that "Jews are people too."

MOVIE THAT REFLECTED LEAST FAVORABLY ON THE JEWS: *Lord of the Rings*—A bunch of short, hairy, persecuted people fight the biggest battle the universe has ever seen over a piece of jewelry. Don't think we didn't catch that one, New Line.

MIRAMAX

FOUNDED: 1979 by Harvey and Bob Weinstein (Jews)

CURRENT PRESIDENTS: The Weinsteins, but they were acquired by Disney in 2005

MOVIE THAT REFLECTED MOST FAVORABLY ON THE JEWS: *A Price Above Rubies*—Renee Zellweger plays a badass Chasidic who tells her husband, "It's my way or the Chai-way."

MOVIE THAT REFLECTED LEAST FAVORABLY ON THE JEWS: *Life Is Beautiful*—Nazi concentration camps are made to look like a trip to Disneyland.

20th CENTURY FOX

FOUNDED: 1915 by Willam Fox (originally William Fried—Jew)

CURRENT PRESIDENT: Thomas Rothman (Jew)

MOVIE THAT REFLECTED MOST FAVORABLY ON THE JEWS: *Star Wars*—Jewess Carrie Fisher plays Princess Leia and shows that Jewish American Princesses, when called upon, can kick serious intergalactic ass.

MOVIE THAT REFLECTED LEAST FAVORABLY ON THE JEWS: *Cocoon*—A bunch of old Jews in South Florida ditch their families for the opportunity to live forever with a bunch of aliens on another planet.

DREAMWORKS

FOUNDED: 1994 by Steven Spielberg, Jeffrey Katzenberg, David Geffen (Super-Jews)

CURRENT PRESIDENT(s): Spielberg, Katzenberg, Geffen

MOVIE THAT REFLECTED MOST FAVORABLY ON THE JEWS: *Meet the Parents*—Nebby Jew charms scary Gentile dad and wins himself HBS (Hot Blonde Shiksa).

MOVIE THAT REFLECTED LEAST FAVORABLY ON THE JEWS: *Cast Away*—Tom Hanks, a Gentile, not only becomes a castaway on a deserted island, but builds a home, a boat, learns how to catch crab and cook them over a fire that he made, loses 60 pounds, looks fantastic, and survives. Enough said.

TOTALS

NUMBER OF MAJOR STUDIOS DISCUSSED HERE: Ten

NUMBER OF STUDIOS CREATED BY JEWS: Nine

PERCENTAGE: 90%

NUMBER OF STUDIOS CURRENTLY RUN BY JEWS: Ten

PERCENTAGE: 100%

CONCLUSION: Yes, we do control the movie studios. All Jews please report to the World Conspiracy Headquarters immediately (don't forget to bring your pass code).

HBO

FOUNDED: 1972 by Gerald Levin, Jew

CURRENT PRESIDENT: Carolyn Strauss, Jew

SHOW THAT REFLECTED MOST FAVORABLY ON THE JEWS: *Sex and the City*—Sarah Jessica Parker shows that even when wearing $700 Manolo Blahniks, Jewish women aren't above having a one-night stand.

SHOW THAT REFLECTED LEAST FAVORABLY ON THE JEWS: *Curb Your Enthusiasm*—Bald, nebbishy Jew Larry David plays himself and pisses off everyone he comes into contact with.

CBS

FOUNDED: 1939 by Arthur Judson, Gentile who quickly sold to Jews Jerome Louchheim and Ike and Leon Levy

CURRENT PRESIDENT: Les Moonves, Jew

CEO: Sumner Redstone, formerly Sumner Murray Rothstein

SHOW THAT REFLECTED MOST FAVORABLY ON THE JEWS: *Good Times*—One of the most accurate portrayals of a family of Reform Jews ever seen on television.

SHOW THAT REFLECTED LEAST FAVORABLY ON THE JEWS: *M*A*S*H*—Jamie Farr, the one Jew in the platoon, would run around like an idiot dressing in drag so they would send him home.

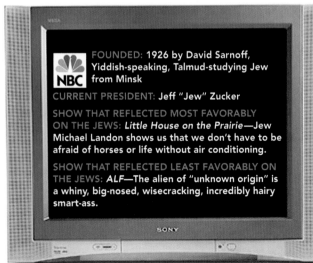

NBC

FOUNDED: 1926 by David Sarnoff, Yiddish-speaking, Talmud-studying Jew from Minsk

CURRENT PRESIDENT: Jeff "Jew" Zucker

SHOW THAT REFLECTED MOST FAVORABLY ON THE JEWS: *Little House on the Prairie*—Jew Michael Landon shows us that we don't have to be afraid of horses or life without air conditioning.

SHOW THAT REFLECTED LEAST FAVORABLY ON THE JEWS: *ALF*—The alien of "unknown origin" is a whiny, big-nosed, wisecracking, incredibly hairy smart-ass.

abc

FOUNDED: 1943 by Edward Noble, Gentile

CURRENT PRESIDENT: Ann Sweeney, Gentile

SHOW THAT REFLECTED MOST FAVORABLY ON THE JEWS: *Happy Days*—Let it never be forgotten that the Fonz, at one time the coolest person on TV who could even fix a broken jukebox by smashing it with his elbow, was played by Henry Winkler.

SHOW THAT REFLECTED LEAST FAVORABLY ON THE JEWS: *MacGyver*—Jews feel inadequate enough that they're bad with tools, and it only made matters worse to see a Gentile on TV every week who could build a nuclear weapon out of chewing gum, tin foil, and liquid Tide.

FOUNDED: 1980 by Robert L. Johnson, Gentile
CURRENT PRESIDENT: Deborah Lee, Gentile
SHOW THAT REFLECTED MOST FAVORABLY ON THE JEWS: *BET Style*—Fashion program where basketball jerseys ten sizes too big encrusted with 40 carats of diamonds and gold are proclaimed as cool, making the tacky outfits of old Jewish women in Palm Beach tame in comparison.
SHOW THAT REFLECTED LEAST FAVORABLY ON THE JEWS: *Black College Football*—Fast, coordinated, and strong black athletes playing football confirm that Jews have absolutely no business partaking in professional sports.

FOUNDED: 1995 by Paramount Television Group
CURRENT PRESIDENT: Les Moonves, Jew
Co-President: Dawn Ostroff, Jew
SHOW THAT REFLECTED MOST FAVORABLY ON THE JEWS: *WWE SMACKDOWN*—Starring Jewish wrestling champ GOLDBERG, who could jump 20 feet off the ropes and somehow not throw out his back.
SHOW THAT REFLECTED LEAST FAVORABLY ON THE JEWS: *America's Next Top Model*

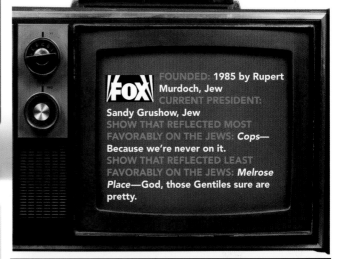

FOUNDED: 1985 by Rupert Murdoch, Jew
CURRENT PRESIDENT: Sandy Grushow, Jew
SHOW THAT REFLECTED MOST FAVORABLY ON THE JEWS: *Cops*—Because we're never on it.
SHOW THAT REFLECTED LEAST FAVORABLY ON THE JEWS: *Melrose Place*—God, those Gentiles sure are pretty.

FOUNDED: 1995 by Jamie Kellner, Jew

CURRENT PRESIDENT: Garth Ancier, Gentile

SHOW THAT REFLECTED MOST FAVORABLY ON THE JEWS: *Buffy the Vampire Slayer*—Jewess Sarah Michelle Gellar could kill vampires with her bare hands and never even mess up her hair.

SHOW THAT REFLECTED LEAST FAVORABLY ON THE JEWS: *Seventh Heaven*—Look how pretty and close and happy and perfect the nice religious Gentile family is!

TOTALS
NUMBER OF NETWORKS DISCUSSED HERE: Eight
NUMBER OF NETWORKS FOUNDED BY JEWS: Six
PERCENTAGE: 75%
NUMBER OF NETWORKS CURRENTLY RUN BY JEWS: Six
PERCENTAGE: 75%
CONCLUSION: While this is the tip of the iceberg of TV stations, it is safe to say that the majority of shows you are seeing on TV were put there by Jews. We would like to formally apologize for the following: *T.J. Hooker, American Idol, Mr. Ed, Fantasy Island, Battle of the Network Reality Stars, Britney and Kevin: Chaotic, BJ and the Bear, Wife Swap, Dog the Bounty Hunter, Bridezilla, Doogie Howser, M.D., Saved by the Bell,* and *I Want to Be a Hilton.*

CONSPIRACY THEORY #1: JEWS CONTROL HOLLYWOOD
Part III: Jews and the Black Sitcom

Researching the conspiracy of Jewish-controlled Hollywood, we must share another startling conspiracy that we've uncovered. All of the most popular black sitcoms of the '70s and '80s were created by...that's right, you guessed it, Jews! This could be part of another Jewish conspiracy to control black people along with everyone else in the world, or to sneak subversive messages into seemingly innocent entertainment. Or maybe it's simply because if there's one thing that the Jewish writer in Hollywood knows, it's what it's like to be black and living in America.

The Fresh Prince of Bel-Air

JEWISH CREATORS: Andy Borowitz and Susan Borowitz

THE PLOT: Underprivileged inner-city youth gets shipped from his mother's house in Philadelphia to his uncle's mansion in Bel-Air to whip him into shape. He learns valuable life lessons that enable him to eventually go out into the world and defeat evil aliens and robots.

HOW YOU CAN TELL JEWS CREATED THIS SHOW: Who better understands the plight of living in Bel-Air?

Good Times

JEWISH CREATORS: Norman Lear and Bud Yorkin (Writers: Garry Shandling, Saul Turtel-taub, Bernie Orenstein, Arnie Rosen, and James Stein—the Jewish equivalent of the "Dream Team")

THE PLOT: An impoverished family of African Americans trying to figure out how they were going to eat every week. Every now and then Janet Jackson would show up playing an abused neighbor. Laughs aplenty.

HOW YOU CAN TELL JEWS CREATED THIS SHOW: Aside from a family trying to figure out when their next meal was going to be, we have absolutely no idea.

What's Happening!!

JEWISH CREATORS: Eric Monte (What was "happening" was that Eric was black but the four head writers were Barbara Berkowitz, Mary Farrell, Joseph Neustein, and James Stein.)

THE PLOT: Rerun, Dwayne, Roger, and their best friend Shirley get into various high jinks. This is a landmark in black entertainment as it is the first time there are three three-hundred-plus-pound black actors on the same show. (Don't forget Momma!)

HOW YOU CAN TELL JEWS CREATED THIS SHOW: Jews hanging around in delicatessens all day kvetching was the inspiration for Rerun, Dwayne, and Roger hanging out at the diner. Even Dwayne's catchphrase, "Hey! Hey! Hey!" sounds almost identical to a Jew choking "Chach! Chach! Chach!"

The Jeffersons

JEWISH CREATORS: Norman Lear and Bud Yorkin

THE PLOT: Wealthy African American New Yorker George Jefferson owns a chain of Laundromats throughout the city. He works all day, makes all the money, then comes home to find Weezy and Florence fucking all his shit up.

HOW YOU CAN TELL JEWS CREATED THIS SHOW: Successful NY businessman is driven crazy by his spendthrift nagging wife and his slacker housekeeper. Sound familiar?

The Cosby Show

JEWISH CREATORS: Michael Leeson and Ed Weinberger
THE PLOT: Bill Cosby plays a New York doctor doing the best he can to raise his family of five children. Each week Bill Cosby imparted a valuable family lesson to the nation and then went to a Motel Six and had unprotected sex, fathering countless illegitimate children who pop up out of nowhere and sue him.

HOW YOU CAN TELL JEWS CREATED THIS SHOW: The father was a doctor, the mother was a lawyer, and they put a lot of pressure on their children to succeed...Not to mention that the grandparents were over **ALL** the time.

Diff'rent Strokes

JEWISH CREATORS: Jeff Harris and Bernie Kukoff

THE PLOT: A rich old white guy adopts the two poor black kids of his dead housekeeper and puts them up in a fancy New York townhouse. Even though the children are surrounded by rich whites, they demonstrate they've kept their blackness by saying things like, "Wat chew talkin' about, Willis?"

HOW YOU CAN TELL JEWS CREATED THIS SHOW: Wealthy Jews adopting the little midget black child with a kidney disorder and his Afrocentric older brother of their dead housekeeper happens every day on the Upper West and East sides of Manhattan.

Sanford and Son

JEWISH CREATORS: Norman Lear and Bud Yorkin

THE PLOT: Father and son live together in a shithole, and try to get along with each other while owning and operating a junkyard.

HOW YOU CAN TELL JEWS CREATED THIS SHOW: Sanford's signature move was feigning a heart attack and pretending that at any moment he could die so he could guilt-trip his son, Lamont, into making him do whatever he wanted. Sound familiar again?

Webster

JEWISH CREATORS: Jewish network execs spotted Emmanuel Lewis doing a Burger King commercial, hunted down his little black ass, and promptly signed him to his own TV show. The problem was that they didn't have an idea about what the show would be. The answer: Bring in Fred Rubin and Barry Gold.

THE PLOT: The token black friends of a wealthy white family die in a car accident and the rich white married couple inherit Webster. Desperate to compete with the success of *Diff'rent Strokes*, the Jews at ABC had to find their own cute little black kid with a kidney disorder who looked ten years younger than he actually was.

HOW YOU CAN TELL JEWS CREATED THIS SHOW: Wealthy Jews adopting the cute little midget black child with a kidney disorder of their token dead black friends happens every day on the North Shore of Chicago.

CONSPIRACY THEORY #2: JEWS CONTROL THE MEDIA

When Johann Gutenberg invented the movable type printing press in 1440, this hapless German probably had no idea he was creating yet another tool Jews could use to covertly control the hearts and minds of people and push our liberal views on the entire world. But 550 years after his invention, is there any truth to hate groups' claims that Jews control the media?

 LOOK AT THE NEWSPAPERS AND MAGAZINES BELOW. CAN YOU TELL WHICH ARE RUN BY JEWS AND WHICH ARE RUN BY GENTILES?

THE WALL STREET JOURNAL.

Morgan Stanley raises ratings on Manischewitz: CEO states, "It's time to put your money into Matzoh"

☐ JEW
☐ GENTILE

Chicago Tribune

CHICAGO PROFESSOR PROVES THEORY OF INTELLIGENT DESIGN, "HOW ELSE COULD WE HAVE GOTTEN HERE?"

Hospital regulator targets infections

Citing criticism, watchdog plans to toughen rules

Bitter cold grabs Chicago in its icy grip

☐ JEW
☐ GENTILE

The Washington Post

Halliburton wins 20 billion dollars in Iraqi contracts— Cheney's response: "That's all?"

Bush Plans Coulter to Replace Rehnquist

Limbaugh to High Court

Failed to Receive Ten Percent of Vote

• MacAuliffe Suicide

GOP Rules Senate With Seventy-one Seats

☐ JEW
☐ GENTILE

The New York Times

U.S. Continues to Successfully Spread Democracy

Release Given To McDougal; Health is Cited

Clinton Starts Visit to China By Answering Critics in U.S.

☐ JEW
☐ GENTILE

NATIONAL EDITION
Los Angeles Times

FRIDAY, OCTOBER

Scientific Research Links Asian Tsunami and Gulf Coast Hurricanes to Bush Administration

NEWS ANALYSIS
Will N.Y. M.O. Work in L.A.?

☐ JEW
☐ GENTILE

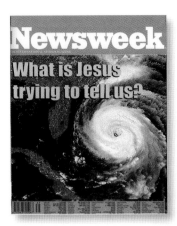

Newsweek

What is Jesus trying to tell us?

☐ JEW
☐ GENTILE

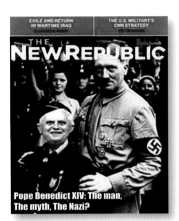

THE **NEW REPUBLIC**

EXILE AND RETURN IN WARTIME IRAQ | THE U.S. MILITARY'S CNN STRATEGY

Pope Benedict XIV: The man, The myth, The Nazi?

☐ JEW
☐ GENTILE

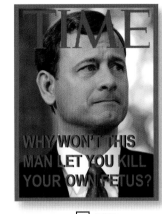

TIME

WHY WON'T THIS MAN LET YOU KILL YOUR OWN FETUS?

☐ JEW
☐ GENTILE

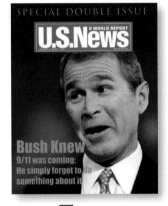

SPECIAL DOUBLE ISSUE

U.S.News & WORLD REPORT

Bush Knew
9/11 was coming:
He simply forgot to do something about it

☐ JEW
☐ GENTILE

PLAYBOY

Girls of the top
10 yeshivas:
All wigs are off!

☐ JEW
☐ GENTILE

ANSWER KEY

NEW YORK TIMES
Jew—Chairman and publisher, Arthur Sulzberger

WASHINGTON POST
Jew—Chairman, Donald E. Graham

LOS ANGELES TIMES
Gentile—Liberal publisher Jeffrey Johnson (trick question)

CHICAGO TRIBUNE
Gentile—Editor, Ann Marie Lipinski

WALL STREET JOURNAL
Jew—Chairman, Peter R. Kann

TIME
Jew—Editor in chief, Norman Pearlstine

NEWSWEEK
Gentile—Chairman and editor in chief Richard M. Smith

U.S.NEWS & WORLD REPORT
Jew—Editor in chief, Mort Zuckerman

NEW REPUBLIC
Jew—Editor and CEO, Martin Peretz

PLAYBOY
Jew founder—Hugh Hefner, the most awesome Jew of all time!

TOTALS

NUMBER OF PUBLICATIONS
DISCUSSED HERE: Ten

NUMBER OF PUBLICATIONS RUN BY
JEWS: Seven

PERCENTAGE: 70%

CONCLUSION: Jews have lots of opinions that they to love to write about and charge you money to read! Cool.

CONSPIRACY THEORY #3:

JEWS CONTROL THE BANKS

In order to write about Jewish conspiracies, it is important to compile only the most accurate and concise data. That is why in order to answer the question of whether Jews control the world's

banking, we went right to the source of trusted and true information: The Imperial Klans of America International Headquarters newsletter. No other organization could have such an impartial,

unbiased, and unprejudiced understanding of the Jewish people. Below is an actual article we found in a recent edition of their incredibly illuminating and surprisingly well-written monthly newsletter.

Imperial Klans of America Newsletter
June 2004

INTERNATIONAL ZIONIST BANKERS WHO RUN THE WORLD
(Otherwise Known as the International Private Jewish Banking Cartel)

by Peter Kershaw, I.G.W.
(Imperial Grand Wizard)

Peter Kershaw provided the answer to who owns the Federal Reserve System of America in "Economic Solutions" where he lists the ten primary shareholders in the Federal Reserve banking system.

1) The Rothschild Family* - London
2) The Rothschild Family* - Berlin
3) The Lazard Brothers - Paris
4) Israel Seiff* - Italy
5) Kuhn-Loeb Company* - Germany
6) The Warburgs* - Amsterdam
7) The Warburgs* - Hamburg
8) Lehman Brothers* - New York
9) Goldman & Sachs* - New York
10) The Rockefeller Family - New York."

> Sounds good, where can we sign up?

> What the fuck? He's not even a Jew!

Through their banks, they control, and/or own outright, most of the Corporations of America, and in the entire world. In fact two Jewish families, control all the American food exports, to the Communist Nations.

These Jewish Banking family dynasties, own or control, through their hidden holding companies, the news media, the radio and television networks, the newspapers, and most of the publishing houses in the world. They control, and rule over all the Governments of the World.

These Jewish banking families have secret occult organizations that descend from the original "Illuminati," formed May 1, 1776. Their descendant organizations are for example, The Council on Foreign Relations, The Trilateral Commission, which is headed by David Rockefeller.

These Jewish banking families have many other secret organizations, whose purposes are mysterious, and secret. Through massive liberal campaigns through

> The entire world? Cool!

> Which nations are these? Cuba and China?

> Come on, guys, you know we've got nothing to do with Zimbabwe.

> No duh. That's why we call them "secret organizations."

continued on page 4

...merica Newsletter, June 2004

...ontinued from page 1

the Atheist-Jewish organization World Council of Churches and related organizations, Jewish communism has been made the main doctrine of all the churches.

The U.S. Federal Reserve banking system is, like many things in America, a Jewish-invented fraud, yet few people know it. Further, this banking system is American but the problem is actually global, a Jewish octopus "attacking" various targets worldwide from its American base, using your non-Jewish-created dollars.

Because of this, the power of our Congress to control the nation is largely illusionary, since no matter whether Republicans or Democrats are in the driver's seat, the power of control remains in the hands of the bankers. This means that we have been under alien control since at least 1913.

The Chief Executive Officers of the Federal Reserve have always been known publicly as Jews, with Alan Greenspan being the latest. Every year these business vultures, inured by the Babylonian System of Jewish "gelt," deliberately ruin thousands of people's lives. Small businessmen and farmers by the hundreds of thousands have been ruined by these unscrupulous rapists and many have been driven to suicide, drink, and dope, as the result of the usurious interest rates which a subservient Congress always approves.

Most Americans believe that THE FEDERAL RESERVE SYSTEM is part of the American Government. They have no idea that it is governed by Federal banks, whose heads are aliens, who are members of the International Illuminati conspiracy. Who are these bankers, you may rightly ask? According to reliable sources in Switzerland say the ten banks listed above hold the controlling interest in the FEDERAL RESERVE SYSTEM. They are all Jewish owned and/or controlled.

All the details of this are available, with documentation, in a book written by Eustice Mullins titled: "The Federal Reserve Conspiracy." We would very sincerely suggest you get this book and study it.

But if you believe that these conspirators are content with the mere control of your money, you are sadly mistaken, and you are in for another shock. These foundations funded the rights of civil disobedience; the rights of the filthy minded to spread the poison of pornography; the rights of Jew doctors to murder millions of unborn babies; the rights of homosexuals to spread their filth; The Women's Liberation Movements. Almost without fail all of these were headed by Jews. ∎

Annotations:

The Athiest-Jewish organization? World Council of Churches? What the fuck are they talking about?

A Jewish octopus? That's not kosher.

As does the book reviewer for storm-front.org, which gives it a 3.5 burning crosses out of a possible five. Go Eustice!

That's right, as we all know, the Bush family members are, in fact, aliens.

Hey, you left out the evil lawyers that manipulate the courts. That one was ours too!

This is a new one. We've now been blamed for the suicide of a drunken-drugged-out farmer.

Switzerland? The same country that hid all the money and art that the Nazis stole from the Jews? They're trustworthy.

CONCLUSION:
If you are a fan of Eustice Mullins, have stormfront.org on your computer "favorites," or attended Hammerfest 2005, then yes, we control and own ALL the banks.

CONSPIRACY THEORY #4:
JEWS CONTROL THE WORLD'S MONEY SUPPLY

This is simply not true. Only one Jew controls the world's economy. And that Jew is Ben Shalom Bernanke. Big Ben controls the Federal Reserve, which means he decides when to raise or lower interest rates and when to put more or less currency into circula-tion, thus affecting all consumer and banking loans. By setting the economic policy of the most powerful and richest country in the world, his decisions affect the pocketbook of every person on the planet. His mother must be kvelling!

Name: Benjamin Shalom Bernanke

Age: 53

Height: 5'6"

Weight: 157

Hair: Balding

Eyes: Brown

Turn-ons: Low interest rates, butt plugs, and masturbating with a sock on his hand while watching Maria Bartiromo on CNBC.

Turn-offs: People who are so self-involved that they think the world revolves around them.

Favorite color: Fuchsia

Favorite food: Chicken tikka masala

Hobbies: Making President Bush pull dingleberries out of his ass while flipping a coin to decide which way interest rates should go.

Pets: A thirteen-year-old Cambo-dian boy named "Bokpantu-poo" that he keeps locked in his wine cellar.

And now the former Jew who controlled the world's money supply for 18 years, Alan Greenspan, offers up some advice to Ben Shalom Bernanke about how to handle the pressures of his new job.

SHALOM, BEN SHALOM, ALAN G HERE, RECENTLY RETIRED AND NOW CHILLIN' OUT FULL-TIME WITH MY TWO HOT LATINA MOMMAS HERE ON ISLA MUJERES. I KNOW THAT YOU'RE PROBABLY TRIPPIN' HARDCORE BEING THAT YOUR JEW ASS NOW CONTROLS THE WORLD'S ECONOMY! BUT DON'T SWEAT IT, ALL YOU GOT TO DO IS FOLLOW THESE TWO RULES.

RULE #1: EVERY TIME THE ECONOMY HEATS UP, RAISE INTEREST RATES.

RULE #2: EVERY TIME THE ECONOMY SLOWS DOWN, LOWER INTEREST RATES. SEE, YOU DON'T NEED A HARVARD DIPLOMA TO FIGURE THAT SHIT OUT! NOW IF YOU'LL EXCUSE ME, I'M GOING TO HAVE MARIA AND CLARITA RUB SUN-TAN LOTION INTO MY BALD JEW-HEAD WHILE I DO SOME ONLINE STOCK TRADING. PEACE OUT! MY FELLOW ECONOMY MANIPULATOR.

LOVE AND KISSES,
THE G-MAN

HOW ALAN GREENSPAN BANKRUPTED ME

BY BRYAN FOGEL

In 1999, as the NASDAQ stock market soared to new highs, Alan Greenspan coined the phrase "irrational exuberance" to define people's optimism in technology stocks. Over a period of a year, Alan continually raised interest rates, quenching the monetary supply, and thus caused the technology stock bubble to burst. Finally, Alan succeeded. Between March of 1999 and early 2000, the bubble burst leaving millions of investors reeling from losses comparable to the crash of 1936.

Soon after the crash, with the world's economy collapsed, Alan orchestrated another breathtaking scheme: By lowering the interest rates that he had just raised, he would spur people to now buy underpriced real estate and to get cash by taking second mortgages on their homes. Over the next few years Alan would lower rates again and again until interest rates were at their lowest level in the history of the United States. All the while

the real estate market has gone up and up and up, setting the stage for the next major bubble to burst.

Unfortunately for me, I had invested all of my savings in Oracle, Cisco, and Microsoft, which dropped over 80% during this time. The money that had grown over 1000% during the past fifteen years that I was going to use to make a down payment on a home was gone.

Thanks, Alan. Great job.

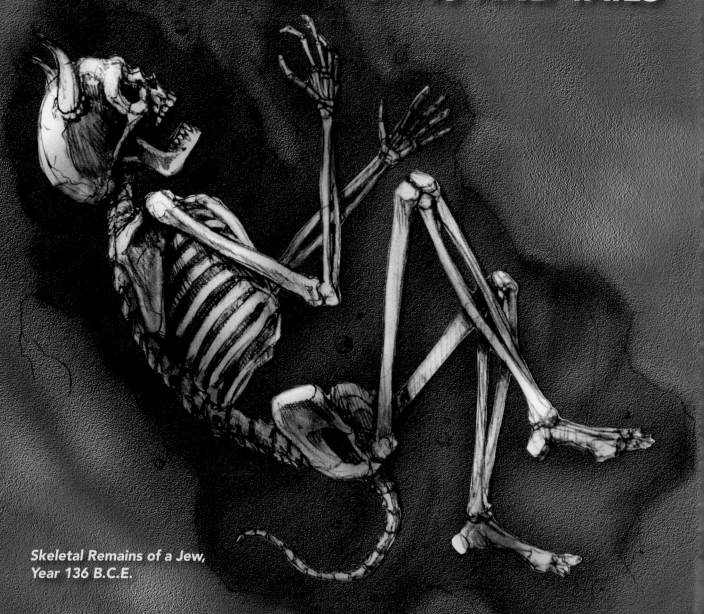

CONSPIRACY THEORY #5:
JEWS HAVE HORNS AND TAILS

Skeletal Remains of a Jew,
Year 136 B.C.E.

Undecided.
Stemming from the belief that Jews are direct descendants of Satan, it comes as no surprise that anti-Semites believe Jews actually have horns and tails. This conspiracy was thought to be ridiculous until a group of archeologists recently uncovered this skeleton in a remote cave in Israel. While we can't vouch for its authenticity, we do feel that it is our obligation to present the facts as they have been presented to us.

Co-author Sam Wolfson in a scene from *Jewtopia* the play: This can't be helping matters.

CONSPIRACY THEORY #6: JEWS ARE PLOTTING TO RULE THE WORLD

If you've ever wondered why this particular conspiracy theory exists and how it is perpetuated, you don't have to look much further than a little gem of a book called *The Protocols of Zion*. Without spoiling too much of the plot, *The Protocols of Zion* is the heartwarming tale of the Jews' secret plan to achieve complete global domination.

The Protocols is widely considered to be the beginning of contemporary conspiracy theory literature. It was first published abridged in 1903 as a series in a daily newspaper in St. Petersburg, Russia. It was so popular, it was later turned into a published book for sale. But could one book really have such a profound impact on why people think Jews are out to control the world?

LET'S BREAK IT DOWN:

- Many Arab governments fund the publication of new printings of *The Protocols*, and teach them in their schools as historical fact.

- It is distributed by Louis Farrakhan to all of his Nation of Islam followers.

- *The Protocols* have been accepted as fact by Islamic extremist organizations Hamas, Islamic Jihad, and Al Qaeda.

- In 1927, Henry Ford sponsored the printing of 500,000 copies and published excerpts from *The Protocols* in his newspapers.

- The American retail chain Wal-Mart sold *The Protocols of Zion* on its website until it received harsh criticism and finally withdrew it from sale in September 2004!

- *The Protocols* were recommended by Presidents Gamal Abdel Nasser and Anwar Sadat of Egypt, King Faisal of Saudi Arabia, and Colonel Mu'ammar Qaddafi of Libya to their citizens to read and in March 1970, *The Protocols* were reported to be the top nonfiction bestseller in Lebanon!

- In Japan, there have been "self-help" books published expressing admiration for the Jewish conspiracy portrayed in *The Protocols* and suggesting that the Japanese should attempt to emulate it to become as powerful as Jews.

1943 Polish Edition
Sample Chapter: The Jews have brainwashed the world to think that we don't know how to screw in a lightbulb.

2005 Syrian Edition
Sample Chapter: Sand: Why are the Jews trying to steal it from us?

1972 Egyptian Edition
Sample Chapter: The Jews are trying to tear down our pyramids and build condominiums.

1998 Austrian Edition
Sample Chapter: Schwarzenegger's Jewish agent forced him at gunpoint to do *Jingle All the Way*, *Junior*, and *Kindergarten Cop*.

Wow! That's a whole lot of hatin' going on. While we're sure *The Protocols* makes for fantastic beach reading, the truth is that Jews to our knowledge ARE NOT involved in a secret plot to control the world. However, in the spirit of honoring the book that has done so much for our people, please enjoy these *Protocols of Zion* book covers from the different versions of the book that have been printed all over the world. You will also find a few samples of chapter headings for each of the various editions.

1930 Spanish Edition
Sample Chapter: The Jews are secretly breeding "Killer Bulls" to wipe out all of our matadors.

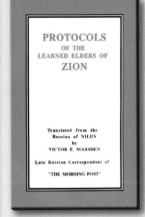

2000 United States Edition
Sample Chapter: Jews are trying to pass legislation to change the phrase, "As American as Apple Pie" to "As American as Bubbe's Cinnamon Noodle Kugel."

1978 United Kingdom Edition
Sample Chapter: Jewish dentists are the reason we have bad teeth.

1934 French Edition
Sample Chapter: The Jews have stolen all of our deodorant.

1992 Russian Edition
Sample Chapter: The Jews have all the bread and are keeping it for themselves.

1987 Japanese Edition
Sample Chapter: They're the JAPS, not us!

1968 South African Edition
Sample Chapter: The Jews made you black.

PHONE CONVERSATIONS WITH

Linda Fogel

Linda: Did I catch you at a bad time?

Bryan: No, just working on the book with Sam.

Linda: What chapter are you working on?

Bryan: Our last chapter, Jewish conspiracy theories.

Linda: Tell me you're not still planning on doing that page where you're cutting out the noses of famous Jews to create a "match game" where people will have to match the nose with the Jew.

Bryan: Yeah, but it's in the stereotype chapter.

Linda: Why are you doing that? Do you want Barbra Streisand to be mad at you?

Bryan: Mom—

Linda: What did Babs ever do to you?!

Bryan: Mom, I'm not saying anything bad about her. I'm just cutting out her nose.

Linda: And what does Time Warner think about this? They can't be okay with this.

Bryan: Mom, it was in the proposal for our book that we gave them. Besides, it's our book. We can do whatever we want.

Linda: So what are you putting in this conspiracy theory chapter of yours?

Bryan: Well, we just finished writing a section on how Jews control Hollywood and that all the famous black sitcoms were actually created by Jews.

Linda: Oh great! You're going to piss off Steven Spielberg and he'll stop Time Warner from releasing your book.

Bryan: Steven Spielberg can't stop Time Warner from releasing our book!

Linda: He's Steven Freakin' Spielberg, he can do whatever he wants! And now you're going to get all the black people mad at you too?

Bryan: Mom, I gotta go.

Linda: You better not say anything bad about Emmanuel Lewis!

(Bryan hangs up the phone.)

JEWISH MOTHERS: PART EIGHT

Sam: Hello?

Arlene: What do you have against Emmanuel Lewis?

Sam: What are you talking about?

Arlene: Mrs. Fogel just called me and told me you're doing a piece in your book about how the Jews brainwashed Emmanuel Lewis.

Sam: Mom, we're writing something about how all the famous black sitcoms were created by Jews.

Arlene: You can't write about that! That's just wrong!

Sam: Nothing's wrong with it and besides, it's kinda funny.

Arlene: Why do you want to create tension between the blacks and Jews? Weren't those Los Angeles riots a few years ago enough?

Sam: That had nothing to do with Jews. That was the L.A.P.D.!

Arlene: It doesn't matter whose fault it was. There could be another riot in L.A. and I don't want you to die.

Sam: I don't live in L.A.!

Arlene: Well, your stuff is still in storage there. You don't want that to get burned, do you? (pause) God, I used to love *The Cosby Show*. Did a Jew create that?

Sam: Yes.

Arlene: Come to think of it, that makes perfect sense. Billy Cosby was a doctor, Phylicia Rashad was a lawyer, they were always putting pressure on their children, and the grandparents were always over.

Sam: Mom—

Arlene: You better not say anything bad about Bill Cosby!

Sam: I gotta go—

Arlene: He always wore those great Coogi sweaters!!!

(Sam hangs up the phone.)

Arlene Wolfson

BOX NO. _____

```
┌─────────────────────────────────────────────┐
│                                               │
│            EXAMINATION BOOK                   │
│                                               │
│   Name _____   │
│   Subject _Jewtopia 101_____       │
│   Class _Final Jew Review_ Section _____    │
│   Instructor _Fogel and Wolfson_ Date _____ │
│                                               │
└─────────────────────────────────────────────┘
```

No. 44789
8" x 8"
6 Leaves 5 Pages

THE FINAL EXAM: *HOW GOOD A JEW ARE YOU?*

While there are many branches of Judaism, the majority of today's Jews generally divide themselves into one of two categories: Good Jew or Bad Jew. But what makes a Good Jew good? What makes a Bad Jew bad? While being a Good Jew entails going to temple and having a Bar or Bat Mitzvah, this is just scratching the surface. Now that you've reached the end of our book, it's time for you to take our final exam and discover once and for all how good or bad a Jew you really are.

1) ON AVERAGE, HOW OFTEN DO YOU CALL YOUR MOTHER?

A. 5–10 times a day.

B. 5–10 times a week.

C. Once a month, and always two minutes before you walk into a movie so you have an immediate out.

D. Once a year on her birthday after 9:30 P.M. because you know she's already asleep with the ringer off and you can just leave her a message saying, "Sorry I missed you, Mom! Happy birthday!"

2) WHAT ARE THE MEMORIES OF YOUR BAR/BAT MITZVAH?

A. A defining moment in your young life that solidified your commitment and love for Judaism.

B. A fun weekend getting to hang out with relatives, eat some great food, then by Monday it was as if the whole thing never happened.

C. Your first time fingering someone/getting fingered in the parking lot during the party.

D. No memories because you never had one.

3) TO YOU A MEZUZAH IS:

A. Hung at an angle in every doorway and kissed when passed.

B. Hung on the front door in an effort to keep the Angel of Death away.

C. Made of platinum with diamonds and worn as a lovely necklace on the High Holidays.

D. That thing your mom gave you for your apartment that you now stash pot in.

4) WHAT ARE YOUR MEMORIES OF VISITING ISRAEL?

A. Never felt so connected to your homeland and proud to be a Jew.

B. Never felt so connected to your homeland and proud to be a Jew, but still petrified that you could be blown up at any second and cut your trip three days short.

C. You accidentally went there because you thought that's where the pyramids were.

D. Tons of hot Jew ass.

5) HOW OFTEN DO YOU PERFORM AN ALIYAH?

A. Every week and you have a reserved seat with your name on it next to the Torah Ark.

B. Once a year, until the time you lifted the Torah out of the Ark, threw out your back, and sued God unsuccessfully.

C. Once, when you were Bar Mitzvahed.

D. Bought an Aliyah CD after her plane crashed.

6) WHEN YOU PRAY, WHAT DO YOU PRAY FOR?

A. A safe Israeli state that is respected and loved by all of its Arab neighbors.

B. A Democratic president who is pro-choice and pro-Israel.

C. A Democratic president and for Clay Aiken to get the respect he deserves.

D. That thing you just found is not herpes.

7) HOW OFTEN DO YOU USE TEFILLIN?

A. Every morning as commanded by the Torah.

B. Once when Bar Mitzvahed.

C. Frequently use it to tie up your sex partner.

D. Isn't that what they make non-stick pans out of?

8) HOW WELL DO YOU SPEAK HEBREW?

A. Fluently, Biblical and Modern.

B. You can only recite the most common prayers.

C. You can hum along to "Dayenu."

D. You can make the *chhh* sound.

9) WHEN SOMEONE CALLS YOU LAST MINUTE TO TAKE PART IN A MINYAN, WHAT DO YOU DO?

A. Drop whatever it was you were doing and rush over to the home of your grieving friend in need.

B. Say you'll be right there, finish the football game you are watching, arrive at your friend's two hours later and say there was an accident on the highway.

C. Lie and tell them you're sorry, you'd love to help, but you are already booked at another minyan on the other side of town.

D. Start to speak Spanish and pretend like your friend dialed the wrong number.

10) WHAT DO YOU TYPICALLY DO ON HANUKAH?

A. Light the menorah all eight nights and recite the appropriate prayers.

B. Light a menorah candle for five nights and recite the appropriate prayers.

C. Light the menorah candle the first night and recite the prayer, plan on doing it the second night, forget to do it, skip third, fourth, fifth, sixth, seventh nights, feel guilty and light candle on the eighth night, skip the prayer because you're late for a movie.

D. Go dressed as Santa Claus to your Gentile friend's Christmas party, get drunk off eggnog, photocopy your ass on the Xerox machine, make out with a Gentile in a supply closet, go home, barf on menorah.

11) HOW OFTEN DO YOU EAT KOSHER?

A. Every meal of every day no matter where you eat.

B. At home, but not when you go out to eat because the rules don't apply when you're at Red Lobster.

C. Just once, when American Airlines screwed up and gave you a kosher meal.

D. After a night of drunken debauchery, you go to a deli at 4 A.M. because it's the only restaurant still open and you eat a bowl of matzoh ball soup so you won't throw up.

12) HOW HAS BARBRA STREISAND AFFECTED YOUR LIFE?

A. Went to see her live 10 times, and once paid 5,000 bucks a ticket to sit in the front row.

B. No longer will enter the state of Colorado.

C. When she walked past you in Malibu, you wept openly and yelled out, "I love you, Babs!"

D. Own *Meet the Fockers* on DVD.

NOW TALLY UP YOUR SCORE!

YOUR SCORE

A = 8 points, B = 5 points, C = 2 points, D = 0 points

Out of a possible 96 points, how did you do?

96–73: THE ULTIMATE JEW: Congratulations. You are as good as a Jew gets! God brags about you all the time, and he has a special favorite troll-doll pen he uses just to inscribe your name in the Book of Life each year. What are you doing reading this book? You should be in temple praying for the rest of us!

72–49: THE GOOD JEW: While you might not be winning any prizes for being the World's Best Jew, you're still a pretty good addition to the tribe. If THE ULTIMATE JEW is a Rolls-Royce, you're a really, really, nice Audi with the sports package and leather interior.

48–25: THE AVERAGE JEW: You're a completely mediocre Jew in every way. You do just enough to still be considered a Jew, but not so much that it cuts into your spin class and XBox playing time. This is how you've lived out your entire average existence, which is why you are now, and forever will be, an assistant manager at Bed, Bath & Beyond.

24–12: THE BELOW-AVERAGE JEW: Not only are you a pretty bad, non-practicing, apathetic Jew, you're probably eating a ham-and-cheese panini as you read this. On the other hand, you did have a Bar/Bat Mitzvah, and you did cry when you watched *Sophie's Choice*. Any other religion would have kicked you to the curb a long time ago, but seeing as how Judaism is dying out, we'll keep you around just to keep our numbers up.

11–0: THE BAD JEW: You live out of a Winnebago Itasca Horizon, you gargle with eggnog every morning, and you read *The Protocols of Zion* as a bedtime story to your children.

Afterword

During the course of this book, you probably asked yourself the following questions: "How did Bryan Fogel and Sam Wolfson come up with such a fresh and hilariously funny take on being a Jew? Where did they come up with all of their material? And why do I find myself getting aroused when I look at their bio pictures?"

The answer might lie in the fact that the two of us grew up in two completely different homes, practicing two completely different branches of Judaism, in two completely different cities. Bryan grew up Modern Orthodox in Denver, Colorado, and Sam grew up Reformed in Jacksonville, Florida. Yet when we sat down to write our play and our book, we both found ourselves laughing at our nearly identical crazy Jewish upbringings.

And if there's one thing we've learned over the course of writing our book and performing in our play *Jewtopia* (still running in New York City, tickets at www.jewtopiaplay.com), it's that Jews are Jews! And whether you keep kosher and were brought up Orthodox in Paris or eat lobster every day and were brought up Secular Humanistic in Tel Aviv, culturally, we're all the same. And if you don't believe us, all you have to do is take a look at the radically different ways in which we were Bar Mitzvahed, yet we were still able to write this book together.

Bryan's Bar Mitzvah Photos

VENUE: Temple BMH, Denver, and the Wailing Wall, Jerusalem, 1986

THEME: Bryan's parents didn't believe in themed Bar Mitzvahs

NOTE: These are the only THREE known pictures from Bryan's Bar Mitzvah, as Orthodox Jews do not allow photography on the Sabbath

PICTURE #1—While there are no photos of the actual ceremony, this is the single photo taken the day before while Bryan practiced at the Bimah. Note the wonderful lighting conditions, as flashes are not allowed in the sanctuary.

PICTURE #2—Bryan and younger brother, Glen, get ready to party!

PICTURE #3—Bryan chanting his haftorah at the Wailing Wall with his grandfather Jimmy. Linda Fogel flew 6,000 miles to peek through the "protective anti-female screen" in hopes of catching a glimpse of her son becoming a man.

Sam's Bar Mitzvah Photos

VENUE: Temple Etz Chaim, Florida, 1986

THEME: Come dressed as your favorite movie star

NOTE: These are just 5 of over 500 pictures from Sam's Reform Bar Mitzvah

Aunt Marion—Michael Jackson
Aunt Rita—Boy George
Aunt Helaine—Tina Turner
Cousin Ira—Eddie Murphy

PICTURE #1—The entire Wolfson clan dressed as their favorite celebrities. Notice that 3 out of 18 relatives are dressed as blacks and that one of them is dressed as a gay transvestite.

PICTURE #2—After taking out a second mortgage to pay for the party, Sam's parents, a.k.a. Humphrey Bogart and Ingrid Bergman, fake a smile for the party's photographer, Annie Leibovitz.

PICTURE #4 AND #5—Sam and his sister, Stacey, hop aboard the "Magical Mystery give your relative a hernia chair ride." No yarmulkes required!!!

PICTURE #3—Sam "Sonny Crockett" Wolfson strikes a lethal pose. What does this have to do with becoming a man?

Acknowledgments

We can't believe that we actually finished writing this book! What was going to be a kitschy little paperback turned into us being holed up in our house for nine months working 16 hours a day with a team of illustrators and graphic artists to turn our idea of creating the craziest illustrated book of Jewish culture in the history of the world into life.

First, we'd like to thank Adam Chromy, our book agent, for approaching us with the idea of "Hey, you guys should write a *Jewtopia* book—it'll be easy, I promise!" and not letting up until we stupidly said, "OK."

Second, none of this would have happened if not for the incredible support of Jason Pinter and everyone else at Warner Books for believing in us enough to let us create the book that we truly wanted to create.

Our amazing creative design team: Drew Beam, whose original sketches, drawings, and photography are true works of art. Amy Marrin and Kim Schuman, who laid out and designed every page from nothing more than words and ideas in our heads. They managed to do all of this while literally working at the kitchen table in our NYC apartment.

Amy Shearn: The Wind Beneath Our Wings. How the hell did we find someone as talented as you on Craigslist???

Special thanks to Adam Markowitz, Deirdre MacNamara, and Aryeh Cohen-Wade for bringing us the extra funny when we needed it. And Hannah Seligson for all the great research and endless Googling direct from the couch in our den.

James Rothbart: Our friend, our attorney, and the most honest and good person in all of Hollywood. Thank you for always believing in us.

Andy Fickman: Our original L.A. director and now big-time Hollywood Superstar. For believing in us long before anyone else did and for helping turn our little show into a huge hit. Soylent Green is People!

Roy Ashton, Michael Cardonick, Jared Hoffman, Peter Jacobs, and Adam Kanter: Our bad-ass team at CAA.

To our friends and families: Arlene, Dennis, and Stacey Wolfson; Linda, David, Jill, and Glen Fogel. Goldye Radetsky, Bill Franzblau, and George Pitt, the man whose lavishly furnished home we sublet while we wrote the book—if you had truly known how many people were working out of your home (plus Drew's dog, Stuart), you would have come back from Italy a lot sooner. And to Charlotta and Kate…for waiting up!

Photo Credits

Introduction/Foreword:
vi–vii: *Jewtopia* production photos: Carol Rosegg
viii: Herbie Hitler: iStockphoto/*Jewtopia*

Chapter 1:
1: Moishe: Photos.com
2: Abs: Ablestock; Hebrew: iStockphoto
3: Sega Genesis: *Jewtopia*; Eve: Clipart
4: Steven Polansky: Getty; Islam flag: iStockphoto
5: Abraham and Isaac: Ablestock; Donny Osmond: Getty
6: Joseph: Clipart; Charleton Heston: Corbis
7 & 8: Noah's ark spread: *Jewtopia*; Boy band: iStockphoto
10: Slingshot: iStockphoto
11: Solomon's Temple: Clipart
12: Japanese girl: Ablestock; Burning bush: Clipart
13–16: Moses: *Jewtopia*
17 & 18: Timeline: Egypt: Photos.com; Lasagna: Ablestock; Castle, torture device: iStockphoto; Rat: Getty; Hitler: Corbis; Palestinian: Associated Press; *Jewtopia* poster: *Jewtopia*
19 & 20: Moms: Screen capture from *Jewtopia* commercial spot

Chapter 2:
21: Ventriloquist Jesus: *Jewtopia*
22: Jerusalem: iStockphoto
23: Masada: iStockphoto; Blonde: *Jewtopia*
24: Bishop, Ladder: Clipart
25: Crusades: Clipart
26: Ted Neely: Getty
27 & 28: Jesus spread: *Jewtopia*; Britney Spears, David Lee Roth, Kenny G: Corbis; Michael Bolton, Virgin Mary underpass, Virgin Mary underpass crowd: AP
29: Martin Luther, Chinese guy: Clipart
30: Scribes: Clipart
31: Theodor Herzl: Library of Congress; Star of David: Public domain; *Sound of Music*: Getty
32: *The Producers*, Menachem Begin, Bill Clinton: Getty; George W. Bush: AP
33 & 34: Six-Day War: *Jewtopia*
40: Wailing Wall: Getty
41 & 42: Herzl: Library of Congress; Gene Simmons: Corbis; Golda Meir: Getty; Abraham, Albert Einstein: Clipart; Bugsy Siegel, Alan Dershowitz, Dr. Ruth Westheimer, Son of Sam: AP
43 & 44: Moms: Screen capture from *Jewtopia* commercial spot

Chapter 3:
45: Bubbe: *Jewtopia*
46: Serious Jews: Clipart
47: Shoe tie: iStockphoto
48: Shabbat Shalom: *Jewtopia*
49: Spock hand: *Jewtopia*
50: Osama bin Laden: Getty
51: Guy in makeup: iStockphoto
52: Shofar: iStockphoto
53 & 54: Propaganda campaigns: *Jewtopia*
55: Etrog and Shofars: Clipart; Sudoku: *Jewtopia*
56: Sukkah: *Jewtopia*
57: Purim characters: *Jewtopia*
58: Hamantaschen: iStockphoto; Persia map: Clipart
59: Carpy: Clipart; Dollar bills: iStockphoto
61: Seder plate: *Jewtopia*
62: Alternate Uses for Matzoh: *Jewtopia*; Sunbather: Getty
63: Glen Fogel: Courtesy of the Fogel family; Judah Maccabee album cover: *Jewtopia*
64: Jewish toys: http://www.jewishtoy.com/
65 & 66: Christmas vs Hanukah: *Jewtopia*
67: Torah guys: Clipart; Miriam Goldberg: iStockphoto
68: Fogel family, Pushke box: *Jewtopia*; Tree: iStockphoto
69 & 70: Moms: Screen capture from *Jewtopia* commercial spot

Chapter 4:
71: Sweet and sour carp: *Jewtopia*
72: Sandwich: *Jewtopia*
73: Bacon: iStockphoto; Sir Francis Bacon: Clipart
75 & 76: Unkosher treats: *Jewtopia*
77 & 78: Bagel, Challah, Smoked fish: Clipart; Sandwich: iStockphoto
79 & 80: Chinese food: Clipart; Latkes, Blintz, Gefilte fish, Soup, Mandelbread: iStockphoto
81 & 82: Food: *Jewtopia*
83: Mee-Maw: Courtesy of the Wolfson family
84: Cheeseburger: iStockphoto
85 & 86: Actually Bryan's mom's freezer: Courtesy of the Fogel family
88: *Jewtopia* poster: *Jewtopia*
89 & 90: Restaurant: *Jewtopia*
93 & 94: Moms: Screen capture from *Jewtopia* commercial spot

Chapter 5:
95: Kwanzaa: Getty/*Jewtopia*
96: Sam: Courtesy of the Wolfson family; Old couple: iStockphoto
99 & 100: Baby's room: *Jewtopia*
101 & 102: Bar Mitzvah family: Corbis
103 & 104: Gentile bachelor party: *Jewtopia*
105 & 106: Jewish bachelor party: *Jewtopia*

107 & 108: Christmas family, NASCAR party, Baptism: Corbis; Kwanzaa: Getty

109 & 110: Manscaping: *Jewtopia*

111 & 112: Chutes and Ladders: *Jewtopia*

113–116: Kama Sutra: *Jewtopia*

117 & 118: Holes in sheets: *Jewtopia*

119 & 120: Good poo spread: *Jewtopia*; Pills, Toilet: Clipart; Bran castle: Wikimedia Commons Public Domain Photography

121 & 122: Moms: Screen capture from *Jewtopia* commercial spot

Chapter 6:

123: Dennis Wolfson: Courtesy of the Wolfson family

124: The Wolfsons, Rose Weissman: Courtesy of the Wolfson family

125: Airplane: iStockphoto

126: Gurney: iStockphoto

128: Michael Jackson: Getty; Uncle Harold: Courtesy of the Wolfson family

129: Airplane seats: *Jewtopia*

130: Inside airplane: iStockphoto

132: Flight attendant: Getty

133 & 134: Hotel, Bathroom: iStockphoto; Bacteria: Getty; Skull: Clipart; Uncle Harold and his toilet nest: Courtesy of the Wolfson family

135: Guidebook girl: Clipart

136: Suitcases: iStockphoto

137 & 138: USA: Mount Rushmore, Hot tub, St. Louis arch, Beach, Statue of Liberty: Getty; Hollywood star, Sears Tower, Hancock Building: iStockphoto; Harvard sweatshirt: *Jewtopia*; George W. Bush, Jewish men: Clipart

139 & 140: Central & South America: Child: Getty; Chichen Itza, Machu Picchu, Hat, Maracas guy, Jews Gone Wild face: Clipart; Mario Kreutzberger: Wikipedia; Carnivale lady, Jesus: iStockphoto; Mule equation: *Jewtopia*

141 & 142: Africa: Fur coat, Congo River: Getty; Mask, Diamonds, Machete, Tribal fellow, Border Pattern: Clipart

143 & 144: India: Indian woman, Henna hand, Goa, Ganges bathers, Taj Mahal: Getty; Elephant, Yogi: Clipart; Bollywood, IT guy: iStockphoto

145 & 146: Eastern Europe & Russia: Sexy blonde, Bear, St. Basil's: Getty; Taxi driver: iStockphoto; Prague, Siberia cold guy: Clipart; Flags: CIA Factbook

147 & 148: Europe: British Museum, OktoberFest: Getty; Flags, British guard: Clipart; Stonehenge, Louvre, Gladiator, Netherlands: iStockphoto

149 & 150: Asia: Peep show: *Jewtopia*; Malaysia, Dalai Lama, Caning: AP; Great Wall, Closed sign, Forbidden City, Tattooed man, Steak, North Korean seal, Chopsticks, Take-out box, Lions, Great Wall background: Clipart; Mount Fuji: Wikimedia Commons Public Domain Photography

151 & 152: Israel: Galilee, Pita: *Jewtopia*; Tree planting: Courtesy of the Fogel family; Tel Aviv: Getty; Kibbutz: Wikimedia Commons Public Domain Photography; Israel map and flag: CIA Factbook; Matzoh, Beach,

Torah scrolls, Megiddo, Temple Mount, Knesset, Background flag: Clipart

153 & 154: Middle East: Camel ride: Courtesy of the Fogel family; Scorpion, Snake, Camel toe, Burka, Camel, Kaffiyeh, Table: iStockphoto

155: Stove, SWAT guy: iStockphoto

156: Crazy doctor: Getty; Kidnapping: iStockphoto

157 & 158: Moms: Screen capture from *Jewtopia* commercial spot

Chapter 7:

159: Bryan in gas mask: *Jewtopia*

160: Trevon: Getty

161: Fake nose: iStockphoto

162: Albert Einstein, Barbra Streisand, Ben Stiller, Bob Dylan, Adam Sandler, David Schwimmer, Gene Simmons, Jon Stewart, Sarah Jessica Parker, Owen Wilson: Corbis

163–165: Neurotic illustrations: *Jewtopia*

166: Hammerfest flyers: http://www.stormfront.org

168: Penny: iStockphoto

171 & 172: Sheds: Clipart; Actual drawer in kitchen: *Jewtopia*

173 & 174: Bryan's old car: *Jewtopia*

175 & 176: Watch: *Jewtopia*

177: J.A.P.s: iStockphoto; Smile: Clipart

178: Joseph Lieberman, Barbra Streisand, Franz Kafka, Marv Albert, David Berkowitz: AP; Albert Einstein: Clipart; Ben Bernanke: Getty

180: Bald Ben Bernanke: Getty

181: Gorilla: Ablestock

182: Hairy Jew face: iStockphoto

183 & 184: Moms: Screen capture from *Jewtopia* commercial spot

Chapter 8:

185: Gary Coleman: Getty

186: Hall & Oates: Corbis; Neo-Nazi: AP

187 & 188: Studio logos: Websites

189 & 190: TVs: Clipart, iStockphoto, Photos.com

191 & 192: *Fresh Prince of Bel-Air*: Corbis; *What's Happening!!*: Getty; *Good Times, The Jeffersons, Sanford and Son*: Corbis; *The Cosby Show, Webster*: AP; *Diff'rent Strokes*: Getty

193 & 194: Covers: *Jewtopia*; John Roberts: AP

197 & 198: Ben Bernanke, Party girls: Getty; Alan Greenspan: Corbis

199: Skeleton: *Jewtopia*

200: Devil Sam: *Jewtopia*

201 & 202: *The Protocols* covers: Wikipedia

203 & 204: Moms: Screen capture from *Jewtopia* commercial spot

Afterword:

209 & 210: Bar Mizvah photos: Courtesy of the Fogel and Wolfson families

Final Photo: Bryan, Sam, and their moms: Getty

The real Linda Fogel (left) and the real Arlene Wolfson (right) at the opening night party of JEWTOPIA in New York City on October 21, 2004.